FOR LOVE OF
MAGIC

BAEN BOOKS
by SIMON R. GREEN

ISHMAEL JONES MYSTERIES
The Dark Side of the Road
Dead Man Walking
Very Important Corpses (forthcoming)
Haunted by the Past

Jekyll & Hyde Inc.

For Love of Magic

FOR LOVE OF MAGIC

SIMON R. GREEN

BAEN

A Baen Books Original

Baen Publishing Enterprises
P.O. Box 1403
Riverdale, NY 10471
www.baen.com

ISBN: 978-1-9821-9261-7

Cover art by Tom Kidd

First printing, May 2023

Distributed by Simon & Schuster
1230 Avenue of the Americas
New York, NY 10020

Library of Congress Cataloging-in-Publication Data

Names: Green, Simon R., 1955- author.
Title: For love of magic / Simon R. Green.
Description: Riverdale, NY : Baen Publishing Enterprises, [2023]
Identifiers: LCCN 2022059945 (print) | LCCN 2022059946 (ebook) | ISBN
    9781982192617 (hardcover) | ISBN 9781625799135 (ebook)
Subjects: LCGFT: Fantasy fiction. | Romance fiction. | Novels.
Classification: LCC PR6107.R44 F675 2023 (print) | LCC PR6107.R44
(ebook)
    | DDC 823/.92—dc23/eng/20221213
LC record available at https://lccn.loc.gov/2022059945
LC ebook record available at https://lccn.loc.gov/2022059946

Printed in the United States of America

10 9 8 7 6 5 4 3 2 1

FOR LOVE OF
MAGIC

History isn't what it used to be.

Once upon a time, the world was a better place. Horses had wings and rings granted wishes, animals could talk, there were castles in the clouds, and everyone knew who the real monsters were. True love was everywhere, and happily ever after came as standard. And good things happened every day.
That world is gone, but we all dream of it.

Palimpsest: a manuscript that has been written over, so that sometimes the original writing can be seen peeping through. Also: a useful metaphor when it comes to understanding the past.

History has been rewritten, to take all the magic out of the world. But not all of it has been erased.

CHAPTER ONE
THERE'S SOMETHING IN THE PAINTING

London is a city haunted by its past, by the cold facts of history and the hot fever dreams of legend. A city built on bones and ghosts, dreams and myths, and all the other things that refuse to be forgotten.

I'm Jack Daimon, and it's my job to make the past behave.

I walked through a door that appeared out of nowhere, and just like that I was strolling through Westminster late at night, with a map in my head telling me where I needed to be. The pavements seemed more than usually crowded as I headed for the Tate Gallery at Millbrook, and whatever Bad Thing was waiting for me there. It's my job to defuse the supernatural equivalent of unexploded bombs: all the weird artefacts and infernal devices left behind by forgotten civilisations and peoples we're better off without. I protect the present, from the sins of times past.

I was wearing my usual black goat's-skin leather jacket over a black T-shirt, workman's jeans, and stout walking boots. For me, fashion and style have always been things other people do. I was in my late twenties, in good enough shape, and with the kind of face that doesn't get noticed. A backpack over my shoulder held the tools of my trade: cold iron and cursed silver, fresh garlic and bottled wolfsbane. A mandrake root with a screaming face, a Hand of Glory made from the severed hand of the last politician to be secretly hanged in England . . . and an athame, a witch knife that can cut through all the things other blades can't touch.

When I finally got to the Tate, it was closed. All the windows were dark, like so many empty eyes, and two uniformed policemen stood guard at the front door. Even at this late hour a major tourist attraction like the Tate should still have been open for business, but the few hopeful souls who did approach the police were politely but firmly turned away. No visitors, no exceptions, try again tomorrow.

Since I was here, that had to mean whatever had gone wrong was way out of the ordinary and more than usually dangerous. I wasn't surprised. All art galleries are packed full of things that have been allowed to hang around for far too long. Menaces from the past, preserved in canvas and paint, stone and marble. Just waiting to wake up angry and bite someone's head off.

I headed straight for the two policemen, and they stood a little straighter despite themselves. Walk like an officer and smile like a predator, and the world will fall over itself to be helpful. I crashed to a halt and looked the policemen over like I was thinking of trading them in for something more efficient.

"Hi, guys! You can relax now; I've arrived."

"I'm afraid the Tate is closed, sir," the older policeman said carefully. "The lights have failed, and no one can be allowed in until the problem has been dealt with."

"That's why I'm here," I said.

I flashed them one of the many false IDs I've accumulated from all the various organisations I've helped out. Sometimes they offer me money as a thank you, but I always go for the favour. You get more mileage out of a favour. My Tax Inspector ID opens the most doors, but for the Tate I was a Detective Inspector from New Scotland Yard. One of the policemen quickly unlocked the door, and the other politely offered me a flashlight. I accepted it with a friendly smile, because at the end of the day we're all just working stiffs, and then I strode into the Tate to poke danger in the eye one more time.

The lobby was dimly illuminated by streetlight falling through the windows like half-hearted spotlights. I pointed my flashlight here and there, but nothing moved in the great open space. The air was still, and the silence was heavy enough to cover a multitude of threats. I did wonder if I might have arrived too late, and missed all the excitement . . . But it didn't feel that way. Something up ahead was lying in wait, and watching to see what I would do.

I strode on through the Tate, passing quickly through deserted corridors with tall ceilings and pleasantly decorated stone pillars. Important works of art covered the walls, reduced to shades of grey in the obscuring gloom, and there were any number of statues, ancient and modern. I gave them plenty of room. Never trust anything that can stand that still; it's just waiting for a chance to ambush you.

I finally rounded a corner and someone else's flashlight hit me in the face. I stopped, and held up my fake ID. I'm a great believer in being polite and reasonable, right up to the point when it stops working. After that, I have no problem with becoming suddenly violent and completely unreasonable.

A harried-looking dog handler was dragged forward by his Alsatian as it strained against its leash and growled loudly at me. I showed the handler my ID, and he made his dog sit. The animal didn't want to, but it finally slumped down and glowered at me suspiciously.

"Sorry about that, sir," said the handler. "We still haven't found any of the missing people, and the dogs are getting a bit tense."

"How many teams do you have looking?" I said, as though I understood what we were talking about.

"Six dogs and their handlers, sir. There's more on the way; we understand this has top priority. Then there's twenty uniforms from the local stations, and the entire Tate security strength. If the missing visitors are still here, we'll find them."

"Who's in charge of the operation?" I said.

"Some Government type, sir. Wouldn't even tell us which Department he represents."

"Did he at least give you a name?"

"Oh yes, sir. George Roberts."

"Of course," I said. "It would have to be him."

I could always trust George to be right in the middle of whatever he was investigating. And if I had to deal with an authority figure, I wasn't too upset it was him. I knew where I was, with George.

I followed the dog handler's directions to a large viewing area, and there was George, standing at his ease in a pool of light generated by a circle of battery-powered lamps. He was giving all his attention to two paintings in particular, and didn't even glance in my direction, though I had no doubt he knew I was there. The young woman at his side fixed me with a challenging glare. I gave her my best *Don't you wish you were somebody?* smile, put my flashlight away, and started forward. George finally condescended to turn just enough to nod in my direction.

Well past retirement age, his back was still straight and his gaze was still sharp. Medium height, and rather more than medium weight, George was dark-skinned with close-cropped grey hair, and always wore an Old Etonian tie with his sharp city suit, because wherever he happened to be, he wanted everyone to know he was the man in charge. He didn't move from in front of the paintings, because he was waiting for me to come and join him, so I did. I like to allow people their little victories; it makes them so much easier to work with. George showed me his polite smile, the one that means nothing at all because it never touches his eyes.

"So good of you to grace us with your presence, Jack. I can always use another warm body to throw to the wolves."

I just nodded. "If you're happy to see me, this must be a really bad one."

"There are . . . complications."

As Head of the Department For Uncanny Inquiries, George dealt with the kind of threats most people don't even know exist. He had power beyond the dreams of politicians, and only abused it when he felt like it. I've known George on and off for years. We're not friends, but we can fake it enough to get the job done.

"I do feel easier for you being here, Jack," he murmured, as we shook hands just long enough to get it over with. "How much do you know?"

"Only that visitors to the Tate have gone missing, and can't be found."

George considered me thoughtfully. "We should work together more often. Your father and I often joined forces, to pull the world's fat out of the fire."

"I'm not my father."

George just nodded. "I sent a wreath to the funeral, on behalf of the Department. I didn't think it would be in good taste to make a personal appearance."

I shrugged. "It's not as if there was a body to bury." I glanced at the woman standing beside him. "Is this all you brought as backup? You usually travel with enough firepower to intimidate a small nation."

"We got caught with our pants down on this one," he admitted. "By the time word reached me on what had happened here, I'd already dispatched most of my forces to the Orkney Islands, to investigate a ring of Standing Stones that had changed their positions overnight. The locals claimed the Stones had been dancing again."

"Can't be anything important," I said. "Or I'd be there, instead of here."

The young woman at George's side decided she'd been patient long enough and cleared her throat, loudly and just a bit dangerously. She had an athletic build, a horsey face, and jet black hair. Her power-cut business suit gave her an air of someone ready to walk through anything or anyone who got in her way. I just knew we weren't going to get along. George nodded politely in her general direction.

"Allow me to present my new second-in-command, Miriam Patterson."

I gave Miriam my best *We don't have to be enemies; it's up to you* smile. She sniffed loudly, and scowled at George.

"Why has this person been granted access to such a restricted area?"

"Because he's Jack Daimon, and we need him," George said patiently.

"What makes him so important?"

"Jack is the current Outsider," said George.

Miriam studied me carefully, as though she was thinking about buying me and wondering if I'd break easily.

"I always thought the Outsider would be scarier," she said finally.

"I am," I said. "When I need to be." I looked reproachfully at George. "She's your new second-in-command, and you haven't briefed her about me?"

"I thought I'd let you give the speech. You do it so much better than I ever could."

I met Miriam's icy gaze with my most self-assured smile.

"Think of me as a supernatural troubleshooter, keeping a lid on the leavings of history. It's my job to deal with the last remnants of a time when Humanity wasn't even close to being top dog. The old gods may be gone, but some of the things they used to fight their wars got left behind."

"I don't believe in the supernatural," said Miriam.

"It believes in you."

"The paranormal is just science we don't properly understand yet!"

"Whatever gets you through the night," I said diplomatically.

"No squabbling, children," said George. "Jack, Tate security hit the panic button three hours ago, when twenty-two visitors were reported missing. Surveillance cameras confirm they haven't left the building, but we can't find a trace of them anywhere."

"When did the lights go out?" I said.

"The moment people started leaving the Tate," said George.

I nodded thoughtfully, because that helps me look like I know what I'm doing.

"Any clues?"

"The only surveillance cameras to stop working were the ones covering this particular area," said George. "And the only new additions are these two pieces by the Victorian artist Richard Dadd: one quite famous, the other appearing for the very first time."

"Someone used the Orkneys as a distraction," said Miriam. "So we'd have no one to send when people started disappearing into the woodwork."

"Who'd want to piss in your fountain that badly?" I said.

"We police the paranormal," said George. "We're never going to be short of enemies."

I nodded, acknowledging the point, and looked around the open area. I could still feel the Bad Thing watching me, from some unseen hiding place.

"You look spooked, Outsider," said Miriam. "What do you know that we don't?"

"Jack doesn't approve of museums," said George.

"I have a problem with any place where artefacts from the past are on open display," I said. "All the spoils of Empire, brought back from the far corners of the Earth . . . not realising how many of them were Trojan Horses. Pots full of poltergeists, weapons looking for a chance to possess a new owner, and jewels with hidden agendas. The past, forever revenging itself on the present."

Miriam looked at George. "He does like to make speeches, doesn't he?"

"You have no idea," said George.

"And don't get me started on paintings!" I said, aware my voice was rising and not giving a damn. "Take Rossetti's 'The Highgate Lamia.' He made it look like just another pretty face, but the model who sat for him wasn't even a little bit human."

"What was wrong with the painting?" said Miriam.

"If you looked it in the eye, it ate your soul," said George. "Which is why 'The Highgate Lamia' is now a lost masterpiece." He smiled briefly. "It did burn very prettily."

"And let's not forget the Roman statue that walked the British Museum at night, looking for people to strangle with its cold marble hands," I said. "The trouble with history is that it's not always content to stay in the past. All ancient artefacts and works of art should be destroyed. Because you can never be sure when they'll turn on you."

"And how would we explain that to the general public?" said George.

"If people knew the truth, they'd trust us to do the right thing."

"The public?" said George. "Have you met them?"

"You're such a snob, George."

"Doesn't mean I'm not right."

I gave my full attention to the two paintings.

"Do you need me to tell you what they are?" said Miriam.

"The one on the left is 'The Fairy Feller's Master Stroke,'" I said. "The painter was locked up as a criminal lunatic after he murdered his father. His early works were dainty fairy scenes from Shakespeare: Titania and Bottom reclining at their ease. Chocolate box art. But this . . . is like a view into another world. A whole court of fairies, gathered to observe an event of horrible and irrevocable significance. A turning point in history, that no one remembers any more."

"Oh come on!" said Miriam. "There's no such thing as fairies."

"Don't tell them that," said George.

Miriam sniffed loudly. "You'll be looking under the bed for the bogeyman next."

"That would be the first place I'd look," said George. "Provided I had a big enough club."

I gave George my best thoughtful look. "I'm missing something.

You aren't normally this patient with your subordinates. Why are you being so nice to this one?"

"Because Miriam has been chosen to succeed me, as the next Head of the Department," George said calmly.

I took a moment, to consider the implications.

"So she's a political appointment?"

"Aren't we all," said George. "I'm quite looking forward to stepping down. I only hung on this long because I was waiting for someone who could handle the responsibility."

"And you think she can?"

George shrugged. "Other people seem to think so."

"What kind of people?"

"None of your business, Outsider," said Miriam.

I considered her carefully, and she glared right back at me.

"If you don't believe in the supernatural," I said, "what do you believe in, that makes you want to run the Department?"

"Protecting people," said Miriam.

I nodded. It was a good answer.

"Maybe we can work together," I said. "Try to keep up."

"I was going to say the same to you," said Miriam.

We shared a smile, almost despite ourselves, and I turned to the second painting. The title card said simply "The Faerie War." Two huge armies of elves, going for each other's throats in an unknown setting. A living hell of inhuman fury and vicious carnage. You could almost hear the screams. Dadd's style was unmistakable, but this canvas was much bigger than his usual, some twenty feet in length and almost four feet high.

"Where did this come from?" I said, not looking away.

"It was only recently discovered, and donated to the Tate," said George.

"Like dropping a grenade in a fish pond," I said. I moved slowly down the length of the painting, trying to make sense of the staggering amount of detail crammed into one moment of battle. "How could Dadd have painted something this big without his keepers noticing?"

"He couldn't," George said flatly. "There must have been official collusion at some level."

Light and Dark elves slaughtered each other on a great volcanic plain, under a sky of roiling purple. The sun was a fierce white furnace. The Light elves leapt and pounced in their intricately carved bone armour, while the Dark elves were more like jungle cats, malicious and deadly in their armour of jade and coral. Swords and axes burned brightly as they rose and fell, while blood ran in rivers across the broken ground.

"That is not our world," I said finally. "The Fae had to go somewhere else to fight their war, because they knew it would tear the Earth apart."

"You think we're looking at something that actually happened?" said Miriam. "The one thing we can be sure of in this case is that Richard Dadd was barking mad!"

"Sometimes madness helps you see things more clearly," I said.

"I have sent for special equipment," said George. "So we can take a look at what's going on beneath the surface of the painting."

"If you think that will help," I said.

"Why wouldn't it?" said Miriam.

She sounded honestly interested, so I kept my voice calm and reasonable.

"Because science can only take you so far. After that you need people like me. Or possibly Weird Harald."

"Who the hell is Weird Harald?" said Miriam.

George made a quiet embarrassed noise. "A consultant, attached to the Department. Very good at learning secrets by the laying on of hands. Unfortunately, he can't turn it off. Which is why he spends so much of his time in a straitjacket, in the most secure mental institution we could find."

"How long before you could get him here?" I said.

George concentrated on the painting, so he wouldn't have to look at me. "Harald is currently doped to the eyeballs on industrial-strength mood-stabilisers, and chained to the wall of his cell. He was presented with something unusual from a prehistoric burial mound . . . and by the time they could drag him down, he'd killed thirty-seven people just by looking at them. We have exorcists working in eight-hour shifts, but it'll still be some time before we can make use of him again."

I just nodded. I'd heard worse. "And you think this painting is connected to the missing people . . . ?"

"The surveillance cameras are working everywhere else," said George. "That can't be a coincidence."

"Have you tried damaging the painting, to get a reaction?" I said.

"Don't you dare!" bellowed an outraged voice behind us. "You are talking about a newly discovered national treasure!"

I took my time looking round, and discovered two new figures hovering on the edge of the lamplight. I raised an eyebrow at George.

"I was wondering when they'd turn up again to annoy me," he said, not bothering to lower his voice. "Jack Daimon, meet Hugh Wittington and Amanda Fielding."

Hugh strode forward, doing his best to look like someone in charge. Amanda followed on behind, all smiles and good cheer. A tall, untidy scarecrow of a man, Hugh was fighting a losing battle with middle age, in a battered tweed jacket with leather patches on the elbows and a bow tie that was almost aggressively askew. He had a thin face, a heavy scowl, and floppy grey hair. The attitude was the real giveaway; a bureaucrat who wanted us to think he was an academic.

Amanda hit me with a wide smile, and I lost all interest in Hugh. Amanda looked to be in her mid twenties, with long blonde hair, a strikingly pretty face, and startlingly blue eyes. Only a little over five feet tall, her stylish Little Black Dress had been expertly cut to show off her figure to its best advantage, and her spiked stiletto heels beat out a rapid tattoo on the floor.

"Hi!" she said brightly. "What do you think of our new painting?"

"It does draw you in," I said.

"I discovered it," Amanda said proudly.

"Any chance you could put it back where you found it?" I said.

"This masterpiece is my responsibility!" Hugh said loudly.

I looked at him. "Good. We're going to need someone to carry the can for what's happened here."

George cleared his throat loudly, and then did it again until I looked at him.

"You should take something for that," I said. "It sounds painful."

"Mr. Wittington represents the Tate's Directors," said George, just a bit pointedly. "While Miss Fielding has specialist knowledge of Dadd's art."

"I acquired 'The Faerie War' for the Tate," said Hugh. "And I demand that I be included in all decisions regarding it."

George looked at him until he stopped talking. "If this painting really is responsible for the disappearance of twenty-two people, attaching your name to it might not be the wisest decision."

Hugh pouted like a sulky child, and scowled at Amanda. "I should never have let you talk me into displaying it."

"I didn't have to," she said sweetly. "You jumped at the chance to cover yourself in reflected glory."

"I refuse to believe that this important new acquisition has anything to do with today's unfortunate events," Hugh said loudly.

"You didn't even want the authorities called in," said Amanda.

"He actually tried to deny us entry," George murmured to me. "I had to let Miriam reason with him."

"She stuck a gun in my face!" said Hugh, very loudly.

Miriam surprised me then, with a mischievous smile. "Shouldn't have called me a soulless functionary."

"Not on a first date," I agreed.

Hugh stabbed a quivering finger at me. "I demand to know who this person is!"

"He's with me," said George.

"You wish," I said. I smiled at Amanda. She was very easy to smile at. "I'm something of an expert in these matters."

"Me too!" Amanda said happily. "I know all kinds of interesting things!"

"Good," I said. "Why don't you start with how you acquired this painting?"

Amanda shrugged. "Some builders restoring an old section of Broadmoor hospital found the canvas rolled up behind a false wall. One of them recognised Richard Dadd's style and got word to me, and I made arrangements for the painting to be brought here. Hugh was only too happy to organise the extensive publicity that brought so many people to the Tate today."

Hugh started to say something, caught George's eye, and thought better of it. Amanda carried on as though she hadn't noticed.

"We should have shut the whole building down the moment it became clear people were going missing, but Hugh dug his heels in. This was his big day, and he didn't want it ruined."

Hugh thrust both hands deep into his pockets and stared determinedly off into the distance. Miriam scowled at "The Faerie War."

"Share your expertise, Outsider. What are we dealing with here? Is the painting haunted, or possessed, or . . . ?"

"That is not the official position of the Tate!" Hugh said immediately, and then went back to sulking when everyone ignored him.

"It could be some kind of gateway," I said. "Dragging people in, so figures in the scene can get out."

"What are you talking about?" said Hugh, pulled back into the conversation despite himself. "I thought you were here to help!"

"We are," said George. "Now do pipe down, there's a good chap, or I'll let Miriam reason with you again. If you're not comfortable with the way we do things, feel free to go and make yourself useful somewhere else."

The veins stood out on Hugh's forehead, and he started to sputter something. Miriam pulled back her jacket to reveal a holstered gun, and Hugh subsided, but he didn't leave. Interestingly, Amanda didn't seem in the least impressed by Miriam or her gun. I filed that thought away, and nodded to Miriam.

"If some of the elves had escaped from their War and gone walkabout, someone would have noticed. And if people had been sucked into the painting to replace the elves, we'd see them in the scene."

"Then what is going on?" said Miriam.

"Creating a painting is like an invocation," I said. "Calling something into existence that wasn't there before. Sometimes the caller gets more than they bargained for. You'd be surprised what lurks in the background of some very famous paintings."

I started rummaging through my backpack.

"What are you looking for?" said Miriam. "Your magic wand?"

"It's in for repairs," I said. "Clutch kept slipping."

I took out my athame, and shrugged the pack back over my shoulder. My witch knife is two feet long with a leaf-shaped blade, and ancient sigils etched into the steel. Miriam frowned at the sigils as though she recognised them, and not in a good way.

I went right up to "The Faerie War" and moved slowly along the canvas, leaning in close so I could examine individual figures in the battle. Every face seemed unique, every death utterly real, as though the scene had been painted from life. When I finally reached the end of the canvas, I stepped back and considered the composition as a whole. Despite hundreds of elves caught up in the madness of the moment, there were still definite lines of sight built into the scene to guide the viewer's eye to the most significant figures and events.

"Well?" George said quietly, not wanting to break my concentration. "What do you see, Jack?"

"It's what I'm not seeing," I said. I pointed to one particular spot, right in the middle of the action. "There's a gap in the composition where something should be happening, but isn't."

Everyone pressed around me, trying to see what I saw. Amanda squeezed in so close I could smell her perfume, rich and earthy. Her arm pressed familiarly against mine. I didn't move away.

"I suppose that could be a gap," Hugh said finally. "But it's too small to be anything important."

"Big enough to get my hand in," I said.

"Don't you dare!" Hugh raised himself to his full height, the better to look down his nose at George. "I demand you order your man not to interfere with a national treasure!"

"Jack goes his own way," said George. "That's what he's here for."

"It's possible Dadd never completed the painting," said Miriam. "He didn't finish 'The Fairy Feller's Master Stroke.'"

"You can tell that's incomplete because the bottom is just bare canvas," I said. "'The Faerie War' goes right up to the edges. No, there's something very wrong about that gap . . . It feels like there is something there, but we're being prevented from seeing it."

Hugh frowned, trying to keep up. "Are you saying someone has altered this painting?"

"Yes," I said. "From the inside."

"What is this man talking about?" said Hugh, just a bit desperately.

"George," I said. "I need everyone out of here. And yes, that includes you and Miriam."

She bristled immediately. "Why do I have to leave?"

I nodded at the painting. "Because I'm about to punch a really dangerous thing, just to see what happens."

It took all of George's authority to get the others moving, and even then only as far as the edge of the lamplight. I called up my Sight, that lets me see the world as it really is, and focused on the gap in the action; suddenly a deep dark hole was falling away into the painting. I had to brace both hands on either side of the gap to keep from being pulled in. Somewhere at the bottom of the hole, I could hear people screaming. I forced my inner eye shut, and stepped quickly back.

"Jack?" said George. "What just happened?"

I gestured sharply for him to stay where he was, and took a moment before I answered, so I could be sure my voice would sound calm and assured. People really don't like it when the bomb disposal expert sounds worried.

"The missing people are trapped inside the painting. The gap must have pulled them in when they got too close."

"Then why didn't anyone notice?" said Miriam. "Whole crowds of people have filed through this area today."

"Whatever is hiding in the painting was powerful enough to shut down this area's surveillance systems, and turn off all the Tate's lights," I said. "I doubt it would have much trouble concealing the disappearance of a few people at a time."

"Do you have any idea what we're dealing with?" said Miriam. Her hand had dropped to the gun under her jacket.

"It's abducted twenty-two people," I said. "The only thing we can be sure of, is that it's a monster." I looked steadily at George. "I'll do everything I can to get them out, but if that turns out not to be possible, destroy the painting. Before whatever's in there becomes strong enough to force its way into our world."

Hugh's voice rose dangerously high. "You are talking about a priceless work of art! I will not stand for it being vandalised, just because of your lunatic delusions!"

He broke off as Miriam stuck her gun in his ribs. It was a pretty big gun. All the colour dropped out of Hugh's face, and his mouth snapped shut. Amanda looked like she wanted to applaud. George sighed quietly, and nodded to me.

"I can't get my people back from the Orkneys in time, so all I have is you. Don't let me down, Jack."

"You always did fight dirty," I said.

"Whatever works," said George.

I turned back to the painting. The elves were still busy slaughtering each other, with weapons far more dangerous than anything I had. Never mind what else was in there, hiding in plain sight and waiting to see what I would do. I smiled briefly. If being the Outsider was easy, everyone would be doing it. I opened my inner eye, and let the gap drag me in.

For a time there was nothing but darkness, and falling. Like jumping out of a plane without a parachute, or bungee-jumping without the rope. And then suddenly the fall was over. No warning and no impact; I was just standing somewhere, alone in the dark.

The athame's hilt pulsed in my hand like a living thing, and I focused my Sight through it. The steel blade shone fiercely, surrounding me with a pool of vivid azure light. And one by one people came stumbling forward out of the dark, their faces drawn and haggard. They blinked painfully at the new light, tears streaming down their cheeks. The circle of light quickly filled up with missing people, intact and unharmed. They all wanted to talk at once, and it took me a while before I could calm them down enough to get their story.

It seemed they had all moved in close to the new Dadd painting to admire the detail, and then the world disappeared, replaced by utter darkness. And even though they'd called out desperately, and sometimes thought they could hear other voices calling in return, they couldn't find anyone else. The only thing they could be sure of . . . was that there was something else in the dark, with them.

They had no idea how long they'd been gone. They thanked me endlessly, almost delirious with joy at the thought their ordeal was finally over. Which made it that much harder, when I had to tell them that it wasn't.

"I know a way out," I said. "But I can't take you with me. I have to leave you here, just for a while, so I can make arrangements to get all of you home."

The crowd fell silent, staring at me with huge eyes and quivering mouths like disappointed children.

"You'll be safe, as long as you stay in the light," I said quickly. "For now, I need you to form a human chain. Everyone take hold of someone else's hand and, whatever happens, don't let go."

They grabbed each other's hands and held on tightly, gazing at me trustingly. I knelt down and stabbed my athame into the ground, anchoring the circle of light so it would still be there after I was gone. There was some danger in that, because light in a place like this could attract all manner of things, but I couldn't leave them in the dark. That would have been cruel. I jerked the athame free, got to my feet and looked around.

"I'll send you a sign. You'll know it when you see it. And that's your way home."

"Please," said a young woman with fragile eyes. "Don't forget us."

"Never," I said. I showed them my most confident smile. "Hang in there, people. Because saving the day is what I do."

I cut into the darkness with my athame. Blazing blue light followed the blade, outlining a door, making it real and solid. I hit the door with my shoulder, and plunged through.

I staggered and almost fell as light filled my eyes, but George was quickly there to hold me up. Miriam hurried past us to keep a watchful eye on the painting, while Amanda looked anxiously into my face to make sure I was okay. I managed a smile for her. Hugh stayed at the edge of the lamplight, his eyes almost popping out of his head.

"You vanished!" he said loudly. "And then you reappeared again! That's not possible!"

"Congratulations," said George. "You have just taken your first step into a larger world."

Miriam made a seriously upset sound, and we all turned to look. Where the gap in the composition had been there was now just a patch of nothingness.

"What is that?" said Miriam.

"Something just raised the drawbridge," I said.

"What happened while you were inside the painting?" said George. "We couldn't see you anywhere."

"I wasn't in the battle," I said. "There was nothing but darkness, until I conjured up some light. But I did find the missing people."

"Were they all right?" said Amanda.

My legs were starting to feel steady again, so I nodded to George. He immediately let go of my arm.

"They're fine," I said. "Scared out of their minds, of course."

"Then why did you leave them in there?" said Miriam.

"The only exit I could make was one they couldn't use," I said. I gestured with my athame, before slipping it in my belt. "This only works for members of my family line."

"Then how are we supposed to get them out?" said Miriam.

"I have a plan," I said.

"Of course you do," said George.

I stood before "The Faerie War," trying to focus on the new gap. It kept trying to convince me it wasn't there; nothing to see, nobody home. I reached out until my fingertips touched the gap, and then pushed hard until they sank in past the surface of the painting. The gap tried to force me out, but I piled on the pressure until most of my arm had disappeared. And then another hand grabbed hold of mine, and I took a firm hold and pulled back as hard as I could.

First my arm and then my hand emerged from the painting, and then a man burst out of the canvas, followed by a second man hanging grimly onto his hand. I kept pulling with all my strength as I backed away, and one by one the human chain of missing people came flying out of the painting.

They piled up on the floor, sprawling all over each other, exhausted and shaking violently from their ordeal. Still holding hands, terrified to let go in case they might get pulled back into the darkness. They looked around them and then started to laugh breathlessly, clinging to each other like drowning people pulled from the sea. I checked quickly, to make sure all twenty-two had made it out, and then jerked my hand out of the first man's grasp, breaking the link. And then I hurried back to stand before the gap in the painting, witch blade at the ready. Just in case something tried to follow them out.

George, Miriam and Amanda helped the returned men and women to their feet, talking kindly and reassuringly. To his credit, even Hugh came forward to help. The rescued people seemed to be in their right minds, and considering everything they'd been through that was a triumph in itself, but it wouldn't be long before they started asking questions. I called quietly to George, and he came over to join me.

"Don't worry," he said. "I'll make sure they won't remember any of this. It's the kinder option."

"Get them out of here," I said quietly. "We still have work to do."

George went to the edge of the lamplight and called off into the gloom. Half a dozen uniforms quickly appeared, gaped at the returned people, and then snapped to attention when George raised his voice.

"Take them to the nearest hospital. No one is to question them about their experiences until my people arrive to take over. No media access, and watch the hospital staff; everyone's got a camera phone these days. Most importantly, none of these people are to leave the hospital until I say it's all right for them to go."

The security men nodded quickly, because everyone does when George starts giving orders in that tone of voice. They gathered up the returned men and women with professional kindness, and led them away.

"Mr. Wittington, Miss Fielding," said George. "Thank you for your assistance, but we can take it from here."

Hugh looked at him steadily. "I have no idea what just happened here, and I don't want to know. Just deal with this, whatever it is, and give me my gallery back."

He turned on his heel and stalked away. Amanda smiled at me.

"I'll go and make him a nice cup of tea. Very good for shock, tea. I assume someone will be along later, to provide some kind of explanation?"

"Somebody will definitely talk to you," said George.

Amanda shot me one last dazzling smile, and set off after Hugh. I turned back to "The Faerie War." George and Miriam moved in on either side of me.

"Whatever it is," I said, "it's still inside the painting. Watching, and waiting."

"Are you sure you can't get me in there?" said Miriam. "I could reason with it. I have lots of ammunition."

"My ways only work for me," I said. "Which is why I have to go back in and finish this."

George started to say something, but I cut him off.

"I know. Don't damage the national treasure."

I cut a door into the air between me and the painting. The

athame's blade glowed brightly as it sliced through the surface of the world.

"Oh, I want one of those!" said Miriam.

"Not on our budget," said George.

I kicked the door open and strode through, leaving the world behind.

The air was hot and humid, and the fierce white sun blazed in the alien sky as the Faerie War raged around me. Light and Dark elves howled their battle songs as they went to the slaughter like starving men to a feast. Winged elves swooped back and forth over the battleground, throwing themselves at each other like exotic fighting fish. Elves duelled with glowing longswords, or dismembered each other with weapons that shone too brightly for me to look at, but none of them came anywhere near me. Because this was their War; I wasn't a part of it.

Cut-off hands scuttled across the broken ground like pale spiders. Eyes rolled in severed heads, while the mouths shrieked silent threats. Headless bodies stumbled through the fighting, still striking out at everything within reach. Because elves don't die easily.

And then the Bad Thing appeared. Huge and vast, like a mountain walking, it towered so far up into the sky I couldn't even see the top of it. Horrid and malignant, its shape was so complex it was actually painful to human eyes. Some ancient god or devil, from a place where all the rules were different, it strode through the fighting armies as though they didn't exist. As though it was the only real thing in this world, and everything else was just ghosts and shadows.

It was coming straight for me, and I knew I didn't have anything in my pack that could hurt it or even slow it down, so I just turned and plunged back through the door I'd made. Back to the safety and sanity of my own world.

I staggered away from the painting, never taking my eyes off it. George and Miriam shouted questions at me, alarmed by the expression on my face. I raised a hand to stop them, and took a deep breath to calm myself.

"What happened?" said George. "You were only in there for a few moments. What did you see?"

"And why do you look like you're about to fill your trousers?" said Miriam.

"I don't know what I saw," I said. "It was like a mountain of flesh, vile and awful..."

"Okay," said Miriam. "Somebody needs a time out and a stiff drink."

"It's in the painting and it wants out!" I said sharply. "Something so big it could break our world just by walking on it!"

"Perhaps we should destroy the painting after all," said George. "The nation has enough treasures."

"We don't have the time!" I said.

"The only exit point is the gap we saw earlier," said Miriam. "It would have to shrink right down to get through something that small, and then I could just shoot it in the head." She stopped, and looked at me. "Does it have a head?"

"I don't know," I said. "I couldn't see up that high."

"If it's that big and powerful," said George, "why did it need to abduct all those people?"

"To forge a connection between its world and ours," I said.

"But we've taken the people back," said Miriam.

"The connection still exists," I said. "I reenforced it, when I made a door to get me into the painting."

A great force leapt out of the canvas and pulled me forward, slamming me up against the gap in the painting. I stabbed my athame into the canvas and clung to the hilt with both hands, anchoring myself, but the gap was steadily widening. The strength of the pull increased, and George and Miriam hit the painting on either side of me, equally helpless in the grip of that terrible gravity. I yelled for them to grab hold of my arms, and they both clung to me with desperate strength.

"What is it?" Miriam said loudly. "What's happening?"

"The Bad Thing is trying to drag us in!" I yelled. "So it can use us to get out!"

"Then do something!" said George.

The air howled as it rushed past us, drawn in by a gravitational force so strong nothing could resist it. Miriam drew her gun and emptied it into the gap, but the bullets didn't affect the pull at all. And then Amanda Fielding called my name, her voice rising above the shriek of disappearing air. I looked back, to see her clinging to a wall right on the edge of the lamplight.

"Use the painting against the painting!" she yelled.

"How?" I yelled back.

Amanda let go of the wall and allowed the terrible gravity to drag her forward. Her shoes screeched across the marble floor as she struggled to hold herself upright, and angle herself toward the right-hand end of the painting. When she finally slammed into it, she tore the end away from the wall and started rolling up the canvas, one foot at a time, moving steadily inwards. I saw what she was doing, and felt a rush of hope. God bless lateral thinking and all who sail in her.

I yelled to George and Miriam to let go of my arms and grab the athame. Once I was sure they had a firm grip on the hilt, I grabbed the top of the canvas and hauled my way along the painting. I had to fight the pull from the gap with all my strength, my muscles straining, but finally I reached the left-hand end. I yanked it away from the wall, rolled up the canvas, and moved steadily inwards.

Amanda and I closed up the painting like a giant scroll. The fierce gravity kept trying to drag us in, even as we closed in on the gap from both sides, and it began to disappear inside the growing scroll. I yelled for George and Miriam to let go of the athame, and the moment they did I yanked the knife out of the canvas, and Amanda and I forced the two rolled-up ends together.

The pull broke off, and just like that, it was over.

We all took a moment to lean on each other, and get our breathing back under control. Amanda grinned at me, and I grinned at her. The rolled-up painting stood on its end between us, harmless and quiet.

"Well," said George, looking down at his feet as though surprised to find they were holding onto the floor again. "That was interesting."

"Find a really big furnace," I said. "And feed this thing into it until there's nothing left but ashes. Then scatter the ashes in running water, just to be sure."

George smiled. "Hugh really isn't going to be happy."

"That's just a bonus," I said.

Miriam looked at Amanda. "How did you know what to do?"

Amanda shrugged. "The painting didn't pose a threat all the time it was behind that wall at Broadmoor. Rolling it up again just seemed the obvious way to go."

I presented the canvas to George, who accepted it with good grace.

"I'll take care of whatever clean-up may be necessary," he said.

I raised an eyebrow. "Are you trying to tell me I'm no longer needed?"

"For the moment," said George.

I met his gaze squarely. "Destroy the painting, George. Don't get clever, or ambitious. You didn't see what was in there."

"Do feel free to visit us at Department Headquarters," George said easily. "You'd be made very welcome, just like your father."

"I'm not my father," I said.

"More's the pity," said George.

He turned away to talk to Miriam, indicating that our conversation was at an end. Amanda tapped me lightly on the shoulder.

"Jack, I have seen some incredible things this evening... And I want to know more."

I smiled at her. "I could use a nice sit-down, and a whole bunch of drinks."

"I know a bar," she said demurely.

"Of course you do," I said. I looked at her thoughtfully. "Why did you come back?"

She grinned. "Because I hadn't seen enough."

"Hold it!" said Miriam. "You can leave, Outsider, but she's not going anywhere until I've had a chance to debrief her."

Amanda looked at me. "Does that mean what I think it means?"

"Almost certainly not," I said.

"Wouldn't make any difference," said Amanda. "I never wear any."

Miriam grabbed Amanda by the arm, and hauled her off to one side. I looked at George.

"Why was Miriam chosen to take over the Department?"

He shrugged. "She wanted the job enough to fight off all the other contenders. Which is usually a good sign. She'll spend the next few months shadowing me, and then I'm off to Cornwall to grow roses. Or possibly bees."

A raised voice caught our attention. Miriam was firing questions at Amanda, who was doing a lot of shrugging. I got the feeling that Amanda was prepared to go on shrugging until the cows came home and trampled all over Miriam.

"How do you feel about her taking over?" I asked George. "Do you think she's up to it?"

"No," said George. "But then neither was I, when they first dropped me in the deep end and threw a shark in after me. The Head of the Department is always going to be a political appointee, but the job has a way of making you its own."

"You say that like it's a good thing."

We realised it had suddenly gone quiet. Miriam had given up and had turned her back on Amanda so she could stare off into the gloom and sulk. Amanda smiled at me expectantly.

"Get out of here, Jack," said George. "Take that nice young lady for a drink. You're entitled to a life, outside your work."

"A life?" I said. "When have I ever had time for one of those?"

CHAPTER TWO
GETTING TO KNOW YOU.
GETTING TO KNOW ALL ABOUT YOU.

City girls always know the best bars. The White Rabbit turned out to be a pleasant little watering hole tucked away down a side street just a few minutes' stroll from the Tate. The hanging sign showed a humanoid white rabbit in a Victorian smoking jacket, complete with top hat and monocle. Amanda burst through the door like the hunter home from the hill, and people smiled and nodded as she breezed past them. I followed on behind and no one even glanced in my direction, which suited me well enough.

Amanda ordered a bottle of the house red and I paid for it, relieved she hadn't ordered some cocktail with a pornographic name. City girls have their ways, but I don't always have to like them. We settled ourselves comfortably in a booth at the rear of the bar, and toasted each other. I was pleased to see Amanda drink her wine with an honest thirst, none of that elegant sipping nonsense. She emptied her glass, and I emptied mine. Amanda hit me with her dazzling smile as I poured again, mischief dancing in her impossibly blue eyes.

"You didn't accept my invitation for a drink and a chat just because I'm easy on the eye, Jack."

"Not entirely," I said.

"I saw some amazing things this evening. And I'm not just talking about the painting; you were amazing too."

"You flatter me," I said.

"You saved all those people!"

"That's my job," I said.

"I want to know more, Jack. About you, and the kind of things that make someone like you necessary. Why did George call you the Outsider? Is it because you fight monsters from Outside?"

"Partly," I said. "But mostly because the life I lead keeps me outside of normal society. I can't talk about what I do, or why it's necessary, because the truth would only frighten people."

"You're talking to me," said Amanda.

"You're coping surprisingly well. After everything that happened at the Tate tonight, most people would have run away screaming."

"I'm not most people," said Amanda. "When I see something new and marvellous I run toward it."

I had to raise an eyebrow. "You think what happened tonight was marvellous?"

"Of course! It was like being handed a leading role in my very own big budget fantasy movie! Though I could have done with a stunt double at the end. I'm going to have some really colourful bruises tomorrow. If you're very good, I might let you see them."

"Something to look forward to," I said.

Amanda gave me an appraising look. "Do you really think George will destroy that painting?"

"No," I said. "His Department never gives up on anything they think might prove useful in the future."

"What use could they possibly have for a painting that eats people?"

"To eat something even more dangerous."

"You think that's likely?"

I shrugged. "My world isn't all marvels and wonders. Sometimes it's monsters and horrors."

"There are bound to be questions if 'The Faerie War' just disappears from the Tate," said Amanda. "Hugh put a lot of money into publicizing the new Richard Dadd masterpiece."

"Oh, 'The Faerie War' will be back on the wall in a week or so," I said. "Along with a plausible excuse for its absence. George's people are probably already hard at work producing a convincing copy. They've done it before, with other works of art too dangerous to be allowed out in public."

"Really?" said Amanda, widening her eyes and smiling bewitchingly. "What other paintings?"

"Sorry," I said, refusing to be bewitched. "Not all my secrets are mine to tell."

Amanda shrugged. "How did you get to be the Outsider? Did you have to attend a school with a sorting hat, or draw a sword from a stone?"

"Are you sure you're not a reporter?" I said. "I'm really not looking for publicity."

"I'm just interested in you," said Amanda.

"That covers a lot of ground," I said.

"I can believe six impossible things before breakfast and still not lose my appetite," Amanda said happily.

"I can believe that," I said. "If I tell you all about me, will you tell me all about you?"

"Of course not!" Amanda said brightly. "But I will tell you just enough to keep you fascinated. So, how did you become the Outsider?"

"It's all about duty," I said. "There has always been an Outsider in my family."

Amanda cocked her head to one side. "Like your father? I heard George mention him. What kind of a man was he?"

"Hard-working. We didn't see much of him, while I was growing up."

"Did you inherit the position as eldest son?"

"No," I said. "I inherited the Sight, that allows me to See all the hidden mysteries of the world. Ghosts from the past, solutions to present problems, and warnings of bad things to come. Only one person in each generation has the Sight, and they get the job. Whether they want it or not."

"And you didn't want it?"

"I saw what the job did to my father, and my family. And yet, here I am."

"You're being very open, Jack," said Amanda, smiling easily. "I was worried I'd have to get you drunk first, but you've barely touched that second glass."

"And you've barely touched yours," I said. "I notice things like that."

"Really?" Amanda said lightly. "Why would you need to?"

"Because I always have to be on my guard. There are people who don't approve of what I do."

"But you're humanity's protector! Who could object to that?"

"Treasure hunters, seekers after forbidden knowledge, and people dumb enough to serve forces from Outside. If they could only See what they're worshipping, they'd throw up in their souls."

Amanda nodded slowly. "So . . . you've always been alone? There's never been anyone special in your life?"

"I decided a long time ago that I wouldn't inflict my life on anyone I actually cared about."

"But . . . that's so sad!"

"That's my life."

"What about your family?"

"I'm good to my family. I don't go home much." I smiled, to take the sting out of the old joke. "I don't want them to see how much the job has changed me."

"They coped with your father's absences . . ."

"No, they didn't," I said. "Change the subject."

"Tell me more about the unexploded supernatural bombs," said Amanda.

I launched into one of my prepared speeches, for when I have to explain myself to local authority figures who didn't get the memo.

"History isn't what most people think it is. Our view of the past is always changing, as new facts and interpretations come to light. But there's more to it than that. History is like a palimpsest, one of those old manuscripts where the original text was erased and a new one written on top. Sometimes parts of the original text show through, stubborn remnants from a forgotten era. Our entire existence was overwritten, so that the original history of magic and monsters could be replaced with a sane and rational world."

"And you think that was a good thing?" said Amanda. "Replacing magic with science?"

"Of course! Magic is crazy and unpredictable, and most people have no defence against it."

"Like the thing that got into the painting?" said Amanda. She was leaning forward again, staring at me intensely.

"There are forces in the universe that want humanity dead and gone," I said carefully. "And they're always searching for a weakness in the walls of the world."

Amanda just nodded. Which was interesting.

"You haven't explained what these supernatural bombs are, exactly."

"Flotsam and jetsam from the way things used to be, washed up on the shores of the present. Supernatural land mines from forgotten wars, still waiting for a chance to do their worst long after their original purpose became meaningless. It's my job to make them safe."

"I thought you said magic was lost when history was rewritten?"

"Remember the palimpsest," I said. "Some things just won't go away."

Amanda smiled brightly, trying to dispel my gloom with the sunshine of her gaze.

"Isn't there any fun in your job?"

I smiled back at her, in spite of myself. "I do enjoy making the world a little bit safer every day. Taking care of all the things that pose a threat."

"By killing them?" said Amanda.

"They're monsters," I said. "They'd kill us all, if they could."

"Do you ever wonder whether they see you as the monster?"

"If the things from Outside would leave us alone, I'd be happy to leave them alone," I said. "I like to think of myself as a man who keeps the world safe, not an executioner."

"Of course you do," said Amanda. "You have a good heart."

I toasted her with my glass. "You really are very easy to talk to."

"You're very easy to listen to," said Amanda. "How did you start out, as the Outsider? What was your very first mission?"

"My Sight kicked in when I was eighteen," I said. "No warning: my inner eye just slammed all the way open and showed me the world as it really is. Which came as something of a shock. But I didn't want to be the next Outsider. I'd seen what the job did to my father and my family. But then my father died, trying to defuse a bomb that was too much for him. And I decided that while I didn't give a damn about being the Outsider, I did want to avenge my father's death."

"I thought you didn't care much for him?"

"I didn't. But he was still my father. Afterwards . . . I couldn't put the burden down. These things were killing people, and their victims were always going to be someone's father, someone's son."

I took a long drink. So did Amanda. I was telling her things I'd never told anyone else because I thought she, of all people, would understand.

"What happened when you took on your father's last case?" Amanda said finally.

"The trouble with supernatural bombs is that they can explode over and over again until someone shuts them down. This one was a puzzle box, with more than three dimensions. It tried to talk to me, forcing strange buzzing words inside my head, and then it tried to kill me the same way it killed my father. By pulling me inside it and crushing me down to nothing. But I'd already anchored myself with the athame."

"That thing does come in handy," said Amanda.

"Oh, it does. You have no idea."

"Why did the box try to talk to you?"

"A test. If I couldn't understand it, that meant I didn't belong to the people who made it, so I must be the enemy."

"How did you destroy it?"

"Pounded it to pieces with a hammer," I said. "It isn't always about magical knives, or devious thinking. And it did feel good, to hear it scream."

Amanda nodded slowly. "So . . . how much penance do you have to do, before you can believe your father would forgive you for letting him die?"

"Of course he'd forgive me," I said. "He was my father. I don't forgive me."

"That doesn't even make sense," said Amanda.

"I know," I said. "But it doesn't change how I feel."

Amanda sat back in her chair, and considered me thoughtfully. "You're being very open with me, Jack. Even allowing for my obvious charms, I can't believe you found it easy to bare your soul."

"You're not like everyone else," I said. "You're different."

"That's sweet."

"Not really," I said. "I can tell you these things because you already know most of them. Because you're not human."

All through the bar conversations went on around us, a multitude of cheerful voices rising and falling, unaware that something magical was taking her ease among them. I sat back in my chair and smiled at Amanda. I was pretty sure I could stop her if she bolted for the door, but I didn't think that was going to happen. Amanda had gone to a lot of trouble to set up this meeting. She smiled easily at me, her eyes sparkling.

"What makes you think I'm not human, Jack? Don't I look human?"

"I have the Sight, remember? All living things have . . . let's call it an aura. But not you. Which can only mean you're hiding the truth from me. So, Amanda Fielding, what are you, really? I've never met anyone like you before."

"I'll bet you say that to all the enigmas."

"I notice you're not denying any of this," I said.

Amanda laughed softly. "What would be the point? I put on a pleasing face and came to London specifically to make myself known to you. Because there's something very important that needs doing; I can't do it without your help."

I looked at her steadily. "Did you arrange what happened tonight?"

"I may have pointed a few people in the right direction, so that 'The Faerie War' would end up on display at the Tate."

"You put people's lives in danger!"

She didn't flinch at the anger in my voice. "I knew you'd save them. If you were the kind of man I needed you to be."

"What if you were wrong?"

"George would have coped. Or Miriam."

"You haven't answered my question," I said. "What are you?"

"You're not ready for that," she said calmly.

"Then what can you tell me?"

"That we're both in unknown territory, so we have to go slowly to make sure we don't lose our way." She grinned cheerfully. "You're not going to kill me, are you, for the crime of not being human? That would be a hell of an end to our first date."

"You're not a monster," I said. "Are you?"

"Not as such."

"Why did you go to such lengths to arrange this little get-together, Amanda?"

"You said it yourself, Jack. History has been rewritten. Did you never wonder what could possibly justify such a change?"

"I've thought about it. I even asked George, but no one in his Department has any idea. Do you know why?"

"Think of it this way," Amanda said carefully. "What if everything, from the very beginning of the world right up to its end, was one big Story . . . a Story so wonderful, and with such a glorious ending, that everyone would be able to look back at their lives and say, Everything we endured was worth it, to get here. But after magic was taken away the Story was compromised, derailed from its original purpose. Humanity has been crippled . . . prevented from becoming everything it should have been."

"What does this have to do with me?" I said bluntly.

Her smile disappeared, as she held my gaze with hers.

"We are approaching the point of no return. Our last chance to restore history to its original path, bring back magic, and save the Story."

I took a slow drink from my glass, to give me time to think.

"A Story . . ." I said. "That implies a Storyteller."

"Let's start by wading into the shallows," said Amanda. "Before we head out to where the sharks are."

"But you do know who's responsible for the Story?"

"We've met," said Amanda. "For now, just try to accept that magic doesn't have to be the enemy."

"Every magical creature I've encountered has been a danger to humanity."

"If you approach something as a threat, that's how it's going to react."

I remembered the Light and Dark elves in the painting, driven to destroy each other by a rage and a hatred that didn't allow any room for understanding.

"Let's stick to the basics," I said. "Why are you so reluctant to reveal your true nature?"

"Because I don't want to scare you."

I had to smile. "I don't do scared."

"I know," said Amanda.

Something in the way she said put a chill in my heart.

"You want me to just trust you blindly?"

"Yes," said Amanda.

"Not going to happen."

"I am placing my life in the hands of someone who's spent his life destroying things like me," she said steadily. "I'm ready to take a leap of faith; why can't you?"

I wanted to believe she was sincere. If only because it felt so good not to be alone, for once. I nodded slowly.

"What is it you want me to do?"

"Help me bring back the unicorns and the dragons, the elves and the giants: all the myths and legends and fairy tales that people still cling to. Because they've never given up on them."

"You want to turn the clock back to when armies of peasants worked the land from dawn to dusk? Living short, hard, miserable lives, so the rich and entitled could wallow in luxury?"

"No," said Amanda. "That's how history is now, after the rewriting. Think about it, Jack. If you could grow a thousand-foot beanstalk from a few magic beans, why would you need peasants to raise crops? If a hen can lay golden eggs and a maiden can spin gold out of straw, who can be poor? If everyone could find their heart's desire at the foot of a rainbow, who would be unhappy? In the magical world everyone can have their dreams come true. It's time to bring colour back to this grim grey existence."

She could see I was moved but not convinced, so she changed tactics. She clasped her hands together on the tabletop, and fixed me with an earnest look.

"You don't have to commit yourself right now. Just help me get to the truth about why history was rewritten, and then decide whether the change was a good thing."

I nodded slowly. "That does sound like something I ought to know. Where do you suggest we start?"

"With the Department For Uncanny Inquiries," said Amanda. "They have the biggest library I know of."

"It is supposed to be pretty impressive," I said. "My father always thought of it as his second home. Which was a bit much, considering how little time he spent at his real home."

"Is that why you've never wanted to visit the Department's headquarters?" said Amanda.

"Partly," I said. "But mostly I just didn't want to end up working for George. The Department is a government office, so it tends to worry more about what's politically expedient rather than what needs doing. I'm pretty sure that's why George is so keen to have an Outsider on his team. To be his conscience . . . or his scapegoat, if things go wrong."

"We need to access the library," said Amanda. "It contains knowledge and secrets even the Department doesn't know it has."

I raised an eyebrow. "And you know that how?"

She just grinned.

"George isn't going to let us just help ourselves to whatever books take our fancy," I said.

"But you're the Outsider," Amanda said sweetly. "He wants you under the Department's wing. He'll be only too happy to use the library as bait, to lure you in."

"You're forgetting Miriam," I said. "She's on track to be the next Head of the Department, and she doesn't give a damn about the Outsider."

"Then you'll just have to distract her, while I search the library."

"Me?"

"Of course," said Amanda. "Miriam likes you."

"No, she doesn't!"

"Men never notice anything," said Amanda. "She was flirting with you all the time we were at the Tate!"

"You call that flirting?"

"What would you call it?"

"Intimidation and death threats!"

"She was just trying to impress you."

And then we both looked up as a shadow fell across our table. A tall, unnaturally thin figure was looming over us. His dark suit was defiantly old-fashioned and disturbingly dusty, as though it had been kept in storage for a really long time. Something about the man suggested he might have been too. His face was inhumanly gaunt, the colourless skin stretched taut like ancient parchment. His eyes were deep set and unblinking, and his smile showed more teeth than humour. He was a figure of menace, and he gloried in it.

No one else in the bar paid him any attention. He knew how to move unnoticed in the world.

"This is one of the legendary Men In Black," I said to Amanda.

"Don't look impressed, he'll only give himself airs. He's really nothing more than a glorified messenger boy. What name are you using this week, Man In An Ill-fitting Suit?"

"Call me Mr. Slender," he said, in a harsh grating voice designed to alarm and intimidate.

"You haven't gone back to those Slender Man sites, have you? They are so last decade."

He bent almost in two as he sat down with us. His joints made loud creaking noises, as though only operating under protest. I've never been sure whether the Men In Black are recruited or constructed. Or possibly just grown in oversized flower pots, with plenty of manure. Mr. Slender nodded to Amanda, and she nodded back.

"You two know each other?" I said.

"We move in the same circles," said Amanda.

"There is such a thing as too much mystery in a woman," I said. I fixed Mr. Slender with my best hard stare. "Why are you here, Spooky Boy?"

"You were never supposed to meet her," said Mr. Slender. "I have been sent to instruct both of you to go your separate ways. And you, Outsider, are forbidden to interfere with the way things are."

"Or?" I said.

He fixed me with his unblinking gaze. "Or, there will be consequences. Don't meddle in things beyond your comprehension, Outsider. Just do what you were designed to do."

I looked at him sharply. "What do you mean, designed?"

"Did you never wonder why the world needs an Outsider?" said Amanda. She wasn't smiling any more. "After history was rewritten, those responsible decided they needed a janitor. To clear up the mess they'd left behind."

Mr. Slender ignored her, his cold gaze locked on mine. "You are not to listen to her, Outsider. She is dangerous."

"She must be," I said. "You've never been dumb enough to threaten me before. Do you know what she really is?"

"No, he doesn't," said Amanda. "He only thinks he does."

"Who is sending me this message?" I said to the Man In Black.

"No one you'd know," said Mr. Slender. "And no one you need to know. Just do as you're told."

"Really not going to happen," I said.

Mr. Slender's smile stretched unnaturally wide, revealing a hell of a lot of pointed teeth. "Perhaps I should break a few of your bones... make you scream. Just to underline the serious nature of my instructions."

"I think it's time you were leaving, Slender Boy," I said calmly. "Because if you don't, I will open my inner eye and See exactly who and what you are, and what it would take to unmake you."

The Man In Black rose jerkily to his feet, turned stiffly, and strode out of the bar. I kept a watchful eye on him all the way to the door, and then turned back to Amanda. She was looking at me thoughtfully.

"Were you bluffing, Jack?"

"I'll never tell. But you should be grateful. That messenger boy with delusions of thuggery convinced me where you couldn't. If someone doesn't want me to know something that badly, I'm pretty sure I want to know what it is. So let us go visit George, and ransack his amazing library."

Amanda smiled at me dazzlingly. "Let's."

CHAPTER THREE
YOU'D BE AMAZED
WHAT YOU CAN FIND IN A LIBRARY.
OR WHAT CAN FIND YOU.

When we left the White Rabbit I half expected to find some kind of supernatural Uber waiting for us, but instead the moment I stepped outside I found myself facing rows of bookshelves retreating into the distance for just that little bit further than my mind could comfortably cope with. I glanced behind me and the door to the bar was gone, replaced by yet more bookshelves. I turned to Amanda.

"This is the Department's library?"

"Yes! Isn't it fabulous?"

"How did we get here?"

She smiled winningly. "I know all the short cuts."

I shook my head. "So we are now trespassing inside the most secret and heavily guarded Library in the known universe. I can't help feeling we should have at least tried knocking on the front door. I do have an invitation."

"I don't," said Amanda. "And places like this can get very stuffy when it comes to plus ones. You're not scared of the Department, are you?"

"I don't get scared," I said. "I'm the scary one."

"Hang on to that attitude. It'll come in very handy, some of the places we're going."

I gave the bookshelves my full attention. Some of the stacks looked tall enough to give experienced mountain climbers nosebleeds, their topmost shelves leaning so far out they actually met over our heads.

39

Narrow passageways went darting off between the stacks as though they couldn't wait to take us somewhere interesting, but there didn't seem to be any signs or directions, let alone a map with a helpful *You are here*. The library was like a massive hedge maze, designed by someone with a vicious grudge against the kind of people who used mazes. Every shelf was packed with books ancient and modern, and I was hard-pressed to see how some of them stayed in place given how far out their shelves jutted.

"Well?" said Amanda. "What do you think?"

"I think this is where books go after they die, if they've been good."

"You can find the answers to any question you can think of here. Though of course there's no guarantee you'll like the answers."

I peered around me, straining my eyes against the gloom filling the gaps between the stacks.

"Where is everyone? Places aren't normally this empty without a really good reason."

"This is the last great repository of dangerous and suppressed secrets," Amanda said calmly. "Books so extreme they don't need guarding, because they can look after themselves."

"But how are we supposed to find what we're looking for?"

"Just concentrate on what you need, and the right book will make itself known to you," said Amanda. "In fact, the more aggressive or affectionate volumes will actually jump off the shelves and come looking for you. Some of them take rejection very badly, so don't let your thoughts wander. Unless you want to end up with some unexpurgated volume humping your leg."

I looked at her. "Please tell me you're being metaphorical."

"Not even a little bit."

"You are really not selling this to me."

"We're where we need to be, Jack."

There comes a point when you just know asking questions isn't going to get you anywhere, and all that's left is to jump in with both feet. I approached the nearest bookshelf and studied some of the titles. *Immortality On Two Farthings A Day. How To Get The Best Price For Your Soul Or Someone Else's. Where All The Missing People Are.*

Amanda looked at me kindly. "That is a serious frown, Jack. What's the matter?"

"I had no idea so many magical books still existed," I said. "Why didn't George tell me?"

"Why do you think he kept pressing you to come and visit?" said Amanda.

All the alarm bells in the world suddenly started ringing, loud enough to wake the dead and the recently embalmed. I started to raise my hands to my ears, but the deafening racket stopped as suddenly as it began.

"That's better," I said, and then caught the look on Amanda's face. "Isn't it?"

"They'd only shut down the alarms that quickly if security already had a lock on us," she said. "Which means a whole bunch of heavily armed guards are currently speeding in our direction. Almost certainly not in a calm or forgiving mood."

I glared at her. "We are going to get shot to death and buried in unmarked graves and it is all your fault!"

She shrugged. "So much is."

Two huge bookshelves swung back as though they were weightless, and a dozen security guards came charging through the gap. They were all wearing long black scholars' robes complete with mortar boards, and carrying seriously impressive automatic weapons. I put my hands in the air to show I wasn't a threat, and all the guards opened fire. Amanda thrust out a hand, and every single bullet slammed to a halt in mid-air. The cloud of expended ammunition hung in place for a moment, as though embarrassed, and then dropped to clatter quietly on the polished wooden floor.

The guards looked at the fallen bullets, and then at each other. I grabbed Amanda by the arm and hauled her out of sight between the nearest stacks.

"They just opened fire on us!" I said.

"I know, Jack. I was standing right there when it happened."

"But I had my hands in the air! They never even gave us a chance to explain!"

"They're not paid to listen," said Amanda. "All that matters to them is: we shouldn't be here."

I held onto my calm with both hands. "I just saw you stop bullets in mid-air."

"Are you complaining?"

"You did magic!" I said. "Real magic!"

"Of course. I'm magical."

"Well," I said. "I wouldn't argue with that."

"You are such a sweetie, Jack."

"So," I said. "You're a witch?"

"Oh please, nothing so vulgar."

"Then what are you, really?"

"The guards will be coming in after us the moment they've reloaded," said Amanda. "Don't you think we should be concentrating on the deadly danger at hand?"

I growled under my breath, rummaged quickly through my backpack, and finally brought out an old bone amulet on a cord fashioned from plaited human hair. I slipped it round my neck and smiled despite myself. I was back in the game. Another quick rummage turned up two pairs of brass knuckle-dusters: one blessed and one cursed. I slipped them on, and nodded to Amanda.

"You stay put, while I go teach those wolves in lecturers' robes the error of their ways."

She looked at me sternly. "I do not need looking after."

"But I can't concentrate properly on handing out beatings if I'm worrying about you getting hurt."

"Testosterone," she said sadly. "It's such a curse."

"I have to do this," I said. "I can't allow myself to be killed by just anyone. I have my reputation to think of."

"Oh well," said Amanda. "As long as there's a rational explanation for running head on at a dozen heavily armed security guards..." She stopped, and looked thoughtfully at the bone amulet hanging over my heart. "What is that thing? It feels seriously old, but I don't recognise the markings."

"It makes other people see me where I'm not."

"Oh. One of those. Does it work on bullets as well as people?"

"It works on the people firing the bullets."

"Oh, go on, then," said Amanda. "Have your fun, but don't take too long. We have a lot to do."

I stepped out of the stacks and into the open; immediately all the guards raised their weapons and opened fire again. Bullets flew past me on either side, but didn't even come close. The guards couldn't hit me because I wasn't where they were aiming. I showed the guards my most confident grin, the one that really upsets people, and charged straight at them.

I was in and among the guards before they had time to react, and they had to stop firing for fear of shooting each other. They lashed out with their gun butts, but I was never where they thought I was. Fists sailed harmlessly past my head as I moved among the guards, lashing out with my knuckle-dusters. Blood spurted from a man's nose as it broke, but I was already turning away to hit another guard in the side of the head, and slam a punch in under a third man's sternum. Guards went crashing to the floor, one after another; none of them got anywhere near me.

I put the hard word on the last man standing with a little extra vim and vigour, and he measured his length on the floor with a satisfyingly loud thud. I lowered my armoured hands, took a few deep breaths, and surveyed my fallen enemies. They never stood a chance, but I couldn't find it in my heart to feel sorry for them. They shouldn't have fired on someone with their hands in the air.

And that was when a whole new crowd of security guards came charging through the gap in the bookshelves, gowns flapping and guns at the ready. I wasted a moment thinking *This really isn't fair*, and then I went to meet them with my knuckle-dusters raised. The odds were really not good, but I needed to keep their attention fixed on me, and not Amanda.

A small part of me was quietly asking *Are you really ready to die for her?* And the answer came back *Hell, yeah.*

"Lower those guns and stand down!" said a loud and thankfully familiar voice. "That's an order!"

The guards stumbled to a halt and lowered their guns as George came striding through their ranks. They avoided his gaze like children who'd been caught doing something they knew they shouldn't, while George took in the semiconscious bodies lying scattered across the floor and allowed his mouth to twitch in a brief smile. He nodded to me, and then glared at the guards.

"This is the current Outsider. He is here at my express invitation."

"He didn't enter the library in the approved manner," muttered one of the guards. "We only discovered the intruders were in here when one of the books informed on them for talking too loudly."

"I am aware of your failure to pay proper attention," said George.

"We will be discussing that later in great detail and you are not going to enjoy it at all." He turned his back on the guards and looked at me reproachfully. "I am pleased to see you, Jack, but the front door is there for a reason."

"I don't like to be predictable," I said. "And I hope you don't mind, but I brought a friend."

Amanda emerged from the stacks, smiling demurely, and slipped her arm through mine. George nodded politely.

"Good to see you again, Miss Fielding."

"Call me Amanda," she said brightly.

Some of the fallen guards were starting to get to their feet, and making really hard going of it. George glared at the second batch.

"Assist your fallen comrades, and then return to your posts. And check the defensive perimeters are still intact! It's always possible someone else could have sneaked in here while you were distracted."

It took the guards a while to get everyone on their feet and moving, accompanied by groans and whimpers and not a little bad language, but eventually they disappeared back through the slowly closing stacks. The last one hurried around gathering up fallen mortar boards, while carefully avoiding our eyes, and then scuttled out after the others. I nodded to George.

"You've got them very well trained."

"Yes," said George. "But unfortunately, training isn't everything."

"Can I just ask: why the black gowns and silly hats?"

"Tradition, Jack. When an institution has been around as long as the Department, it can't help but accumulate a whole raft of weird customs. You wouldn't believe what I have to go through at the changing of the guard."

I shook some blood off my knuckle-dusters, and dropped them into my pockets. Just in case I might need them again.

"Sorry if I damaged some of your people."

"Good experience for them," George said briskly. "For when they have to fight a real enemy."

I put my hand to the amulet on my chest, and concentrated on the disabling words. It turned back into a piece of old bone, and George made a relieved sound.

"Thank you. Damned thing was giving me a headache."

"It saved my life when your guards opened fire on me, after I surrendered!" I said loudly. "Is that standard procedure here?"

"Pretty much," said George. "But I am glad to see you here, Jack. Can I ask what finally persuaded you?"

"I've been trying to explain my life to Amanda," I said. "And it seems I don't know nearly as much about my job as I should. I thought I might find some answers here. If you have no objections..."

"Don't give it another thought," said George. "We have books on every subject under the sun, and some that can only be read in the dark."

He turned his professional smile on Amanda, and she smiled dazzlingly back. George nodded, acknowledging that he'd been out-smiled.

"Tell me, Jack. Why did you bring this charming young lady to such a highly restricted location?"

"Because she's with me," I said.

"Ah..." said George. "So this is like bringing a new girlfriend home to meet the family?"

"Not really, no," I said.

Amanda hugged my arm, and beamed happily at George. "We're still in the getting-to-know-you phase of our relationship."

George met her gaze steadily. "Miriam and I did wonder why you disappeared from the Tate in such a hurry."

"I'm not big on answering questions," said Amanda.

"I can vouch for that," I said.

George shrugged. "She can stay. As long as she doesn't touch anything."

"Never on a first date," said Amanda.

"Now, Jack," said George. "If you'll just tell me the kind of books you're interested in..."

I looked around. "I don't suppose this is a lending library?"

"Hardly," said George. "Removing any book is strictly and violently forbidden. Though you couldn't drive some of them out the door with an electric cattle prod. They know when they're on to a good thing." He smiled at the look on my face. "Fill a book with really weird information, and you shouldn't be surprised when you end up with a really weird book. Some of the older volumes contain so much esoteric knowledge you can hold conversations with them. While others are so paranoid about sharing what they know we have to pry the covers open with a crowbar."

"I thought magic had gone out of the world," I said. "Why didn't you tell me there was so much weird stuff left, George?"

He didn't look apologetic, because that wasn't his way. "I have been inviting you here for some time, Jack."

"We're supposed to be living in a world of science," I said accusingly.

"You'll have to ask Miriam about that," said George. "She's the scholar. Though I should warn you she'll undoubtedly use words like *quantum*, and *experimenter's intent*, until you're ready to accept anything as long as she'll just stop talking at you. Basically . . . some things still insist on being real, despite every argument that they shouldn't."

"These books are the last of their kind," said Amanda. "And you keep them locked up in a zoo for people to stare at."

"Because they're too dangerous to be allowed out in the world," said George.

"Even though they're in danger of becoming extinct?" said Amanda.

"Better them than us," said George. "Especially when some of them will keep trying to escape."

"Knowledge wants to be free," said Amanda.

I cleared my throat loudly, to remind them I was still there. George gestured expansively at the rows of shelves.

"It's all yours, Jack, but I will need some kind of reference point before I can advise you where to start looking. People have been known to venture into the stacks and not come out again. We have to send in search parties."

"We're interested in the history of the Outsider," said Amanda. "And why people stopped believing in magic, in favour of science."

"If only they had," said Miriam.

The next Head of the Department came striding out of the stacks, and glared at me challengingly.

"How did you get in, Outsider?"

"I was invited," I said mildly.

"And what's she doing here?" said Miriam, indicating Amanda with a quick flick of the hand so she could keep on glaring at me.

"Thought I might need a bodyguard," I said.

Miriam smiled. "Yes . . . She looks like she could be scary, in the right light."

"What can we do for you, Miriam?" I said.

"I've just been talking to the security guards."

"As if they hadn't suffered enough," murmured George.

Miriam looked at him. "What?"

"Nothing," said George. "Do continue."

Miriam went back to scowling at me. "How did you get past our defences?"

"I'm the Outsider," I said. "Impossible is what I do before I get out of bed in the morning. Now what were you saying, about people believing in magic?"

"They always have," Miriam said flatly. "Despite every attempt to educate them. Think how far civilisation might have advanced, if it hadn't had to waste so much time battling ignorance and superstition."

"You know magic is real," I said. "You saw it in action, at the Tate."

"That was just a pocket dimension, trapped inside a psychically charged image!" Miriam said loudly.

"Told you," said George.

"What are you muttering about?" said Miriam.

"Nothing," said George. "Carry on explaining things. You do it so well."

Miriam turned back to me. "How were you able to take down so many of our armed guards?"

"I'm the Outsider," I said calmly. "I eat scarier things than them for brunch."

Miriam smiled suddenly. "Good for you. I like a man who sticks up for himself."

She walked right up to me, and it was all I could do to stand my ground. It felt like being approached by an attack dog that had unexpectedly started wagging its tail.

"You were very impressive at the Tate, Jack. Did you go to all this trouble to break in, because you knew I'd be here?"

"I just need to do some research," I said.

Miriam leaned in close. "When you're done, see me afterwards." She stepped back, and was immediately all business again. "Good thing you waited for me, before you went into the stacks. Some of those books would eat you alive."

I looked at George. "Is she joking?"

"Hardly ever, in my experience," said George. "I find it helps to think of the library as a jungle full of predators."

"Speaking of which," I said, "before I came here I received a visit from a Man In Black."

"Nothing to do with me," he said immediately. "They answer to a different authority."

"Anyone I might have heard of?"

George didn't quite glance at Amanda. "Not in front of the civilians, Jack. Did you happen to recognise this particular Man In Black?"

"We worked together in the past," I said. "He's calling himself Mr. Slender these days."

"The horror, the horror," George said solemnly.

"I know," I said. "Some online sites should come with a mental health warning."

"What do you have in common with the Men In Black?" said Miriam.

I shrugged. "Sometimes they know things, about the bombs I have to defuse." I looked coldly at George. "And sometimes they just turn up out of nowhere to intimidate witnesses and make sure they won't say anything."

"There are times when that's part of the job," George said calmly.

"That attitude is what's kept me out of the Department," I said.

"You worked with this Mr. Slender?" said Miriam.

"He was assigned to me, when I first became the Outsider. To show me the ropes, and teach me how to move unnoticed through the world. Can't say I ever warmed to him. Men In Black weren't designed to have people personalities."

Miriam nodded slowly. "So they are artificial. I did hear rumours..."

"What business did Mr. Slender have with you?" said George.

"He wanted me to stop asking questions."

George frowned. "About what?"

"Anything and everything. Apparently I'm supposed to just do my job and keep my mouth shut." I smiled. "He should have known that was never going to fly."

"Couldn't agree more," George said briskly. "Can't have those jumped-up messenger boys getting above themselves. You name the book or the subject, Jack, and we'll find it for you."

"Hold it right there," said Miriam, turning her glare on George. "You're allowing him unrestricted access, on his first visit?"

"If that's what it takes, to bring the Outsider into the fold," said George.

Amanda surreptitiously squeezed my arm. I nodded apologetically to George and Miriam, and moved Amanda off to one side so we could talk quietly.

"We can't allow ourselves to be distracted," she said sternly. "We need to identify which parts of magical history led to the rewriting."

"Let me have a quiet word with George," I said.

"Make it quick," said Amanda. "Miriam is getting suspicious."

"I'm pretty sure she was born that way," I said. "Probably came out of the womb interrogating the midwife about her qualifications."

I went back to George and indicated that we needed to talk privately. Miriam glowered at both of us as we moved away, annoyed at being left out. I told George what I was looking for and he nodded immediately.

"You mean historical anomalies . . . what they used to call damned data: events that refuse to fit into the accepted scheme of things. Why are you interested in things like that?"

"I'm not, really," I said confidentially. "But Amanda is, and I'm trying to make a good impression."

When in doubt, muddy the waters. George loved the idea, and did everything short of wink at me roguishly.

"Of course, Jack. Let me see . . . We have a whole section on Cryptids: strange and unusual creatures that science and evolution can't account for. Or there's Timeslips: places where the past manifests so strongly you can walk around in it. But I think your best bet is going to be Superimpositions, where the way things were can still sometimes overwhelm our reality. The past, haunting the present."

I looked at him accusingly. "You've been keeping a lot from me, George."

"You needed to concentrate on what was in front of you," said George. "And leave the big picture to the Department."

"Because the big picture is far too important to be trusted to loose cannons," said Miriam.

George and I took our time turning around. Miriam was standing right behind us.

"Moves quietly, doesn't she?" I said to George.

"You have no idea."

"Come with me, Jack," said Miriam. "I'll make sure you find everything you need."

"I thought you didn't approve of me?" I said.

"Which is why I want you out of this library as soon as possible." She glanced back at Amanda. "But she stays where she is."

Amanda smiled easily. "You two toddle off and have fun. I'm sure George and I can find lots to talk about."

I thought George looked a bit worried about that, but Miriam was already marching forward into the stacks, so I hurried after her.

"Don't go wandering off," she said over her shoulder. "We have guard dogs patrolling the more sensitive areas. Well, I say dogs... More like big hairy things with attitude, that don't get fed often enough."

The stacks towered over us like great jungle trees, and the narrow passageways were full of shadows. I looked up, and found the out-leaning shelves had come together to form a long book-lined tunnel. As we moved deeper into the library I could feel the pressure of unseen watching eyes. I hoped it was only the books.

"So," said Miriam, almost casually. "How well do you know Miss Fielding?"

"We're just colleagues," I said.

"She knows a lot of things she shouldn't."

"Lot of that going around at the moment."

"Coming here was her idea, wasn't it?" said Miriam.

"She raised some important questions that I couldn't answer," I said carefully. "It seemed likely I'd find the information here."

"After she put the thought in your head."

I nodded, conceding the point.

"You must know you can't trust her," said Miriam.

"I don't trust anyone," I said.

She favoured me with a quick smile. "Good attitude. Hang on to it. You'll live longer."

She came to a halt before one particular stack and gestured proudly at hundreds of books, all of which seemed to be staring back and daring me to come and have a go if I thought I was hard enough.

"This entire section is devoted to places and things that have no business existing in the modern world," said Miriam. "The past is another country, and we're at war with it. You do understand you can't remove any of these books?"

"Of course," I said.

"There are reading rooms, available for a very reasonable fee."

I looked at her. "I have to pay to read these books?"

"State-of-the-art security doesn't come cheap," she said. "And our budget's under review again. It was either that, or a gift shop."

I craned my head all the way back, and still couldn't make out the furthest reaches of the bookshelves. I wouldn't have been surprised to find them sprinkled with snow and hidden in clouds.

"What's the plan?" I said. "Start at the bottom and work our way up?"

"Just climb the ladder and see where it takes you," said Miriam. "The book you need is waiting for you."

"How can you disbelieve in magic, when you're surrounded by it?"

She shrugged. "Self-defence, mostly. You'd better let me take the lead. The books know me."

She started up the ladder and I followed after her. I kept a careful eye on the books I passed, but none of them called out to me. Shelf after shelf fell away behind us, in a mountainside of cracked and faded volumes. I looked down once, and immediately wished I hadn't. The shelves were leaning so far out I was actually hanging over an extremely long drop. I made myself concentrate on the books in front of me.

Miriam stopped suddenly, and I banged into her feet with my head. She didn't apologise.

"Have you found something?" I said, just a bit pointedly.

"I think something has found us," said Miriam.

"You shouldn't have come here, Outsider!" said a harsh voice I knew only too well. "You were warned!"

I leaned cautiously back from the ladder so I could look past Miriam, and there was Mr. Slender, standing at right angles to us, as though the shelves were his floor. Not so much defying gravity as completely indifferent to it. He smiled unpleasantly, as though he was contemplating all the really horrid things he was going to do to me, and looking forward to it.

"How the hell did you get in here?" said Miriam.

"No one can keep us out," said the Man In Black. "Now get out of my way or suffer the consequences."

"Screw you, you over-stretched laboratory freak!"

Miriam drew her gun and opened fire. Mr. Slender swayed back and forth, effortlessly dodging the bullets, and then dropped on all fours and scuttled down the shelves toward us, his long limbs pumping like some huge black spider. Miriam kept firing until she ran out of ammunition, and then cursed flatly.

"Hug the ladder and keep your head down!" I yelled to her. "He doesn't want you, only me!"

"Well, he can't have you! You're under my protection!"

"He's a Man In Black. He doesn't care about things like that."

"Tell me you've got a plan."

"Of course I have. It's a really good one, with bells and whistles and everything."

Miriam shook her head disgustedly, put away her gun, and wrapped both arms around the ladder. I thought quickly, trying to come up with some kind of plan. Men In Black were famously hard to kill, so . . . stick to what I do best. Treat Mr. Slender as an unexploded bomb, and work out the best way to make him harmless. If I couldn't kill or hurt him, what did that leave?

Out-think him, of course. Men In Black were designed to be unstoppable, not smart.

"I thought we were partners!" I yelled.

"You thought wrong," said Mr. Slender.

"Just as well; I never liked you."

"That will make this even more amusing."

"Oh, please," I said. "I'm the Outsider, and you're just a functionary in a shabby suit. You couldn't take me on the best day you ever had and you know it."

He crouched down, compressing his long limbs, and threw himself at me, clawed hands reaching for my throat, but I'd already activated my bone amulet. Mr. Slender sailed through the space where he thought I was and just kept on going. He screamed with rage as he plummeted toward the distant floor, grabbing desperately at bookshelves as he fell past them, but they seemed to suck themselves back in and out of his reach. He finally hit the floor really hard, and stopped screaming. Miriam leaned precariously out from the ladder for a better look.

"I didn't know anything could kill a Man In Black," she said finally. "I thought that was the point of them."

I shut down my amulet. "Do you want to hang on to him, as a souvenir?"

"I suppose we could always have him stuffed and mounted, as a dreadful example." Miriam looked at me. "You just saved my life. He would have killed me as well as you, to make sure I couldn't tell anyone what he did here. George would have just found the two of us dead at the foot of the ladder, and assumed we'd fallen."

"No one gets killed on my watch," I said.

Miriam started to say something, and then stopped herself.

"We'd better go down and check he isn't going to pull a Michael Myers on us."

"Don't be so impatient," I said. "I didn't climb all the way up the north face of this bookshelf just to go back down without finding something useful."

And then I broke off, as something nudged my arm. One of the books was edging itself off the shelf. I reached out a hand, and the book jumped into my grasp. More than two-foot square, and thick enough to stun a rodeo bull if aimed between the eyes, the book was bound in a strange golden leather. The raised title said simply: *Things That Shouldn't Be*. There was no author's name. I could take a hint when it came looking for me, so I hugged the book to my chest with one arm and started back down. Miriam followed quickly after me.

George and Amanda were waiting at the foot of the ladder, contemplating Mr. Slender's unmoving body. His long arms and legs were shattered, and his back was twisted so badly it had to be broken. One side of his bony head had been smashed in by the impact, the eyeball forced half out of its socket. And yet for all the Man In Black's injuries, there wasn't a spot of blood anywhere. George gave me one of his *more in sorrow than in anger* looks.

"Self-defence," I said. "He was sent here to kill me, along with any witnesses."

"Rest assured I shall be having some very stern words with his masters," said George.

"I want to know how he got in here," said Miriam.

"It is starting to feel like an open day," said George. "Why don't you go and ask the guards some pointed questions?"

"Love to," said Miriam.

She stalked off, back straight and chin up, and I just knew that being yelled at was in someone's future.

"Why did the Man In Black want you dead, Jack?" said Amanda. She sounded more curious than concerned.

George looked at me sharply. "That's an excellent question. What are you up to, Jack, that a Man In Black had to be tasked to stop you?"

I gave him my best innocent look, and he sighed.

"It doesn't matter. No one threatens one of my people and gets away with it."

"I thought the Men In Black answered to a higher authority?" I said.

George snorted, amused. "Who told you that? This was probably just a shot across the bows, to test the Department's strength and resolve during the transition from me to Miriam. See if we could defend ourselves against a hostile takeover."

"And you wonder why I don't want to be part of your world," I said. "I can handle unexploded bombs; it's the politics that'll kill you."

I handed Amanda the book that chose me. She leafed quickly through it, nodded happily, casually tucked the oversized volume under one arm, and smiled dazzlingly at George.

"This has all been very pleasant, and we really mustn't do it again. Time we were on our way, Jack."

And then a series of loud cracking noises drew our attention to Mr. Slender's broken body, as it put itself back together. The long arms and legs straightened themselves out, the broken back untwisted, and the crushed skull reformed itself. The protruding eyeball made a wet sucking sound as it was pulled back into its socket.

"They really are built to take punishment," I said, for want of anything better to say.

"Stand back," said George. "I'll summon the guards."

"We don't need them," I said.

George looked at me. "We don't?"

"I can handle this," I said. "But you and Amanda should probably disappear into the stacks for a while, just in case."

"Run, from a Man In Black?" said Amanda. "I wouldn't lower myself. Go ahead, Jack. Show the elongated window dummy who's in charge."

"Quite right, Jack," said George. "I can't wait to see what you're going to do."

I was already searching through my backpack, keeping a watchful eye on Mr. Slender as he lurched up onto his feet: a bag of bones in a black suit, driven by spite and revenge. He wasn't smiling any more.

"You can't stop me, Outsider. I was created to take down far more dangerous things than you." His neck bones popped loudly as he turned his head to glare at George and Amanda. "Watch closely. What I'm about do to this troublemaker will make an excellent object lesson."

"Nasty little man," said Amanda, entirely unmoved.

"They're not programmed for diplomacy," said George.

Mr. Slender turned his back on them, so he could concentrate his glare on me. He flexed his long-fingered hands hungrily, and the heavy knuckles cracked like gunshots.

"Your amulet won't save you this time, Outsider. I've adjusted my eyes to compensate for it."

George produced a gun. I shook my head quickly.

"Miriam already tried that."

"Her gun only fires bullets," said George.

The Man In Black wagged a bony finger at him. "Interfere with my mission, and my masters will take it as an act of war."

Give George his due, his aim never wavered. "I can live with that."

"I appreciate the thought, George," I said. "But I've got this."

I took the witch knife out of my pack. Mr. Slender sneered at it.

"What are you going to do with that? Cut out a door so you can run away? There's nowhere you can hide that I can't find you."

"Then come and get me," I said. "You long, miserable streak of piss."

He surged forward, but I side-stepped at the last moment and swept my athame round in a vicious arc. The Man In Black stumbled on, caught off balance, and the witch knife sliced clean through his neck and out the other side. Because sometimes a knife is just a knife. Mr. Slender's head fell away to bounce across the floor, and the body lurched to a halt, making small helpless gestures. I picked up the head and smiled into its furious eyes.

"I could cut off the top of your head, rip out your brain, throw it on the floor and stamp on it," I said. "Or you could agree to return to your masters and tell them not to bother me again. Blink twice for *Yes I'm a good boy and I'm going to do the sensible thing.*"

There was a pause, and then the eyes blinked twice. I tossed the head back to its body, and the hands caught it awkwardly. The body tucked its head under one arm, because even Men In Black have a sense of tradition, and then walked off through the stacks with as much dignity as it could manage. I dropped the witch knife back into my pack, and nodded calmly to George and Amanda.

"You have to know how to talk to these people."

Amanda clapped her hands loudly, grinning all over her face. George shook his head resignedly and put away his gun. I looked at him thoughtfully.

"How long have you been going armed in your own library, George?"

"Times change," he said. "Thank you for dealing diplomatically with what could have been a very unfortunate situation."

"Would you really have gone to war over me?"

"Of course," said George. "No one gets the better of me in my own library."

Miriam came striding back out of the stacks to join us. She was smiling, and not in a good way.

"I just passed the Man In Black. Love the new look." She nodded briskly to me, her gaze entirely cool and businesslike. "I'll take you to one of the reading rooms, Jack, but your little friend won't be joining you." She glared coldly at Amanda. "I had security run a check on you, and officially you don't exist. So stay right where you are until the guards arrive to haul you off to a nice secure location, where I will find out everything there is to know about you."

Amanda met Miriam's gaze calmly. "Sorry, but I can't hang around."

Miriam's gun was suddenly in her hand, aimed right between Amanda's eyes.

"You're not going anywhere," Miriam said flatly. "I know a threat when I see one."

"Bless you," said Amanda.

Miriam wrinkled her nose, and then sneezed explosively. She tried to say something, but another sneeze interrupted her. She sneezed again and again, until she was bent right over by the force of the explosions. Tears streamed down her cheeks, and her gun waved all over the place. George shook his head sadly, and took the gun away from her.

"You'd better pop off now, Jack. Take the book, and your little friend, and feel free to bring either of them back any time. And remember, you owe me."

"Oh, of course," I said.

Amanda and I headed off into the stacks. Miriam's sneezes continued to detonate behind us.

"She will stop sneezing, won't she?" I said.

"Oh yes," said Amanda. "Eventually."

I shook my head. "Can't take you anywhere."

"You love it," Amanda said cheerfully.

CHAPTER FOUR
THE WAY WE USED TO BE

I'm not used to not knowing where I am. When I pass through one of my dimensional doors, I know immediately where I've come to and where I'm going. But one minute I was walking out of the library with Amanda, and the next I was stumbling across a wide grassy plain with a huge brooding forest lying in wait ahead of us. The trees were tall and broad, weighed down with summer's greenery and packed close together, holding an impenetrable darkness within. The sky was slate grey, the sun half hidden behind ominous clouds. I looked sharply at Amanda.

"Where is this?"

"Welcome to AD 60," said Amanda. "Britain has been a Roman colony for over a century, and I think it would be fair to say that things are not going well. What do you know about this period, Jack?"

"Not much," I admitted. "Are we talking about Boadicea?"

"That's the Latin version," said Amanda. "Her real name was Boudicca."

I didn't like the way the forest was looking at me. A vast, almost primeval presence, it dominated the horizon like the gateway to another world. Just looking at the dark between the trees was enough to put a chill in my heart.

"So, time travel," I said, because I felt I should say something. "Just when I thought my day couldn't get any weirder."

"And our travels have only just started," Amanda said happily.

"That's what worrying me." I looked around, taking my time. "What are we doing here? It's not exactly tourist country."

"We're here because this is where we need to be."

"How very Zen," I said. "A word I have never had occasion to use before, and hopefully never will again. Why do we have to be here?"

"Because this is when history was first rewritten. However, before we go any further, we need to tuck this book away in your backpack. Partly because it's getting very heavy, but mostly because I am going to need my hands free in case I have to hit someone."

I had to raise an eyebrow. "You think that's likely?"

"It's a more primitive time," said Amanda. "Disputes tend toward the physical."

I looked at the oversized volume tucked precariously under her arm. "How am I supposed to cram something that size into my backpack? I'd have a hard time getting it inside a suitcase."

"I'm sure it'll go in if we lean on it," Amanda said cheerfully.

I slipped the pack off my shoulder, and opened it as wide as it would go. Amanda forced one corner of the book in, then gave it a twisting kind of push, and the book disappeared inside as though the pack had swallowed it down. I blinked a few times, and hefted the pack carefully, but it didn't feel any heavier. So I just shrugged, and swung it back into place on my shoulder.

"You see?" said Amanda. "You just need to remind these things who's in charge. Now pay attention, please; lecture mode. Boudicca was Queen of the Iceni, the greatest of the British tribes. She had been promised a free hand by the local Roman authorities, as long as she paid regular tribute and maintained the peace, but the Imperial Senate didn't approve of a female ruler wielding that much power. So they sent in the Legions.

"Boudicca's forces were caught by surprise, and quickly overwhelmed. The queen and her daughters were then publicly whipped and raped by the soldiers. To humble them, and their people, and make them properly subservient to Roman rule. But instead, all the tribes were outraged by this insult. Boudicca formed them into one great army, and then burned and slaughtered her way from one side of the country to the other, wiping out whole settlements for the sin of embracing Roman culture. The Legions were sent to stop her; Boudicca's army cut them down and trampled them underfoot."

Amanda stepped in front of me, so close our bodies were almost touching. She cupped my face in her hands, and when she spoke her words hit my mouth in little puffs of breath, like invisible caresses.

"Open your inner eye, Jack. This is something you need to See for yourself."

Wrapped in filthy furs and covered in tattoos and splashes of woad, Boudicca's army swept through town after town, killing everyone who didn't run for their lives. The queen led from the front, her battle-axe bathed in blood and sanctified with slaughter, marching in triumph from one burnt-out settlement to another, until finally she led her army into Londinium, that great and noble symbol of Roman rule.

Howling like rabid wolves, Boudicca's horde butchered its way through the narrow streets. Swords and axes rose and fell, splashing blood across the smoke-stained walls, as the warriors of the woad butchered every Roman man, woman and child. Corpses piled up in the open squares and littered the streets, while severed heads bobbed in the river Thames, still silently screaming.

This wasn't just war; it was the complete eradication of one culture by another. Boudicca's army hacked a crimson path straight into the heart of the city, and crowds packed the streets as they fled the horror baying at their heels. A city died screaming, and Boudicca laughed in its face.

The horde didn't stop until they ran out of people to kill. And then, finally, they lowered their blood-soaked weapons and looked around them with a sense of a job well done. They looted food and drink from the surrounding buildings, and sat down in the streets among the bodies, laughing happily at the thought of what they'd done. They sang songs celebrating death and destruction, while some of the younger men played football with severed heads. But without their long-hoarded rage to drive them on, Boudicca's army soon lay down where they were and gave themselves up to sleep.

Roman reinforcements arrived not long after, quietly entering the city from a dozen directions. They carefully blocked off all the escape routes, and then fell on the slumbering enemy. The warriors of the woad fought like wolves at bay, but the Legionnaires just kept pressing forward behind the protection of their tall shields. Roman steel rose and fell with merciless precision, taking revenge for Boudicca's revenge.

Her entire army was wiped out in a single night. Finally, cut off and alone, the warrior queen made her last stand surrounded by the corpses of her daughters. Drenched in blood from countless wounds, one eye carved out of her head, she still held her battered axe out before her, daring the soldiers to come to her. In the end she spat a mouthful of blood at the Roman army, and charged straight at them.

After she was dead the soldiers dipped their fingers into what was left of her, so they could smear their faces with her blood to mark their triumph.

Amanda took her hands away from my face, and the vision disappeared. The stench of so much death and horror still filled my head.

"That is your past, now," Amanda said quietly. "After history was rewritten."

I nodded slowly. "So what was here before?"

And just like that we were standing in a wide city street teeming with all kinds of people, and a great many things that weren't even trying to be people. Men on horseback rode casually alongside centaurs: half man and half horse, with barrel chests and noble faces. Both the horses and the centaurs crapped openly in the street, and no one gave a damn. The centaurs conversed cheerfully with the men on horseback, discussing philosophy and wine and war in deep bass voices.

Light and Dark elves walked together, with inhuman poise and grace, and no trace of the bitter hatred I'd seen in "The Faerie War." Whatever had split them apart hadn't happened yet. They moved easily among men of a dozen different races and backgrounds, as though it was the most natural thing in the world.

The street was lined with square solid buildings: single storeys of stone and timber, with trailing vines and flowers for decoration. The various shops had no windows to show off their wares, so the owners stood in their open doorways and sang to passersby of all the marvellous goods they had to offer. Street musicians, conjurers, and the old-time equivalent of fast-food stalls competed for the crowd's attention. It should have been a bedlam of raised voices, but instead there was a cheerful feeling of *We're all in this together.*

A great shadow fell across the street, and I looked up to see a cloud of angels sweep silently by. Huge idealised figures, with widespread wings. Down in the street, everyone just carried on with whatever they were doing until the angels had flown on, taking their shadow with them.

A pack of oversized dogs came racing along the street, darting in and out of the crowd. They suddenly rose up to run on two legs, stretching and twisting until they were men and women wrapped in furs. The werewolves laughed happily, as though this was the best game in the world, and chased each other down the street.

A stone fountain in the middle of an open square tossed its waters high into the air. As they fell back they took on human forms, beautiful nude women who danced with fluid grace, blending in and out of each other. Naiads, I thought dazedly. Water nymphs.

Gods went walking through the crowds, tall and magnificent, a glowing halo surrounding each perfect head. They wore the same clothes as the people they walked among: robes and tunics, furs and armours. Everyone seemed to be taking their presence for granted, and I remembered how ancient writings often told of people talking quite naturally with their gods, as though this was something that happened every day and nothing to make a fuss about.

Some of the gods radiated peace and serenity, while others gave vent to inhumanly fierce emotions. Many were clearly drunk as skunks. Norse, Roman and Celtic deities conversed happily together, as though they were all just toilers in the same vineyard. They moved through the crowd in a not at all mysterious way, mostly interested in intelligent conversation and the pleasures of the flesh. Some of the taller figures had animal or bird heads, like the gods of ancient Egypt, only there was nothing stylised about them. A god with a jackal's head turned suddenly to look at Amanda and dropped her a sly wink. She smiled and blew him a kiss. The god laughed soundlessly and went on his way.

And that was when I realised I wasn't just Seeing a vision of the past. I stamped my foot on the hard-packed earth and breathed deeply, filling my head with all the rich smells of the street, and then laughed out loud at the sheer wonder of it all. I turned to Amanda, and she smiled happily back at me.

"Welcome to the world that was," she said. "When living itself was magical."

"How did we get here?"

"I'm magical. I did tell you. Try to keep up, Jack."

I looked around at the people streaming past us, entirely unconcerned by our presence. Though a few did pause just long enough to look down their nose at my clothes. People and gods found the time to bow respectfully to Amanda, while carefully maintaining a respectful distance. She took it all in her stride, smiling cheerfully on one and all.

"How can we be here, if history has been changed?" I said.

"The past was overwritten, not destroyed," Amanda said patiently. "Remember the palimpsest."

"But ... all these magical creatures ... and the old gods! How can they be here, while Christian angels are flying overhead?"

"It's all just different masks, on the same face," said Amanda.

I looked at her for a moment. "So Jesus is real, in this history?"

"Oh, he's always real," said Amanda.

There was something in the way she said that. "You've met him?"

"We've talked."

"Well?" I said. "What's he like?"

"Funnier than you'd think."

I shook my head. "Even when I do get answers out of you, they never take me anywhere useful."

"Yes, well, that's life for you," Amanda said briskly. "Now can we please get a move on? We have important work to be about."

"But why do you need my help to do it?" I said.

"Because you're the Outsider. You have more practical experience in dealing with the weird stuff than anyone else I know. That's how I knew I could drop you into a scene like this and be reasonably sure you wouldn't jump out of your skin."

"I'm still considering it," I said darkly. "Why is this version of history so different?"

Amanda smiled. "This is how things used to be, before magic was banished. A more generous time, that had room in it for all kinds. Londinium was a gathering place for all kinds, natural and supernatural, and there never was any rebellion against a tyrannous authority. That new and bloody history was put in place to distract people from noticing that all of this had been wiped from humanity's memory. But people still secretly long for the wonders they used to take for granted."

"I get that," I said. "But why have you brought me here?"

"To meet the real Queen Boudicca. This way."

She set off down the street, and I moved quickly in beside her, but we had to stop again when one of my doors appeared right in front of us, blocking the way.

"What the hell is that doing here?" I said. "Does this mean there's some kind of unexploded bomb that needs defusing?"

"No," Amanda said flatly. "If there was, I'd know. This door was sent to take you back. The secret masters really don't like it when their Outsider steps off the reservation."

"Well, they'll just have to wait until I'm done," I said.

I went to walk around the door, but it shifted quickly to obstruct my way again. No matter how quickly I moved the door was always right there in front of me. I felt like giving it a good kick, just on general principles, but I didn't want to lower myself. So I just gave it my best glare, and turned to Amanda.

"Can't you do something?"

"It's not my job to solve your problems," said Amanda. "Think, Jack: what can you do?"

I racked my brain for an answer. If there was something in this version of history that someone didn't want me to know about, that made me even more determined to find out what it was. I ran through all the useful items tucked away in my backpack, and then smiled as the answer came to me. I reached in and brought out my athame, the old reliable witch knife that could cut through anything.

Everyone around me flinched away. The athame's blade was glowing fiercely, its presence beating on the air like the first rumble of an approaching earthquake. Even the door seemed to back away a little. I stepped briskly forward and stabbed it with my very useful knife, and the door vanished as the athame severed its connection to this place and time. I smiled at Amanda, and put the knife away again.

"I think I just cut all the ties to my old life."

"Do you think you'll miss it?"

"No," I said. "I can't go on without answers, and it looks like you're the only one who can help me find them."

"So it all comes down to who you trust," said Amanda.

I looked at her steadily. "You'd better be right about this."

"Of course I am," said Amanda. "I'm always right."

"I wouldn't put money on it," said a loud voice from the crowd ahead of us. A large overbearing man dressed in modern clothes was heading straight for us. The crowd fell back to give him room, the looks on their faces suggesting they weren't at all happy about his presence among them.

"At least it isn't a Man In Black this time," I said.

The newcomer crashed to a halt before us. He'd crammed his oversized figure into a smart business suit, but style and elegance were beyond him. He had a round face, a shaved head, cold eyes, and the kind of smile that suggested you really wouldn't like the things he found funny. There was no denying the man had presence, but it felt borrowed, like an actor on a stage. He drew his second-hand authority about him and addressed himself solely to Amanda.

"Allow me to introduce myself. Emil Morcata, at your service. Ah, you know the name! I am pleased."

"Don't be," said Amanda. "Your reputation is nothing to be proud of."

"You know this person?" I said to Amanda.

"Emil represents a group of supernatural treasure hunters," she said, not taking her eyes off the man.

"Would I have heard of them?"

"Unlikely," said Emil, condescending to throw a glance in my direction. "We are a very private group, very select. And since names have power, I don't believe I'll share it with you."

"They're just scavengers, grubbing through the ruins of history," said Amanda. "Looting the past for fun and profit. Digging up things that should never have been disturbed, and generally giving dogs in mangers a bad name."

"At least we know better than to let such things run loose in the world," Emil said cuttingly. "Particularly after the secret masters went to such trouble to remove all traces of them from history."

"Secret masters?" I said. "Are we talking weird rituals and funny handshakes?"

Emil's sudden glare was like a slap across the face. "Hush, boy. Your betters are talking."

"I am the Outsider," I said calmly. "One more word out of you that I don't like and I will use my Sight to discover what you're really scared of, and introduce you to it."

Emil started to say something, and then didn't. He turned back to Amanda.

"We have dedicated ourselves to seeking out lost objects of power, because such treasures only rightfully belong with those who can appreciate them. But we still have enough sense not to do anything that would allow magic to regain a hold on the world."

"Because you're afraid of it," said Amanda.

"Of course we're afraid! Any sane person would be." Emil turned a surprisingly sympathetic eye on me. "You mustn't trust her, Outsider. She's not human. Everything you see in her is a lie."

"Enough!" said Amanda. Her voice cracked like a whip, and Emil actually fell back a step.

"You wouldn't recognise the truth if you tripped over it in the gutter," said Amanda. She shot me a steady look. "I might not have told you everything, Jack, but everything I have said is true. You must believe that."

"I trust you," I said. "As much as I can."

Emil laughed briefly, and it was a cold and bitter sound. "Lord, what fools these mortals be. I can't reach you, because she's already dug her claws in too deep. It doesn't matter. I was sent here to stop this madness and I will, because she can't be allowed to destroy the proper order of things."

"You really think you can stop me?" said Amanda. She sounded honestly curious.

Emil reached inside his jacket and brought out a mummified hand whose fingers had been fashioned into candles. He pointed the withered thing at Amanda and me, and the wicks in the fingertips burst into thin blue flames that rose straight up, untroubled by even a breath of air.

"Be still," said Emil. "Be bound. Be silent. The Hand of Glory will uncover whatever treasure you came here for, and there's nothing you can do to prevent me. The Hand holds you in its grasp."

Amanda leaned forward and blew out the fingers. Emil looked shocked, every bit of his menace gone with the flames.

"This isn't over," he said numbly.

"It is if you've got any sense," said Amanda.

Emil drew himself up, and then turned and hurried off into the crowd. Not actually running, but I knew a retreat when I saw one. I looked thoughtfully at Amanda.

"Why didn't his Hand of Glory work on us?"

"Because he didn't know how to use it properly," said Amanda. "Typical of his group; they never bother to read the instructions because they're always in such a hurry to sell the stuff on."

"He knew you," I said. Not making a point, just letting the comment lie there.

Amanda shrugged. "I've crossed swords with his group. They're unpleasant, but predictable. They just want what they want, and they're incapable of seeing beyond that."

"He seemed very sure that I shouldn't trust you," I said carefully.

"He was trying to drive a wedge between us."

"But how did he get here?" I said. "Into this past that doesn't exist any more?"

Amanda frowned. "His group leases dimensional doors from the Department, but for him to arrive right after you dismissed the door they sent to bring you back . . . can only mean Emil's people and the Department are a lot closer than they used to be. Which means they must have found a common purpose."

"Like what?"

"Stopping us," said Amanda. She looked quickly around her. "We need to get a move on, Jack. Before someone else turns up to get in our way."

She set off down the street again, and I strode along beside her. It quickly became clear that we were heading for a large hall, set some way back from the main drag. It was the biggest structure I'd seen so far; still just the one storey, but constructed on a much larger scale. The walls were basic timber, with gaps for windows, but the whole thing looked solid enough to survive being hit by an earthquake and a stricken angel plummeting from the sky. I frowned as I took in half a dozen chimneys spouting smoke into the sky. I was pretty sure chimneys hadn't evolved yet in this period, but given that the main street was full of centaurs and jackal-headed gods, I didn't feel like arguing the point.

We'd almost reached the main entrance when a very tall woman suddenly appeared out of the crowd and planted herself right in front of us. She dismissed me with a glance, before smiling coldly at Amanda. A good eight feet high, and built like an Amazon on steroids, she was wearing a white dress sheer enough to show off everything she had. Her face was so beautiful it bordered on the inhuman, and if that wasn't enough to suggest she was one of the old gods, her long red hair waved languorously around her shoulders as though disturbed by some underwater tide. Her fierce green eyes blazed like headlights from oncoming traffic.

A dog big enough to give a wolf serious inadequacy issues sat down heavily at her side, without having to be told.

"Amanda, darling," said the goddess, in a deep rich voice like clotted cream that had gone off. "Fancy bumping into you, in old Londinium town. What brings you to this cosmopolitan corner of the supposedly civilised world?"

She stared down her long nose in a way that suggested we were supposed to bow and scrape in the presence of our betters, but Amanda just smiled easily back at her.

"I'm showing my new friend the sights. I do like the new frock, sweetie; it's very you. I thought you said you'd never lower yourself to return here, after that unfortunate business where you got caught trying to fix the bear-wrestling contest with a rather obvious ringer."

The goddess shrugged, and looked me over as though considering making an offer.

"Pretty enough, I suppose; like most of your toys."

"The name is Jack," I said coldly. "And I'm not anyone's toy."

"Good for you," said the goddess. "Now hush, there's a dear. Grownups are talking."

"Really?" I said. "Where?"

The goddess drew herself up to her full height and I got ready to leap up out of the way, because I knew an oncoming lightning bolt when I saw one. Perhaps fortunately, Amanda stepped forward and fixed the goddess with a cold stare.

"Hands off, sweetie. He's mine."

Surprisingly, the goddess backed down immediately. "You always did have lousy taste in men, darling."

Amanda looked at the patiently sitting dog. "You can talk."

The goddess shrugged. "Trust me, he makes a much better pet than a boyfriend."

Amanda smiled sweetly. "I never did understand your fondness for submissives."

The goddess turned on her heel and strode off into the crowd. "See you later, darlings," she threw back over her divine shoulder. "Things to see, people to do, you know how it is. Come along, boy!"

The dog grinned widely, dropped me a disturbingly human wink, and sauntered off after his mistress.

"Be seeing you, Circe," said Amanda.

I looked at her sharply. "The ancient sorceress, who turned men into animals?"

"Bit of a one-trick pony," said Amanda.

"So that dog was . . . ?"

"Oh yes."

I looked at her steadily. "I am not your toy. Or your pet."

"Just as well. I need a hero."

"I don't do that, either," I said firmly.

"You will," said Amanda.

I sniffed loudly. "How can this be a golden age, if goddesses are allowed to turn people into animals whenever they feel like it?"

"This is a golden age," said Amanda, "But it's not heaven on earth. Despite, or because of, all the gods. People are still people, whether they're human or inhuman. Which is just as well or the world would get terribly boring, wouldn't it?"

"Are we really going to let her just walk off, and leave that man as a dog?"

Amanda grinned. "Don't be so judgemental. He seemed perfectly happy as he is. Though he does seem to be taking the term mistress somewhat literally."

I remembered the smile and the wink and didn't feel like arguing, so I changed the subject.

"How was Circe able to speak such modern English?"

"She didn't," said Amanda. "Instant translation is part of the transportation package. This isn't my first time-travelling rodeo."

I shook my head slowly. "Conversations I never thought I'd be having..."

Amanda headed for the front door of the hall, and I fell in beside her. The wide slab of solid oak looked heavy enough to stop a charging rhino in its tracks, and leave it with a headache to remember. It was guarded by two oversized warrior types, splashed with blue woad and covered in great whorls of intricate tattoos. They were both wearing battered leather armour, and carrying double-headed battle-axes that looked heavy enough to chop down a tree if the guards so much as waved their axes in the tree's general direction. They stepped together as we approached, placing themselves firmly between us and the door. I made a point of nodding casually, to make it clear I wasn't at all impressed or intimidated, but they kept their gaze fixed on Amanda. It was clear they recognised her, and not necessarily in a good way. She nodded easily, and they bowed respectfully in return.

"We're here to see the queen," said Amanda.

The guards looked at each other, as though debating which of them was going to bite whatever passed for a bullet in this period, and finally the taller of the two addressed Amanda in a polite growl.

"Does she want to see you?"

"No one ever does," Amanda said wistfully. "But she knows it's always going to be in her best interests."

The guard carefully worked his way through that, and then nodded glumly to his companion. They pushed the massive door open, and the wooden hinges made loud grinding noises, as though to warn everyone we were on our way. Amanda strolled cheerfully past the guards, and I stuck close beside her. I gave the guards my best *I'm somebody too* look, but if they gave a damn they were doing a really good job of hiding it.

Inside the hall, honey-coloured candles and brass oil lamps provided a rich golden light. Two huge fires blazed fiercely, cooking entire wild boars on slowly turning spits. Hundreds of people packed the hall from end to end, and the smell from so many people packed together was almost overwhelming. It was distressingly clear that the Roman fondness for communal bathing had never caught on here.

The walls were decorated with latticeworks of hanging vines, tangled greenery, and a profusion of brightly coloured flowers. Everyone in the hall wore simple but colourful robes, assorted bits of leather armour, and a sword or an axe on their hip that didn't look the least bit ceremonial. Men and women alike were tall and well made and happily larger than life, eating and drinking and laughing together in loudly raucous company. Nothing like the savages I'd Seen in the other history.

The roar of conversation quickly fell away as Amanda and I made our way through the hall. Most people seemed to recognise Amanda, and those nearest drew back to give her plenty of room. The few who looked at me apparently only did so they could point disbelievingly at my clothes. I was getting a bit tired of that. I leaned in close to Amanda.

"If Londinium is such a marvellous place, and men and gods and everything else are all such good chums, why is everyone here carrying a really big weapon?"

"Remember what I said, about politics tending to be a bit boisterous?" said Amanda. "In this period, fighting your corner isn't just an expression."

"How do they feel about unwanted guests?"

"Just keep smiling," said Amanda. "And act like you have every right to be here. That should keep the flies off."

"Story of my life," I said.

I couldn't help noticing that while everyone seemed ready enough to bow to Amanda, no one seemed that pleased to see her. I also noticed that the crowd had closed in behind us, blocking our way to the only exit. I made a point of smiling easily about me, as though I didn't have a care in the world, and got ready to pull out my witch knife if anyone got too close.

We finally reached the far end of the hall, and came to a halt before a large woman sitting at her ease on a very large throne. I didn't need to be told that the warrior woman happily stuffing her blue-painted face with food and drink, and not giving a damn about the grease and wine dripping onto her leather breastplate, was Boudicca.

Amanda tapped me surreptitiously on the arm. "I am about to introduce you to the Queen of the Iceni," she said quietly. "Be respectful."

"I don't do respectful," I said. "Especially with authority figures. It only encourages them."

"I had noticed," said Amanda. "But these people take their honour very seriously, and she will quite definitely cut your head off if you annoy her."

"I won't start anything if she doesn't."

Amanda shook her head. "This can only go well ..."

"I can do polite," I said helpfully.

Boudicca gnawed the last bit of meat from the heavy bone she was holding, and tossed it to one side. She scratched her ribs unselfconsciously, drained her wine cup and held it out for a refill. Only then did she nod easily to Amanda, and look me over as though wondering if I was worth taking an interest in. Her gaze was like being hit by a truck, and her sheer presence was so overwhelming I was impressed in spite of myself. I bowed politely, and felt Amanda relax just a little.

Boudicca was handsome rather than pretty, with dark brown skin and a proudly broken nose. Her night-dark hair had been packed with clay to give it spikes, under a simple iron crown. Her leather armour had seen a lot of use, and her bare arms showed serious scars on the bulging muscles. A battle-axe large enough to unnerve a Viking berserker lay casually across her lap, as though it belonged there. There was nothing of the feral viciousness I'd seen in the other Boudicca, but this queen's cool and measured gaze made her seem even more dangerous. Her heavy eyebrows descended into a frown, as her gaze settled on me.

"I'm not accustomed to being stared at," said Queen Boudicca, in a deep and only incidentally threatening voice.

"I did bow," I said.

"Most men kneel."

"I'm not most men."

She surprised me then, with a loud and earthy chuckle. "Of course not, or you wouldn't be hanging out with Amanda. Most men would run a mile, rather than risk their heart and their soul loving a power like her."

I smiled. "You don't know her like I do."

Boudicca's smile widened. "It's not often I can find someone with the brass balls to argue with me. How refreshing. Of course, I usually end up cutting their heads off."

I nodded. "It can be difficult for a woman to find a man who gives good head."

Queen Boudicca laughed raucously, and everyone in the hall joined in. Amanda refused to look at me.

"Can't take you anywhere..."

While Boudicca gave herself up to laughter, and beat on the arm of her throne with her fist, I took the opportunity to study exactly what her seat of power was made of. It appeared to be thick vines threaded together, with heavy rugs to act as cushions, and presumably draught excluders in the winter. The vines were punctuated here and there with white roses, and as the general laughter finally died down I realised the roses had started singing in harmony with each other. I took a step forward to try and make out what the song was, and all the roses broke off to hiss at me ominously.

"Knock it off, boys," said Boudicca. "I like this one. Play nicely or it's pruning time again."

The roses subsided reluctantly, like guard dogs convinced they knew better than their mistress.

"Should I offer them a biscuit, or something?" I said.

"Not if you like having fingers," said Amanda. She nodded to the queen. "Hello, Boo. Good to see you again. Allow me to present Jack Daimon, the Outsider. I vouch for him."

"Good," said Boudicca. "That means I can give him some leeway. Now why have you returned to my court, O little gore crow and bearer of bad tidings? Didn't you panic everyone sufficiently the last time you were here?"

"I have to warn you that really bad things are on their way," said Amanda. "In fact, they should be crashing your party any time now."

I looked at her sharply. "You never mentioned that to me."

"It wasn't time yet."

Dozens of my dimensional doors suddenly appeared up and down the length of the hall. Men and women fell back, clawing for their weapons, and then all the doors swung open and an army of Men In Back spilled out. Long spindly shapes in shabby black suits, with unpleasant smiles on their bony faces. Boudicca jumped to her feet, battle-axe in hand, and some of her larger warriors moved quickly to stand between the invaders and their queen. The Men In Black stood unnaturally still, ignoring the raised swords and axes. They didn't even look at Boudicca. Their attention was fixed on Amanda and me.

"I've never seen so many Men In Black in one place," I said quietly. "Why are they giving us the stink eye?"

"They serve the secret masters," said Amanda. "Emil must have ratted us out to the Department."

"Any chance we can negotiate our way out of this?" I said.

"You know better than that."

"There must be something we can do! Boudicca's people have no idea how hard these things are to kill, or the damage they can do."

"What about all the things in your pack?"

"It's a backpack, not an arsenal. Wait a minute, what about the book? Could that help us?"

"I suppose you could hit them over the head with it," said Amanda.

The Man In Black nearest to us suddenly took a step forward, and fixed us with an unblinking gaze. "You will die first, and then everyone else in this place. That's what you get, for being trouble-makers."

Queen Boudicca cleared her throat loudly, just to remind everyone that this was her hall. "Amanda, Jack, you know these demons?"

"Unfortunately, yes," said Amanda. "They have no hearts, no conscience, and they are very hard to kill."

"Then they should make excellent sport," said Boudicca, and a low growl of agreement ran through her people.

The Men In Black flexed their clawed fingers and bared their pointed teeth, anticipating the rending of flesh and the blood and horror to come. I took out my athame, and its presence beat on the air like the wings of a dark angel. But for all the fierce glow of its blade, it was still just one knife against an army of Men In Black.

"Can't you do something?" I murmured to Amanda. "You're the great magical power."

"I brought you here to save the day," Amanda said calmly. "So get on with it."

I gave her my best hard look, and then turned to face the hall and raised my voice.

"I am the Outsider! Everyone here with a long bony head and a shabby outfit is advised to go home before I have to do something I won't regret in the least. No one threatens innocent people on my watch!"

The nearest Man In Black smiled slowly. "Every living thing in this place has been marked for death because you have contaminated them with your presence. So you could say everything that's about to happen is all your fault."

Boudicca's hand whipped forward, and her battle axe flashed through the air to bury itself in the Man In Black's forehead. He fell back a step, and then recovered himself and reached up to tug the axe out of his head. The blade left a deep fissure in his skull, but there wasn't a drop of blood. He let the axe fall to the floor, and wagged a bony finger at the queen.

"Don't be impatient. We'll get to you."

"Your masters shouldn't have sent that door to fetch me," I said. "It's given me a really good idea."

I brought my athame swinging round, and cut through one particular aspect of the Men In Black. All their clothes vanished in a moment, and what had been a vicious and deadly army was suddenly just a bunch of pale and spindly naked creatures.

"Hey!" I said to Amanda. "They don't have anything between their legs!"

"They never did," said Amanda. "They were made that way."

"No wonder they're always in such a bad mood."

"They're homunculi," said Amanda. "You can tell because they don't have navels either."

"I can't help feeling they've been rather short-changed," I said.

"Don't start feeling sorry for them," said Amanda.

"Really not going to happen." I raised my voice again. "Everything in this hall that never had a mother or a father, go home! Or I will think of something even more amusing to do to you."

For a moment I thought my bluff might actually work, and then the nearest Man In Black smiled at me.

"We will savour your screams."

The Men In Black surged forward, and Queen Boudicca and her people went to meet them. Swords and axes flashed in the candlelight as they slammed into bony bodies, but even though the blades sank deep, no blood spurted. Clawed hands lashed out savagely, slicing through throats and guts, and men and women crashed to the floor to stain the rushes with their life's blood. The warriors of the woad howled like wolves as they cut and hacked at the intruders, but the

Men In Black refused to fall. They had been built to take damage and feel no pain, and once set in motion they would not stop until everything in their path was dead.

One young warrior leapt up to bounce off a wall, so he could drop onto a Man In Back from above. But even as his sword hacked deep into the creature's neck, the Man In Black grabbed him out of mid-air and slammed him to the ground with such force his bones shattered. His friends rushed forward to avenge him, and the Man In Black went to meet them with a death's-head grin.

Queen Boudicca stood her ground before her throne, swinging a new battle-axe with both hands. The sheer strength of her blows sent bony creatures flying through the air to crash and flail on the floor, where howling warriors crowded in to take them apart with vicious sword and axe work. But even though Boudicca's guards did their best to protect her blind spots, they couldn't be everywhere. I saw a Man In Black rise up unnoticed behind Boudicca's throne and yelled a warning to her, but the sheer din of battle drowned me out.

I opened up a path through the struggling crowd, my glowing athame slicing through the Men In Black without even jarring on their bones, but even then some of the spindly things refused to fall. One loomed up before me, and I had to duck a blow that would have ripped my face right off. I moved in close, and gutted the creature. Something fell out that I didn't even recognise, and I stepped quickly to one side as the Man In Black stumbled on. I slammed the athame into the back of its skull, and the creature dropped to the floor and didn't move again.

I got to the throne just in time to see a clawed hand reach out to tear through the back of Boudicca's neck. I screamed a warning so loud it hurt my throat. Boudicca started to turn, but the Man In Black was already too close. I lifted the athame for one last desperate throw, and a crowd of white roses erupted from the throne. Thorny stems wrapped around the Man In Black, pinning his arms to his sides while the flowers gnawed at his face. Until Boudicca's swinging axe took his head clean off.

I turned to see how Amanda was doing. A Man In Black was heading straight for her, clawed hands reaching for her face. She leapt lithely into the air, spinning as she rose, and one foot came sweeping round in a kick that crushed the creature's throat and broke its neck.

It dropped to the floor, and Amanda's heel came hammering down with enough force to stamp right through its skull. I fought my way through the press of bodies to join her.

"Nice moves," I said, just a bit breathlessly. "But the Men In Black are still winning! You have to do something!"

"No," she said. "You have to make the Men In Black respect you, Jack, or they'll never stop coming after you."

My thoughts raced, and then I hacked a path through the Men In Black to reach the nearest dimensional door. It was still standing open. I slammed my witch knife deep into the wood and twisted it, cutting the ties that held it in the past. The door actually shuddered, and then an unseen force grabbed hold of all the surviving Men In Black and sucked them back through the doors, all of which slammed shut and disappeared. And just like that, the battle was over. Boudicca and her people slowly lowered their weapons, and then everyone in the hall started cheering and applauding. Boudicca strode over and hugged me so fiercely my knees actually buckled for a moment. She laughed and let me go, dropping a heavy arm across my shoulders.

"Well done, Outsider! I should have known you had some serious magics, if you were keeping company with the likes of her."

"Isn't he marvellous?" said Amanda, beaming happily.

"I'm sorry so many of your people got hurt," I said to Boudicca. "I brought this on you; they followed me here."

"Never blame the enemy for its own actions," said Boudicca. "And what the hell; there's nothing like a good scrap to brighten up a dull day."

The whole hall burst into laughter. The warriors of the woad put away their weapons, and set about congratulating each other on their exploits. Boudicca went back to her throne, spoke soothingly to the roses until they relaxed, and dropped heavily onto her seat. Someone thrust a side of roast boar and a cup of wine into her hands. All around the hall men and women were tending to their hurts, and seeming quite cheerful about it. They appeared more upset over the fact that the dead Men In Black had disappeared along with the living, so there wouldn't be any trophies. I looked at all the dead warriors, lying crumpled on the blood-soaked floor, and couldn't see anything to celebrate. Amanda put a comforting hand on my arm.

"You did well, Jack."

"People died here, because of us," I said.

"It's sweet of you to think that," she said. "But none of this is your fault. Concentrate on all the people you saved, because you had a good head on your shoulders."

"Good thing I didn't cut it off after all," said Boudicca.

"I did vouch for him," Amanda said reproachfully. "You can trust him as you trust me."

Boudicca knocked back her wine, and held the empty cup out for a refill. "What makes you think I ever trusted you, little gore crow?" She turned her gaze to me. "You saved my people from those demons, Outsider, so it seems I owe you a boon. Ask for anything."

She studied me carefully over the rim of her refilled cup, and I didn't need Amanda to warn me this was a test. I raised my voice, and every eye turned to me.

"I could ask for gold or jewels," I said loudly. "I could ask for titles, or land. But I'd rather have something of greater value. The finest gift of all, if it's freely offered. I ask for your friendship, Queen Boudicca of the Iceni. As I offer you mine."

She looked at me for a long moment, and then a smile spread across her blue-painted face, and she nodded approvingly.

"Well played, Outsider. If you ever need me, or my people, call, and we will be there."

"Very generous of you, Boo," said Amanda. "But now, if you'll excuse us, we really must be going."

I looked at her. "We must?"

"You can't leave!" said Boudicca. "We're having a feast!"

"You heard the queen," I said to Amanda. "Feast!"

"You really wouldn't like their idea of delicacies," said Amanda. "And, we have work to be about."

She took me firmly by the arm, and urged me back to the main entrance. The warriors of the woad cheered and applauded me all the way to the door, and I did my best to smile as though I thought I deserved it.

"Did we actually achieve anything?" I said to Amanda.

"We've done what we came here to do," she said.

"Why did you bring me here, really?"

"Partly so you could see what the original Londinium was like, compared to the horror show that replaced it, but mostly so you could make friends and influence people." Amanda smiled at me. "I knew you'd rise to the occasion, given a chance."

"So this was really all about me?" I said.

"It's always all about you," said Amanda. "The one man who can help me put the world back the way it should be. The old you couldn't do that; I have to teach you to be a better man."

"I saved lives as the Outsider!" I said.

She met my gaze unflinchingly. "Think of all the last chances you threw away when you defused the things you thought were bombs. All the magics you destroyed, to help prop up your grey and joyless world."

"What has that got to do with this?" I said.

"The original Londinium was written over and replaced, because it contained magical beings living happily alongside humanity, and one group of humans didn't like that. They thought they were special and should be in charge, but the only way the secret masters could achieve that was if they were the only ones."

I looked at her. "They rewrote all of history, just to get rid of everything that wasn't them?"

"They thought big, for such small-minded people," said Amanda. "But now we have the book to tell us where to go and who to see, we can undo the terrible wrong that was done to the world, and the Story."

"I'm still not convinced bringing magic back is such a good idea," I said.

"Where we're going next should help you make up your mind," said Amanda.

"And where is that?"

"Somewhere . . . interesting."

CHAPTER FIVE
THE PRINCESS AND THE BEAST

Suddenly it was evening, and I was splashing through ankle-deep waters while treacherous mud did its best to slip out from under my feet. Amanda was walking ahead of me, having no trouble keeping her balance. A gusting wind had the feel of winter on its way. Wide-open marshland stretched off into the distance, in shades of bile and bitter green, under a grim grey sky. Everywhere I looked it was stubby grass and mud flats and half-submerged land, with large areas of standing water. Patches of weeds thrust up like drowned men's fingers. A cold, empty, desolate scene. I glowered at Amanda's back.

"Where the hell are we, this time? And what are we doing here?"

"I thought you should see the other side of the magical world," she said, without so much as a backward glance. "It's not all rainbows and unicorns."

"I would have been perfectly happy to take your word for that," I said, and she laughed.

There was no road through the marshes, but we soon came to a series of flat stones, heading off in something that aspired to be a straight line. Amanda skipped lightly from one stone to another, leaving me to follow on behind as best I could. The stepping stones were only marginally less slippery than the muddy waters, and I had to fight to stay upright.

"Where exactly is this, Amanda?" I said, just a bit plaintively.

"The eighth century," she said. "In what will eventually be part of England."

"But not the history I know?"

"Got it in one," she said cheerfully. "This is an age of magic and monsters, when people learned how to become great, by overcoming great difficulties. But even with the best will in the world, people can still make mistakes. And then someone has to come along to put things right."

"And that's why we're here?" I said.

"There's someone I want you to meet," said Amanda. "You'll find it very instructive."

I waited, until it became clear she had nothing more to say.

"You're just full of secrets, aren't you?" I said finally.

"Oh, lots and lots," she said brightly. "Don't worry; all will become clear as we go along. Apart from the bits that don't."

"You know," I said, "at some point you're going to have to start trusting me."

She stopped abruptly, and turned to face me. The gusting breeze wrapped her hair about her face, hiding her expression.

"I do trust you, Jack," she said. "More than you know."

"Then tell me something," I said. "Throw me a bone! Like, why choose me of all people to help you change history back?"

She smiled suddenly. "Because you're worth it."

And in that moment I felt a spark between us, an attraction I had no right to expect given how short a time we'd known each other. I'd never felt anything like it before, and never expected to, but I thought, I hoped, she felt the same way about me. We stared at each other, and I never wanted to look away. For a moment I thought she might be about to say something, but instead she turned and set off again, skipping lightly across the stepping stones. And I followed after her, as best I could.

Some time later I looked out across the marshes and spotted my first sign of civilisation. A great stone hall, standing on its own in the middle of nowhere, half silhouetted against the lowering sky. A stark and brutal structure that made no effort at all to blend in with its surroundings. Bright lights shone through barred windows, and the only door was closed. The whole affair looked about as welcoming as a fist in the face. Amanda waited patiently for me to catch up with her, and then gestured grandly.

"Behold, the hall of King Hrothgar. His people are currently being plagued by a monster called Grendel. It comes to this hall again and again, to kill the people it finds there, and so the king has sent for a great hero to come and slay it."

"Beowulf," I said. "I know the story."

"You know the legend," said Amanda. "This is the history."

"Is it very different?" I said.

"The past that used to be was always magical," said Amanda. "But never perfect. Magic has its dark side. Monsters, as well as marvels."

"Then why should I help bring things like that back?" I said.

"Because people need monsters to fight."

"To prove they can win?"

"To prove they have what it takes to stand against them," said Amanda. "Sometimes, it takes a monster to make a hero."

She set off again, heading for the hall. It had the look of a place under siege, but when Amanda and I finally came to a halt before the closed door the first thing I noticed was that there weren't any guards.

"If there's a monster lurking in the neighbourhood, shouldn't someone be minding the store?" I said.

"All the armed guards in the world couldn't keep Grendel out," said Amanda. "The only protection these people have is safety in numbers."

She snapped her fingers at the door, and there was the sound of locks unlocking and heavy bolts sliding back. The door swung open on its own and I nodded to Amanda, careful not to seem too impressed.

"Nice trick."

"I practice," said Amanda.

"Why would you need to?" I said.

"People aren't always pleased to see me."

"I can't think why."

Inside the hall, a great crowd of people were standing very still, struck silent by our unexpected entrance. Open hostility filled their faces, and quite a few drawn swords were pointing in our direction. Everyone seemed to be wearing long woollen robes under heavy leather armour, which couldn't have been very comfortable given the muggy atmosphere filling the tightly packed hall. I thought they'd all relax once they realised we weren't the Grendel monster, but everyone was staring at Amanda as though they knew her, and not in a good way.

She walked straight at them, and the crowd separated and fell back to form a narrow avenue. My back muscles crawled with tension as I walked alongside Amanda. I wasn't seeing any of the grudging respect we'd found at Queen Boudicca's court; instead, the complete lack of welcome at Hrothgar's hall seemed to have its roots in some deep-seated anger. As though Amanda was an infamous criminal who had dared to return to the scene of her crimes. The few glances that came my way were simply accusing, for daring to be with Amanda. So I made a point of smiling easily about me and bestowing a convivial gaze on one and all, because a confident *I know something you don't* smile can be better protection than any armour.

Amanda and I finally came to a halt before a great stone throne, set on its own raised dais at the far end of the hall. A basic stone seat with a tall back, it looked like it had been carved from a solid block rather than constructed. Angels and demons had been crudely etched into the stone, so they could glare ferociously at everyone who appeared before them. Amanda nodded pleasantly to the old man sitting stiffly on the throne.

"Hello, Hrothgar. Been a while, hasn't it?"

A tall stick-figure of a man hovering protectively beside the throne leaned forward to glare at Amanda. He was wearing a long apron of mail over leather armour and had the kind of face that leant itself to scowls.

"You will address the king with proper respect! Kneel, and bow your head!"

"Not on the best day you ever had," said Amanda. "Hello, Mathias; how's your back these days?"

The man dropped a hand to the sword at his side, and I got ready to leap up onto the dais and do something undiplomatic, but the king silenced his man with a gesture.

"Enough, Steward. The lady Amanda will go her own way, because she always does."

"It's part of the job description," Amanda said calmly.

The king studied her for a while. "I wondered if I would ever see you again. Didn't you do enough damage, the last time you were here?"

"I did what you asked," said Amanda.

"But not what I wanted."

"Yes, well, that's life," Amanda said briskly.

"Where have you been, these last twenty years?" said the king.

"Keeping busy."

"I have lost good people to the beast Grendel! I could have used your help long before this."

"Kings are supposed to solve their own problems," said Amanda.

Hrothgar slumped back on his throne, as though just the force of the argument had worn him out. He had a deeply lined face, and strands of thin grey hair poked out from under his plain golden crown. He looked like he might have been a big man once, but time and hard use had scoured most of that away. His long white robe looked like the finest cloth, and he wore a heavy gold medallion over his breast, but otherwise he was just a tired old man worn down by years and circumstance.

The steward hovering at his side looked to be much the same age, but a stubborn energy kept his back straight and his gaze fierce. He sniffed loudly, and produced a heavy fur cloak from behind the throne.

"Lean forward, so I can wrap this around you," he said to the king. "You know the draughts in this place play merry hell with your joints. I'll have to get the rubbing alcohol out after we're done here."

"Stop fussing, Steward," said the king. "I'm not an invalid."

"One of us has to be sensible and it isn't going to be you, is it?" said the steward. "Do you want some hot soup, to keep out the chill? There's some leftover bits of chicken and bacon I could throw in."

"I don't need anything, Steward! Leave off your mithering, so I can hear myself think."

The steward dropped the cloak over the back of the throne. "Well, it's there if you want it. Catch your death of cold, see if I care."

"You have to excuse him," the king said to Amanda. "Though I sometimes forget why. I suppose I should thank you for showing up at all."

"The last time we spoke, you banished me forever and a day," Amanda said sweetly.

"I had reason," said the king.

Amanda's smile was suddenly a cold and implacable thing. "Always remember, Hrothgar, that I am not one of your people. I was here before you, and I will still be here long after you and your kingdom are gone."

The watching crowd made a low unhappy sound. Amanda shot them a glance, and they all went quiet. The steward started to say something, but the king stopped him with a gesture and stared at Amanda.

"Let the past stay in the past," he said flatly. "My only concern now is the beast. Unseen for centuries, the legendary monster of the marshes has returned to plague us. Can you save my people from the curse of Grendel?"

"No," said Amanda. "But I've brought you a man who can."

All eyes turned in my direction. I did some of my best smiling and nodding, but no one seemed particularly impressed. The king looked me over carefully, trying to see what Amanda saw in me.

"And this is?" he said finally.

"Jack Daimon, the Outsider," Amanda said grandly. "He slays monsters, among other things."

The king nodded to me gravely. "Then be welcome in my court, monster-killer. There is work for you here."

I nodded to him, and deliberately adopted a calm and casual tone, just to make it clear I was my own man. Never give an authority figure an advantage or they'll walk all over you.

"I'll do what I can, but I have to ask: what possessed you to build a hall in the middle of nowhere in the first place?"

The steward looked like he wanted to yell at me for speaking so bluntly to the king, but knew there wasn't any point. The king just nodded judiciously.

"A fair question, Sir Outsider. I needed to make it clear to my neighbouring monarchs that while these marshlands might show as disputed territory on the maps, I still rule here."

"From what I've seen," I said, "there's nothing out there worth fighting over."

"Land matters," the king said heavily. "Because what there is, is all there is. The extent of a king's land defines his power. And besides, this hall was a gift to my daughter, the Princess Jann. She has always loved these marshes, and the wildlife to be found here. It's the one place she seems content, away from the noise and bustle of my court.

"I thought she'd be safe enough, guarded by a handful of my most trusted men. But then Grendel appeared, and killed all the guards. My daughter was lucky to escape with her life. I didn't want her to come back here, but I couldn't leave the hall abandoned in the face of my enemies, so now here we both are, along with the fiercest warriors of my realm. To finish off the beast once and for all."

There was a general growl of agreement from the crowd. I looked them over carefully. They seemed a violent enough bunch, just waiting for the monster to make an entrance so they could jump all over it. I turned back to the king.

"How many people have you lost to Grendel?"

"Too many," the Steward said flatly. "It's pride, not strategy, that brings us here."

"It's up to you, Steward," the king said mildly. "You can hold your tongue, or I'll find someone to hold it for you."

The steward just sniffed. "Do you want some of that soup or not?"

The king sniffed. "I'd rather eat a dog's testicles."

"They are part of the recipe," the steward admitted.

The king almost smiled, and turned his attention back to me. "Brave men died defending this hall. To abandon it now would dishonour their sacrifice. So to aid us I have summoned the great hero Beowulf, fabled slayer of monsters."

A warrior more impressive than everyone else put together came striding through the crowd to join us. Broad-shouldered, with a barrel chest, he was wrapped in well-polished but well-worn mail, and the sword at his side looked big enough to turn any monster into bite-sized chunks. Beowulf had a handsome face, with piercing blue eyes and a great mane of blond hair, along with bulging muscles and more than his fair share of scars. Every inch a fighter, Beowulf gave the impression of being utterly confident in his abilities. He took up a relaxed stance before the throne, nodded briefly to the king in the manner of someone who'd met a lot of kings in his line of work, and favoured Amanda with a winning smile.

"So, you're the famous sorceress who traumatised the kingdom twenty years ago. They've been telling me stories about you that would give white hairs to a rabid wolf. They said you were beautiful, and they were right, but I thought you'd be scarier."

"I am," said Amanda.

Beowulf thought about that, and then turned his smile on me. It was wide and easy and full of bluff charm, and would probably have worked on anyone else.

"Greetings, fellow monster-slayer, and welcome to Grendel's feeding ground. I don't see a sword at your side or an axe in your hand; would you like to borrow a weapon, or are you planning to just throw yourself into the beast's jaws and choke it to death?"

I smiled easily back at him. "I thought I might reach down its throat and rip its heart out."

Beowulf let out a brief bark of laughter. "I'd pay good coin to see that."

"What do you know about this beast?" I said.

Beowulf folded his scarred arms across his massive chest and frowned hard, doing his best to look like an expert. "From what the Princess Jann has been telling me, barriers were no obstacle to Grendel. It just appeared out of nowhere, inside the hall. Inhumanly fast and deadly, none of the guards' weapons had any effect on it. But this time, we will strike it down and trample it underfoot!"

He was talking loudly to make sure everyone in the hall could hear him and take comfort, but the courage and conviction in his voice sounded real enough. He turned back to Amanda, and showed her his most charming smile.

"You really are as comely as they said, lady sorceress."

"While you are everything I imagined you would be," said Amanda.

Beowulf's grin widened. "So, are you doing anything after the battle?"

"Let's see if we're both still here," said Amanda.

Beowulf laughed and Amanda smiled. I felt left out, so rather than watch them get down to some serious flirting I wandered off round the hall, to see what there was to see. And not because I was in any way jealous. Men and women in layers of armour, with heavy swords and axes at their sides, gathered around a series of wooden trestle tables, pounding down the drinks and ploughing through the food. The conversations sounded cheerful enough, and there was a lot of unforced laughter; there was nothing to suggest they were at all worried about the monster from the marshes. They were far too busy celebrating life, in defiance of death.

None of them seemed interested in talking to me, so I was a little surprised when a tall and well-made young lady suddenly emerged from the crowd to plant herself right in front of me and all but force a cup of drink into my hand. Dressed in an elegant green gown, with golden trimmings to match her long blonde braids, she was sharp-faced rather than pretty. She was also one of the few people in the hall who wasn't carrying some kind of weapon. I accepted the cup from her, took a good sip, and pulled a face despite myself. The woman laughed.

"Uisge is a warrior's drink."

"You'd certainly have to be some kind of hero to drink this stuff voluntarily," I said. "I'm thinking of spitting a mouthful of it at Grendel, just to see if it will poison the beast."

The woman nodded solemnly. "I am the Princess Jann. Are you really another slayer of monsters?"

I'd never met a princess before, but I didn't bow. I was the Outsider, after all.

"I've killed my share," I said.

She looked me over critically, taking her time.

"You're not as big as Beowulf."

"Size isn't everything."

"You're not even wearing a sword," said Jann.

I hefted the backpack on my shoulder. "I have other things. I understand you've seen this beast in action?"

All the animation went out of her face, as bad memories haunted her eyes. "It was hard to see much. As though the beast has some power over your eyes, so no one can see it until it makes its move. My father had provided me with the very best guards, and the beast slaughtered them like cattle. Hopefully, my future husband will do better."

"Future husband?" I said politely.

She nodded at Beowulf, still trying out his best smiles on Amanda. "My father has promised him my hand and half his kingdom, if he slays Grendel. The usual deal."

"Don't you get a say in the matter?" I said.

"I know my duty," said the princess. "And he does look rather splendid, doesn't he?"

"Tell me about the beast," I said.

"I only really remember it in dreams," she said slowly. "I saw my guards cut and slice at Grendel, but its wounds healed in a moment. It was huge and terrible, swift and merciless, and its teeth and claws tore through armour as easily as flesh."

"Beowulf seems confident he can kill it," I said.

"He's Beowulf," said Jann. "Because he's always been able to kill monsters, he thinks he always will."

Something in her tone caught my attention. "Would I be right in thinking he's not the brightest button in the box?"

"He's smarter than he looks," said Jann.

"He'd have to be," I said.

"Hush!" said Jann. But she couldn't keep from smiling as she said it.

"Where does Grendel come from?" I said, getting us back on track.

"The beast must have a lair somewhere in the marshes," said Jann. "But no one has been able to find it. My father sent out search parties, and I even led a few myself, because no one knows these marshes like I do, but the beast leaves no tracks and no trail . . . as though it can appear and disappear whenever it wishes." She scowled deeply. "My father wanted to go out after the beast himself, but his advisors wouldn't allow it. They weren't happy about him coming here, but he put his foot down. Perhaps because once it would have been him, not Beowulf, that everyone called on to slay the beast."

She looked at the old man, sitting like a statue on his stone throne. "I appeared late in his life, so I never got to see him in his prime. Everyone says that he and Mathias, the steward, were unbeatable on the battlefield in their day. But now the years weigh heavy on them, and my father and his friend are not what they were. It is a hard thing, to outlive your own legend."

"You're the king's only child?" I said.

"Because he had no sons, I was raised as a warrior," said Jann. "But I never wanted that, so the moment I was old enough I ran away to the marshlands. I have always cared more about the local wildlife than killing people I didn't know just because they were from somewhere else. My father sent men to bring me back, but I kept on running away, until finally he just gave me my head and let me get on with it."

"And you never saw any trace of Grendel in the marshes, before the attacks began?"

She shook her head firmly. "Never. I thought the beast was just another scary story, like the old witch of the marshes, that no one has seen in years."

"Has Grendel ever attacked anyone outside this hall?"

"No," said Jann. "I can't help feeling responsible for what happened to my guards. They were only there because my father built this hall for me."

"Perhaps the beast thinks it's defending its territory," I said.

Jann nodded slowly. "There could be something in that. My father keeps threatening to drain the marshes, to make new land for crops. Even though that would kill off most of the wildlife, and destroy the only place I've ever felt at home."

I thought about the desolate scene under the grey sky, and something must have shown in my face, because Jann chuckled softly.

"I know; it's not for everyone."

"Do you believe Beowulf can kill the beast?" I said carefully.

"He's brave enough," said Jann. "He came all the way here from another kingdom, just for the chance to kill a legend. And he does have a reputation for getting the job done. But, having met the man, I can't help wondering whether he killed all those monsters to protect innocent lives, or for his own glory." She stopped, to look again at the king on his throne. "My father shouldn't be here, risking his life. That's Beowulf's job."

"Why is he here?" I said.

"Because the other warriors wouldn't have come, if he wasn't there on his throne to inspire them."

"Why does he need them, now he has Beowulf?"

"Because even the greatest monster-killer can have a bad day," said Jann. She glowered around the crowded hall. "I just wish they'd finish off the beast and leave, so I can have my life back."

She turned abruptly, and stalked off into the crowd. I turned to look at Beowulf, just in time to see Amanda leave him. She moved over to stand before the throne, and the king leaned forward so the two of them could talk privately. I eased quietly through the crowd, careful to stay out of the king's line of sight, until I was close enough to overhear what they were saying.

"I haven't forgotten what you did for me," said the king.

"I shouldn't have done it, but you wanted it so much."

"My wife died, trying to give me children. If I had died without an heir, the surrounding kingdoms would have devastated this land fighting over it. That's why I had to have your help."

"You were never supposed to have children," said Amanda. "Finding a way to cheat the fates wasn't easy."

"I couldn't believe it when you told me I had to go deep into the marshes, to meet with a woman who lived alone and had a reputation almost as uncanny as yours. But I lay down with her, and she gave me a child." The king shook his head slowly. "I never saw her again, after the child was born."

"Her name was Fritha," said Amanda. "The last time I visited her hut it was empty, and there was no sign of her anywhere."

"Good," said the steward.

Amanda looked at him, and he stopped talking.

"And now here you are, back again," said the king. "I have grown old, while you look exactly as I remember you."

"Why do your people hate me?" said Amanda.

"You are remembered as the sorceress who defied the king by refusing him a son," said the Steward.

Amanda smiled. "I wonder who started that rumour." She fixed her gaze on the king. "Why are you risking your life here?"

"I couldn't keep Jann away from the marshlands," said the king. "Perhaps because something in her blood calls to her. I built this hall so she could have a place of her own. But now Grendel has returned I have to be here, to protect her."

The steward scowled fiercely at Amanda. "There must be something you could do."

"I've already done too much," said Amanda. And she turned and walked away.

Princess Jann burst out of the crowd, to take Amanda's place. She stood tall and proud before the throne, glaring at her father.

"I never asked for any of this! Why can't you just leave me alone?"

"You're all I have," said the king.

"I don't want you here!"

Jann spun on her heel and plunged back into the crowd, and everyone moved quickly to get out of her way as she headed for the front door. The king gestured for it to be unbolted and unlocked, and Jann went out into the night, and the marshes. The door was quickly closed and locked behind her.

I couldn't believe Hrothgar had just let his daughter go. I wouldn't have spent a night alone on those marshes for a bet. I pushed my way through the crowd, to face the king.

"She doesn't even have a weapon! You have to send someone after her!"

"My daughter has spent most of her life in the marshlands," said the king. "And never once come to any harm. Besides, no one has ever won an argument with my daughter."

"Stubborn as a mule," said the steward. "Wonder where she got that from?"

"Now you tell me," Beowulf said loudly.

There were fond smiles, and a certain amount of nodding from the crowd. It was clear from their faces that they all had a soft spot for their wayward princess.

The king carried on speaking to me, though his gaze was fixed on the closed door. "Grendel has never attacked anyone outside the hall. My daughter is probably safer than we are."

"Particularly if she starts talking to the beast," said the steward. "Poor thing would probably rip its own ears off and run for its life."

The crowd laughed, and went back to feasting and drinking. I looked casually around, just on the off chance that Amanda might be somewhere near, and saw she was back talking with Beowulf. She turned suddenly to catch my eye, and waved for me to come and join them. I took my time, just to make it clear I wasn't at anyone's beck and call.

"This is Jack," Amanda said to Beowulf. "A good man and true; I vouch for him."

"Then I accept him, as a fellow slayer of monsters," said Beowulf. We shook hands, or at least mine disappeared inside a huge scarred thing that had to be a hand because it was on the end of his arm. Beowulf released my hand unharmed and nodded easily to me.

"Amanda has been telling me all about you, Jack. How you go from place to place, dealing with supernatural threats; just like me."

"I get around," I said. "How did you get into the monster-slaying business?"

He shrugged. "It's the only thing I was ever any good at. And the pay was excellent. But now I have been promised a princess and a land of my own to rule . . . it's hard to see how I could ever hope to top that."

"Are you thinking about retiring?" I said.

"Be nice to sleep in a bed of my own, for a change," said Beowulf. "Would you ever retire, Jack?"

I glanced at Amanda. "Not as long as I'm needed."

"You're needed here," said Amanda.

"To do what?"

"You'll know, when the time comes."

She smiled absently at both of us and then drifted off into the crowd, lost in her own thoughts. Beowulf and I looked at each other, and shrugged pretty much in unison. We talked weapons and tactics for a while, and to my surprise I found myself warming to the man. Beowulf was pleasantly uncomplicated, a man who killed monsters for a living not because he saw himself as any kind of hero but because it brought him gold, fame, and the adulation of women. I showed him some of the things from my backpack, and he took a professional interest, but nothing really impressed him until I brought out my athame. Beowulf studied the witch knife closely, while being very careful not to touch it.

"There's a power in the blade," he said finally. "But whether it'll be any use against Grendel . . ."

"It's supposed to cut through anything," I said.

"According to the princess, her guards' swords cut into Grendel easily enough," said Beowulf. "But its wounds heal so fast you can hear the edges slam together."

"So how are you planning to kill it?" I said.

He shrugged. "Cut off the head, and then throw it into the fire before the beast can stick it back on."

"I've had some success with that tactic," I said. I looked at him thoughtfully. "Did you know what you were getting into, before you came here?"

"I never ask questions," said Beowulf. "Apart from: how much are you paying? And anyway... I was at a loose end, spent all my coin and outstayed my welcome, so it seemed like the right time to move on. How long have you known the sorceress Amanda?"

"Not long," I said.

"From what I've been hearing, back in the day she had a reputation as a game player," Beowulf said carefully. "Always two steps ahead of everyone else. And only she knew which game she was playing."

"You seemed very taken with her," I said.

He shook his head quickly, showing me a smile with very little humour in it. "Flirting with the ladies is just part of the job. Playing the big hero, so people will take me seriously. But I think your pretty sorceress has serious teeth." He stopped, and looked out across the hall. "And speaking of the scary little she-devil, I think your mistress is summoning you, Jack."

"I am not her dog," I said sharply.

He grinned. "We're all someone's dog."

I made my way through the crowd to join Amanda. She gestured for me to move in close, so we could talk privately, though everyone around us was already going out of their way to ignore us. Amanda looked back at Beowulf, who was busy chatting up a warrior woman even bigger and more scarred than he was. He showed her his muscles, and she giggled like a schoolgirl.

"Charm will get you past more defences than a double-handed battle-axe," said Amanda.

"I get the feeling he might actually be the real deal," I said.

"Oh, he is," said Amanda. "But he's never met anything like Grendel."

I looked at her narrowly. "You're keeping things from me."

"Not all my secrets are mine to share," said Amanda. "You overheard enough of my conversation with the king to know that."

"What is Grendel?" I said bluntly.

"An act of revenge, from out of the past."

And then we both looked round, as Hrothgar raised his voice and called to Amanda.

"I'd better go see what the old boy wants," said Amanda. "He'll only make a fuss otherwise. You see if you can keep Beowulf out of trouble until the beast turns up."

She went over to the throne. I went back to Beowulf, who was looking wistfully after the departing warrior woman.

"I thought you were promised to the princess," I said.

"I'm not married yet," he said cheerfully. "So, eat, drink, and pin someone good-looking up against a wall, because it might be your last chance."

I gestured around me, at the carousing warriors. "I can't believe how happy everyone is. You'd never know they were expecting a demon beast to show up at any moment and gnaw all their faces off."

"These are the finest warriors and back-alley fighters the kingdom has to offer," said Beowulf. "Brought together by a common cause; a chance to be better than they think they are. To defend their land and their princess, and perhaps for the first time in their lives ... to be heroes."

I nodded slowly. "What do you think Grendel is?"

"People have bent my ear with all kinds of stories," Beowulf said slowly. "Some say it's a descendent of Cain, the first killer. Others believe the beast is the result of some magical working that went terribly wrong. But the general feeling is that it's just something big and nasty from the marshlands. There's a lot of wildlife around here that most people never get to see."

"But if it is some legendary beast that hasn't been seen for centuries ... what brought it back now?"

"Beats the hell out of me," said Beowulf. He grabbed a cup of Uisge from a passing tray, and knocked it back without flinching. "There are always mysteries, where monsters are concerned."

Despite all the determinedly raucous partying, it seemed to me that there was a definite tension in the air. Swords and axes had started to appear in people's hands, as they readied themselves for an attack that could come from any direction. Others were casually leaning back against a wall, to make sure nothing could sneak up on them. Beowulf followed my gaze, finished his drink and threw the cup aside, and then raised his voice commandingly.

"Stand ready, my brave warriors! Remember that Beowulf is with you, the legendary slayer of monsters who has never known defeat. When you fight alongside me, you become legendary too!"

The crowd roared their approval, cheering him and themselves. And then everyone broke off as something pounded heavily against the locked front door. A hush fell across the hall, as everyone stood very still. And then a harsh bark of laughter came from the throne.

"Grendel's hardly going to knock, and wait politely for us to open the door, is it?" said the king. "That's my daughter, you damned fools. Open the door and let her in."

The men nearest jumped to obey, and hauled the door open. Princess Jann stormed right past them, heading for her father, and the men rushed to lock and bolt the door again.

"There's no sign of Grendel anywhere," said the princess. "But the beast is getting close. I can feel it."

She looked around for Beowulf, who saluted her with a fresh cup of Uisge.

"You mustn't worry, Princess," he said calmly. "I will rip Grendel's arm off and beat its head in with the wet end."

The princess slapped the cup out of his hand.

"How many of the people here will die, before that happens?"

"It's only a monster," Beowulf said steadily. "And I know all there is to know about killing monsters."

He produced a dagger from his belt, and offered it to the princess.

"When the time comes, stand with me, Princess. You can guard my back."

Jann hefted the dagger and suddenly grinned at him. "Hell with that; you can guard mine."

Laughter ran through the crowd, and they all started talking again. Amanda appeared at my side, and slipped a companionable arm through mine.

"I do like to see everyone playing nicely together."

"I don't know why you brought me here," I said. "It doesn't look like I'm going to be needed."

"You will be," said Amanda. "Stand ready, Jack. You'll get your chance."

The crowd fell silent again, and when I looked round, I realised everyone had stopped what they were doing to stare at the princess. She seemed strangely preoccupied, frowning hard as though listening to something only she could hear. Her eyes were far away. Beowulf watched her carefully.

"It's close," said Jann, her voice strange and fey. "Can't you feel it? The beast is coming for you, and oh, it's so angry . . ."

Beowulf moved in close beside her, his voice low and reassuring. "You're the only one who's seen the beast, Princess. What can you tell us about it?"

Jann's answer was slow and confused, as though she was caught up in a dream. "It's not natural. It's a wild thing, from the night of the world."

I moved quickly through the crowd and eased in on her other side, keeping my voice carefully calm and supportive.

"Do you know why it wants to kill people?"

"To protect its home," said Jann.

The hall was utterly quiet now, everyone's attention fixed on the princess.

"Can we talk to the beast?" I said. "Reason with it?"

"No," said Jann. "There is only rage, and hate; no reason."

"It's just a monster," said Beowulf. "Doing what monsters do. Let it show itself, so I can kill it and be done."

"It's already here," said Jann.

Everyone looked quickly around them, weapons at the ready. The steward called for a defensive circle around the throne, and some of the more experienced warriors hurried forward to create a ring of drawn steel. The king looked as though he wanted to join them, but even as he started to rise from his stone seat the steward put a firm hand on his shoulder and forced him down again. And then he drew his sword and went to join the circle, placing himself directly in front of the throne, so Grendel would have to get through him to get to the king.

"Don't be a fool, Mathias," Hrothgar said sharply. "You're too old for this."

"So are you," said the steward, not looking back. "But my life doesn't matter."

"You know you have always mattered to me," said the king.

"I know," said the steward.

Princess Jann suddenly snapped out of her fey mood, and set her back against Beowulf's. She held her dagger out before her, and her hand was perfectly steady. Everyone was glaring about them, eager for some action at last. I could feel Grendel's presence, as though a cold shadow had fallen across the hall.

"It's almost time, Jack," Amanda said quietly.

"These warriors are ready to lay down their lives to stop this monster!" I said harshly. "But if it really is everything the princess says, it's going to butcher every living soul in this hall. There must be something you can do to help!"

Amanda looked at me steadily. "Would you have me take away their chance to be heroes? I've done what matters. I brought them you. Don't let them down, Jack."

"But what am I supposed to do?" I said desperately.

"What no one else can," said Amanda.

Voices suddenly cried out, thick with shock and horror, as Grendel reared up in their midst. Huge and powerful, the beast had a wolf's ferocity and a bear's bulk, but it stood like a man. Silver fur covered rippling muscles, and its long muzzle gaped wide as though it was silently laughing at us. The nearest warriors raised their weapons and the beast surged forward, tearing out throats and ripping through armour and flesh. Blood spurted thickly as body after body crashed to the floor.

Men and women came charging forward from every side, howling their war cries. They hacked and cut at the beast, but Grendel didn't even try to defend itself. Steel blades sank deep into its flesh, but there was no blood and the beast's wounds disappeared the moment the weapons were jerked free. The beast killed everyone who came within reach, and crimson gore streamed from its grinning jaws.

Beowulf shouted for everyone to get out of his way as he forced his way through the mess of heaving bodies, his face set and grim. Grendel spun round to face him, and Beowulf brought his massive sword swinging down with all his strength behind it. But at the last moment the beast darted to one side, and when Beowulf staggered on, caught off balance, Grendel lashed out with one overlong arm and sent him flying. Beowulf crashed through a dozen people before finally slamming into a stone wall. He dropped to his knees, all the strength knocked out of him, his face slack with shock. But he still clung grimly to his sword, and struggled to force himself back onto his feet.

Grendel headed for King Hrothgar. Howling warriors rushed forward to block its way and rain down blow after blow, but the beast just tore right through them and kept going. It reached the circle of warriors surrounding the throne, and every single one of them fought valiantly, attacking the beast with everything they had, but they had no more chance against Grendel than cattle in a slaughterhouse. The beast sent broken bodies flying in all directions, until there was no one left to face it but the steward. Grendel paused for a moment as the steward stubbornly placed his old body between the beast and the king, defying it to get past him. And then Grendel lashed out with a single clawed hand, and the old man rocked back on his feet as deep furrows opened up in his armoured chest. Blood coursed thickly down the length of his body, but he wouldn't fall. He hacked at the beast with desperate strength, and Grendel actually fell back a step. The steward seized his chance and rammed his sword into the beast's heart.

For a moment they stood facing each other, eyes locked over the steward's extended arm, and then Grendel forced its way along the blade and tore out the steward's throat. When the old man finally fell, it was like a tree toppling. Grendel pulled the sword out of its breast and threw it to one side. Hrothgar rose stiffly to his feet, and king and beast confronted each other, staring steadily into each other's eyes, as though everything that had gone before had been nothing but a prelude to this final meeting.

I was caught on the far side of the hall when Grendel appeared, and it took me some time to force my way through the confusion of heaving bodies. The mass slaughter was so swift most of it was over before I could get involved, and now the last of the warriors were standing very still, afraid to make any move in case it provoked the beast into attacking the king. I eased carefully between them, my witch knife in my hand. And that was when Amanda murmured in my ear, even though she was nowhere near me.

Not the athame, Jack. For this, you're going to need a silver blade.

And with that final clue, I understood what was happening. Grendel could appear out of nowhere, in the middle of a crowd, because it was a werewolf. That was why no sword could stop it, and its wounds always healed. One of the people in the hall had been Grendel, all along. I put away my athame, and took a thin silver dagger from my pack.

I looked around for Princess Jann, but there was no sign of her anywhere. So many bodies were piled up on the blood-soaked floor I couldn't tell which one of them was her. A cold rage moved through me, and my hand tightened on the hilt of the silver dagger as I raised my voice to yell at Grendel.

The long wolfish face turned away from the king. Everyone else hurried to get out of my way as I advanced on the beast. Grendel watched me approach, its eyes fierce and knowing. I breathed slowly and steadily, holding onto my self-control with both hands. I knew I'd only get one chance to avenge the Princess Jann, and all the others who had fallen.

And then Beowulf let out a deafening roar and charged across the hall. The beast's head whipped round, and even as I started to lift my silver dagger Grendel went racing to meet Beowulf. The monster-killer's sword came hammering down, and buried itself deep in the beast's shoulder. The sheer impact drove Grendel down onto one knee, but the beast didn't cry out. Beowulf jerked his sword free, and the terrible wound healed in a moment.

"You can't kill it with steel!" I yelled. "You need silver!"

Beowulf dropped his sword, and pulled a silver knife from the top of his boot. Grendel lashed out with a clawed hand, and Beowulf just managed to duck under it. His silver blade leapt out to cut the beast's throat, but Grendel jerked its head back at the last moment. The knife's silver tip opened up a long thin cut across the beast's face, and Grendel dropped to its knees, howling horribly. But it was Princess Jann who hit the blood-soaked floor.

For a moment, everything was still. The princess knelt before the shocked Beowulf, blood streaming down her wounded face. The king stared at her. Beowulf stood over the princess, his silver blade raised for a killing blow . . . And then he slowly lowered his hand.

"I can't," he said. "Not you."

"You have to," said Jann.

"No," said Beowulf. "There has to be another way."

He opened his hand and let the silver dagger fall to the floor. Grendel burst out of the princess, and threw itself at Beowulf's throat. He got an arm up just in time, and blood spurted as the beast's fangs sank deep into the muscle. Grendel forced Beowulf down onto the floor, jerked its jaws free, and went for his throat again. And I stepped in behind the beast and drove my silver dagger through its ribs and into its heart. Because I was the Outsider, and I have always known my duty.

Grendel reared up, and then fell back against me. Its weight would have pinned me to the floor, but it was Jann who landed on top of me, with my dagger protruding from her ribs. I held her in my arms, and murmured comfortingly to her. She snuggled wearily against me, like a sleepy child. And then she died.

I pulled out the dagger, gently lowered Jann's body to the floor, and got to my feet. The hall was silent. The few remaining warriors stared silently at their dead princess.

"It all makes sense now," I said. "Jann's closeness to the wild animals of the marshland. Her long walks, in the only place she felt at home. She killed her own guards to lure the king here. He had to die, because she knew he was planning to drain the marshes and kill off all the local wildlife." I shook my head. "The only thing I don't understand is how she became a werewolf."

Hrothgar stepped down from his throne, and came forward to join me. He looked small and lost and broken.

"She always did take more after her mother, than me."

I looked at him, and a great many things suddenly made sense.

"You knew," I said. "You knew all along."

"I suspected," he said. "But what could I do? She was my daughter, my only child. None of this was her fault. Grendel . . . was her mother's rage. I promised Fritha that if she gave me a child, I would make her my queen. But how could I? She wasn't human."

"So what did you do?" I said.

"I killed her," said the king. "And buried her body in the marshes. That's why I had to banish Amanda, so she would never find out what I'd done. But something called my daughter back to the marshlands, and brought out the beast in her." He knelt down, and took his dead daughter in his arms. "All my fault. All of it."

Beowulf came over to stand beside me, pale-faced but steady as he tightened a length of cloth around his savaged arm.

"You did what needed doing, Jack. What none of us could have done."

"I wanted to save her," I said.

"You did," said Beowulf. "You saved her from the curse of being Grendel."

I looked around and saw understanding in the eyes of those who'd survived, but no forgiveness. I had killed their princess. Amanda came over to stand beside me.

"Time to go, Jack."

We headed for the door. No one tried to stop us.

Outside, darkness covered the marshes. The stars were out, and a crooked moon shed shimmering light across the standing waters. A cold wind was blowing, sharp enough to cut to the bone. I didn't look at Amanda, as we walked away from the hall.

"If this is what magic does to the world, I don't want anything to do with it."

"You can't have the light without the dark," said Amanda. "I showed you this because I needed you to be sure that I'm not hiding anything from you. But think on this, Jack . . . It was the threat of Grendel that brought those people together, and made them brave enough to fight a monster. It made them heroes. That's what monsters are for."

"Most of those people are dead!"

"I never promised you paradise, Jack, just a better world. Where monsters can be killed."

"You knew Jann was Grendel."

"I knew her mother," said Amanda, looking out over the marshes. "I should never have put Hrothgar and Fritha together, but she wanted a child as much as he did. And I was so much younger then, and thought I knew everything."

"So you brought me here to kill the child you created," I said.

"Together, we put an end to the curse of Grendel. So no more innocent people would have to die. Most importantly, now you know that you are a man who can do what's necessary."

"Get me out of here," I said. "Take me somewhere better."

"I can do that," said Amanda.

CHAPTER SIX
HEARTS OF STEEL

And just like that we were standing on a grassy plain like a great green ocean. The sky was that perfect cloudless blue of high summer, the sun was bright and cheerful, and the air was heavy with birdsong and the buzz of insects. A cloud of vividly coloured butterflies swept past us like an assortment of flags from unknown nations. Amanda smiled about her with quiet satisfaction, as though she was responsible for all of it.

"Well," I said. "This is more like it. Where are we?"

"Just a short walk from King Arthur's Camelot," said Amanda.

I stared at her. "As in the Knights of the Round Table? I love those stories!"

"Most people do. Because everyone wants to believe there was at least one time in history when might stood in support of right."

I looked around me, taking in the glorious summer's day. Everything seemed bursting with life and packed with promise: a whole world just waiting to be explored.

"This is how England used to be?" I said.

"For ages and ages."

"What happened?"

"The secret masters."

I fixed her with my best hard stare. "Are you ever going to tell me who they are? And why they did it?"

"Of course!"

"When?"

"When you're ready."

I considered saying several things, but didn't. It was too nice a day for an argument.

"So, where's Camelot?"

"This way. Shall we go?"

A huge castle stood tall and proud in the middle of a great open plain, approached by half a dozen different roads. As though it was the only place worth going to. The outer wall was a creamy white stone, with crenelated battlements and tall slit windows. Great towers rose up beyond the wall, shining brilliantly in the sunlight, capped with pointed roofs like slanting hats. Flags and pennants fluttered bravely, bearing designs I didn't recognise but were still somehow familiar, as though I'd seen them before in dreams. A blocky stone keep thrust out from the front wall, its entrance left invitingly open. Crowds of people streamed in and out, and the guards on duty seemed perfectly happy to let them get on with it.

I stood and stared, drinking it all in. It was like finding out fairy stories were real after all. When I finally turned to Amanda her smile was full of quiet understanding.

"Camelot," she said. "It really is everything the stories say."

"Thank you," I said. "Wherever we have to go, and whatever we have to do, this sight alone is enough to justify it."

"That's how Camelot affects everyone," said Amanda. "It's why people have never given up on King Arthur and his dream, despite everything the rewriting of history could do to make them forget."

"And we can just . . . walk in there?"

"Camelot is for everyone. That's the point."

"What about the guards?" I said. "They're bound to realise we're not from around here."

"The guards are only there to protect the castle from those who would threaten the dream," said Amanda.

"Who'd want to threaten a place like this?" I said. Just the thought made me angry.

"Arthur believed that the whole point of being king was to protect the innocent from those who wanted to subjugate them. With an attitude like that, he was bound to make enemies."

"Like who?"

Amanda sighed. "It never ceases to amaze me how many things humanity can find to fight over. Come on, let's go and make ourselves known."

"Don't we need an invitation, or something?"

"Oh, I'm pretty sure they're expecting us," said Amanda.

To get to the keep, we had to pass through a small village of tents and marquees that had sprung up outside, along with any number of stalls and booths offering everything from delicate glassware to candied treats to hand-tooled leather boots and gloves. Bargaining was loud and spirited, and equally enjoyed by both sides. The air was thick with rich and nourishing scents, and I would have liked to stop and sample some of the unfamiliar foods on offer, but Amanda linked her arm firmly through mine and kept me moving.

The narrow aisles were packed with people in medieval clothes, chattering loudly about anything and everything. It seemed like everyone had a smile on their face, and a cheerful greeting for all who passed by. Children raced back and forth, raising a racket and getting under everyone's feet, but no one seemed to mind. Dogs ran around like mad things, chasing their own tails when there wasn't anything better on offer, while miniature mammoths chirped happily as they tried to keep up. No one paid Amanda or me any particular attention as we strode through the crowd, except to nod and grin, as if to say *Isn't this marvellous?* And I grinned and nodded back at them, because it really was. Until a thought occurred to me, and I turned to Amanda.

"Why are all these people outside the castle?" I said quietly. "Are they not allowed in because they're trade, or commoners?"

"Stop thinking in terms of our history," said Amanda. "Camelot is one big fortress, home to the Knights of the Round Table, and stuffed to bursting with the small army of people it takes to support them and their mission. These people came here of their own free will, to supply all the little luxuries the castle staff don't have time for. Everyone wants to do their bit, for Camelot."

"Are we really going to meet King Arthur? And his knights?"

"Of course," said Amanda, smiling like an indulgent mother with an overexcited child.

"And Merlin?"

"Oh, he'll be here." Amanda's mouth tightened in a way that was hard to read. "Try not to upset him, Jack. He has a very odd sense of humour."

I took that under consideration. "Why have you brought me here?"

"Because you wanted to see something better."

"Yes, and thank you. But what are we here for?"

"Camelot is the culmination of everything you saw in the original Londinium," said Amanda. "All the peoples of Britain, human and magical, living together in one great society. And that enraged the secret masters. It meant they'd lost the argument, that humankind should be superior to all. They realised the only way to get rid of all the other creatures was to remove the magic that made their existence possible. This is where the rewriting of history was decided."

I looked at the castle looming up before us. For all its fantastic architecture, it seemed very real and solid.

"So is Camelot history? Or legend?"

"This is history," said Amanda. "But it will be reduced to legend. Arthur wasn't supposed to be remembered at all, but Camelot mattered so much to people they simply refused to give it up. It lived on, in the dream of a history so much better than anything people were taught."

"What about Mordred, and the fall of Camelot?"

"Never happened," said Amanda. "Arthur's son was a great hero, and the fall just another attempt to undermine the myth and destroy its power. The same with Sir Lancelot; all that nonsense about a love triangle was added to make those involved seem less admirable. Lancelot was the king's closest friend, and Guinevere would have punched a hole through a wall with anyone who tried to get between her and Arthur. Camelot never fell, in the past that was. It was the inspiration for a Golden Age that should have lasted forever."

"But if everything here is so great, why did Arthur need his knights?" I said. "Why build this great fortress?"

"Not all magical creatures were ready to accept humans as their equal," said Amanda. "There's a constant threat from dragons, ogres, and Dark elves. This is a Golden Age, Jack, not heaven on earth."

We headed for the keep. The two guards on duty recognised Amanda immediately, snapped to attention, and fired off salutes that positively quivered with enthusiasm. She nodded regally in return, and I gave the guards my best hard look, just to make it clear I was somebody too.

"You do get around, don't you?" I said quietly to Amanda.

She grinned. "You have no idea."

Beyond the keep lay a huge open courtyard brimming over with busily working people, most of whom broke off from whatever they were doing to stare at Amanda. She led me on through the sudden hush, and the crowd fell respectfully back to let us pass.

"Wherever you go, you do seem to make an impression," I said.

"I have no idea why."

"That makes you the only person who doesn't."

The clamour of hard work quickly resumed, and no one paid us any more attention. In a deliberate and watchful kind of way.

The cobbled square was covered with straw and mess and all kinds of animal droppings, and I was very careful where I put my feet. Horses bigger than most cars watched us intently from their stables. I supposed they had to be that big to carry knights in their armour, but the look in their eyes suggested they were fierce enough to win most battles on their own. Soldiers in battered mail practiced swordsmanship and archery, while others wrestled bare-chested in front of admiring spectators. Everywhere I looked it seemed like someone was busy sharpening blades on grindstones, or beating dents out of armour.

Just how many enemies did this Golden Age have?

Amanda plunged confidently through an opening in the far wall, and suddenly we were passing through broad corridors and wide-open plazas that were almost as crowded as the courtyard. People inside the castle had a more Shakespearean look: tights and doublets with ankle-length cloaks for the men, long sweeping dresses and high hats and wimples for the women. Styles and fashions that wouldn't appear for another thousand years in the history that would replace them.

We also passed elves and dwarves, yetis and unicorns, and a whole bunch of magical creatures I couldn't even put a name to. The Light elves were inhumanly graceful in their flashing silks and swirling capes, drifting through the corridors like dreams walking. The dwarves were square and solid with stone-grey skins, leather armour and red caps. Their arms bulged with so much muscle they probably didn't need tools to mine their ore, just punched it out of the rock walls. The yetis were huge shambling creatures covered in thick white fur, so tall their heads bumped against the ceilings. They ambled along, smiling shyly at everyone, and being very apologetic when they accidentally stepped on someone. The unicorns, on the other hand, were proud and haughty creatures who expected everyone else to get the hell out of their way, and were perfectly happy to shoulder them aside if they didn't move quickly enough. Everyone smiled on them indulgently, as though they were just fractious children.

Not entirely to my surprise every single magical creature we met recognised Amanda, and bowed their heads to her. She just smiled and kept going.

"This was Arthur's dream," she said. "That all who came here would be equal, and dedicated to protecting those in need. Camelot was a social experiment, to prove the various races could bring out the best in each other, and inspire one another to greatness. And Arthur was right. Camelot is a dream made real."

"I don't see any of the gods we met in Londinium," I said.

"They moved on," said Amanda. And something in the way she said that made it clear I shouldn't ask where, or why.

A harried figure came bustling through the crowds to intercept us, glowering fiercely at one and all. They didn't seem to take it personally. He was dressed more elegantly than everyone else put together, as though he'd put a lot of thought into how to look important. He had a thin body, a thin face, and very thin lips, and while he was careful to bow formally to Amanda, there was a definite grudging feel to it. She smiled graciously back at him.

"Jack, this is the seneschal. Arthur's butler, basically. He likes to think he's in charge here."

"Somebody has to keep the wheels turning, so that things get done," said the seneschal, in a sharp and fractious voice. "If you would care to follow me, Lady Amanda, the king has been anticipating your arrival for quite some time."

"Hold it," I said. "How did Arthur know we were coming?"

The seneschal condescended to look down his nose at me. There was a lot of nose to look down.

"The high sorcerer informed the king yesterday that you would be arriving today."

"Merlin," said Amanda. It was hard to tell whether she sounded more amused, or resigned.

"Quite," said the seneschal.

He led us through wide corridors lined with marvellous hanging tapestries, and paintings so bright and vivid they might have been created just the day before. I would have liked to hang around long enough to pay them the attention they deserved, but the seneschal would have none of it. I quietly considered giving his scrawny backside a good kick when no one was looking, but Amanda caught my eye and shook her head firmly. We finally came to a halt before a huge set of double doors, and the seneschal lifted a hand to knock. The doors swung open on their own. The seneschal's mouth pursed, as though to prevent him from saying what he really wanted, and then he drew himself up and led us into the royal presence.

The huge open chamber had the same scale and atmosphere as a cathedral, and a sense that this was where all the things that mattered were decided. The ceiling was so high you would have needed scaffolding just to dust out the corners. The floorboards had been waxed and polished to within an inch of their lives, but still bore the endless small dents that I supposed were inevitable where men walked around in full armour. Tall pillars had been fashioned from delicately veined marble, while magnificent stained-glass windows depicted armoured knights giving one-eyed giants and fire-breathing dragons a really hard time. But I only had eyes for the Round Table in the centre of the chamber.

It was everything I'd hoped it would be. Big enough to seat a hundred men, the great circle of tawney wood gleamed brightly, as though it burned with some inexhaustible inner fire. I tried to visualise what it must be like when all the knights were assembled around the table, shining in their armour like stars fallen to the earth, debating with their king on subjects of great matter. It must be like God enjoying a chat with his angels.

When I finally paid attention to the knights in armour waiting to meet us, I was a bit disappointed to find there were only four of them. They bowed to Amanda and ignored me, but I was getting used to that. The king stood a little apart from his knights, huge and splendid in his spotlessly polished armour, and smiling at Amanda as though she was the first good thing that had happened to him that day.

A final figure stood at the back of the chamber, staring off into the distance as though concentrating on something far more important. An elderly gentleman with a gaunt face and scraped-back grey hair, he was dressed to the height of Victorian fashion, right down to the gold watch chain stretched across his waistcoat, and the monocle screwed firmly into one eye.

The seneschal bowed to the king and started a formal introduction, but Amanda just talked over him till he gave up.

"Hello, Arthur. It's been a while. Allow me to present Jack Daimon, the Outsider. He's one of the good guys."

Arthur's steel boots made a muted thunder on the wooden floor as he came forward to greet us. A great bear of a man, with a mane of red hair under his jewelled crown, and a heavy jutting beard. I was sure I'd read somewhere that the knights of old were a lot shorter than modern men; something to do with the diet. That's why suits of armour in stately homes always seem so small. But Arthur hadn't got the memo; he stood a good head taller than me, and his shoulders were so broad he probably had to turn sideways to get through doors. His armour was scalloped here and there for style, but still looked like it weighed a ton; yet Arthur moved so easily in it the whole affair might have been made of silk. When he finally crashed to a halt before us his welcoming smile seemed entirely genuine.

"Welcome to Camelot, Sir Jack."

"It's just Jack," I said, too overawed to be properly polite.

The seneschal made a high pained noise behind me, but Arthur didn't seem to mind. He nodded easily to Amanda.

"Welcome back, Lady Amanda. It has been too long since you graced us with your presence."

"Good to be back," said Amanda. "Where's Gwen?"

"It's her day to volunteer at the hospital wards," said Arthur. He shook his head in admiration. "I can honestly say I'd rather fight a pack of werewolves than do bedpan duty. Anyway, allow me to present my knights, Jack. And before you ask, no, we don't normally stand around in full armour. It takes the best part of an hour, and a whole bunch of special helpers, just to get into the damned suits. Unfortunately we're expecting trouble. If Merlin's right."

"I'm always right," said the man at the back of the chamber. "It's my thing. It's what I do. I am Mister Always Right."

"Come and meet my knights, Jack," said Arthur. "They're a lot easier to get on with."

"I heard that!" Merlin said loudly.

"You were meant to," said Arthur.

The first knight I was introduced to turned out to be a woman: Sir Eleanor. A great strapping warrior, she had a harsh driven look but still managed a brief smile for me. Her skin was a deep brown, and it only took me a moment to realise who she reminded me of.

"You're staring," she said, in a not entirely accusing way.

"Sorry," I said quickly. "It's just that you look so much like Queen Boudicca."

Sir Eleanor raised an eyebrow. "My ancestor. How would you know what she looked like?"

"I've met her," I said.

She showed me her brief smile again. "Of course you have. You're with the Lady Amanda."

Next to her stood an elf: Sir Llanfair. Inhumanly tall and slender, even in his armour, his face had been chiselled into sharp angles, with icy blue eyes and tall pointed ears. His shoulder-length hair was so blond as to be almost colourless. He didn't smile, but did favour me with a thoughtful nod.

Sir Guillam was a bluff, hearty, country squire type, and so heavily built his armour must have used up twice as much steel as everyone else. He looked to be well into his forties, and his nose and cheeks had the broken veins of the truly committed drinker. He'd lost most of his hair, and was trying to disguise it with a really unfortunate comb-over.

The final suit of armour looked like it had been through the wars. Someone had put a lot of effort into polishing it, but couldn't disguise all the carefully repaired damage. It was also completely empty. Even though it stood upright on its own, and raised an arm to salute me. The helmet was tucked under its other arm, so I could see right inside, and there was definitely nobody home.

"Sir Brendan was killed in single combat with an ogre, three years ago," Arthur explained. "But he wasn't about to let a little thing like being dead get in the way of doing his duty. So now he haunts his armour and really puts the wind up his enemies. We call him the dead of knight."

The other knights chuckled, in a forced kind of way. It was clear they'd had to hear the joke many times before. The empty suit of armour bent forward a little; the closest it could come to a bow. I nodded back. I was way past the point where I could be unsettled by a ghost in a can.

"You should have seen what he did to the ogre, after he came back," said Sir Eleanor.

"I didn't know you could stick an axe up someone that far," said Sir Guillam.

"Let us be seated," said Arthur.

We all sat down at the Round Table. The king and his knights took a while to settle, because sitting in full armour turned out to be a complicated and somewhat noisy affair. I was just relieved the chairs were able to take the strain. Amanda sat patiently, her hands folded together on top of the table. I looked at Merlin, to see if he would be joining us, but he was completely engrossed in solving a Rubik's Cube. Except he wasn't turning the sides; he just stared at them until they moved on their own. Soon they were spinning so fast that smoke came off them. Arthur started to speak, and I gave him my full attention.

"We're in our armour because Camelot faces a real and imminent threat, and unfortunately most of my knights are away at present. Questing, or removing trolls from under bridges, or just generally keeping busy. I doubt that's a coincidence." He paused, to look steadily at Amanda. "I did hope you might be here to provide us with an answer to our problem."

"I'm afraid not," she said kindly.

"And yet here you are," said Sir Eleanor. "Descending on Camelot like a bird of ill omen, with a companion unknown to any of us."

"You'll have to excuse El," said Sir Guillam. "She's very direct."

"Like an arrow to the eye," said Sir Llanfair.

"Best place for it," said Sir Eleanor.

"I vouch for Jack," said Amanda.

"Then no more need be said." Arthur raised his voice, without looking round. "Come forward, High Sorcerer. Explain the dangers of our current situation to my honoured guests."

Merlin tossed his Rubik's Cube over one shoulder, and it vanished in mid-air. He shot his cuffs, tugged fussily at his waistcoat, and only then slouched over to join us. He didn't sit down, just scowled at the knights like a lecturer facing a more than usually dense audience. I got the impression the knights were used to that.

"As a young sorcerer learning my trade I went walking up and down the land," said Merlin. "Searching out secrets and forbidden knowledge, and spreading joy wherever I went." He glared around the table, to see if anyone wanted to challenge that, and then continued. "One day I happened upon two dragons of quite astonishing bigness making a nuisance of themselves in the North Riding. Terrorising towns, burning settlements, and generally devouring people, livestock, and anything else that didn't run away fast enough. No one had any idea how to stop them, so it fell to me to do something.

"I persuaded the two dragons to enter a great underground cavern with tales of a huge treasure, and then tricked them into fighting over whose hoard it should be. While they were busy getting stuck into each other, I sneaked out and called down an avalanche to seal off the entrance. And that should have been that.

"But it seems the dumb brutes finally stopped fighting, and teamed up to break out of the cavern. Now they're on their way here, to burn down Camelot and piss on the ashes. A bit of an extreme reaction in my opinion, but that's dragons for you."

"We should be able to handle two dragons," Sir Guillam said briskly. "After all, we outnumber them."

"It should prove an interesting test of skill and courage," said Sir Llanfair. "Assuming we don't all get broiled in our armour."

Sir Eleanor carefully didn't look at Merlin as she addressed the king. "The dragons are only coming to Camelot because the sorcerer is here. If he were to leave, on a fast horse that I'm sure someone would be only too happy to provide, the dragons would follow, and the innocent occupants of this castle would no longer be in any danger."

"You do know I'm standing right here," Merlin said mildly. "I can hear every word you're saying."

"Good," said Sir Eleanor. "How fast can you pack?"

"Merlin volunteered to leave the moment he discovered the

dragons were on their way," Arthur said sternly. "I commanded him to stay. Camelot owes its existence to the high sorcerer's wisdom. He is one of us, and we will stand with him against all threats."

"Of course, Sire," said Sir Eleanor. "No matter what it costs us."

"Exactly!" the king said cheerfully. "Besides, it will do us good to get out of the castle for a while, and enjoy some fresh air and good old-fashioned dragon-slaying."

Sir Llanfair raised a pale eyebrow. "Are we to understand that you intend to fight alongside us, Sire?"

"Damn right," said Arthur. "I'm not missing out on the fun."

The knights looked at each other. They didn't seem at all happy. Even Sir Brendan in his empty armour, who didn't have anything to look happy with.

"If we allow anything to happen to you, the queen will have us welded into our armour and thrown into the cesspits," said Sir Eleanor.

"And they're really full of cess at the moment," said Sir Guillam.

"You know she would forbid this, Sire," said Sir Llanfair.

"Then it's just as well she's busy at the hospital," Arthur said happily. "By the time any tattletale can get word to her, it'll all be over."

"This is a really bad idea, Sire," said Sir Guillam.

Arthur looked at him. "Who's king?"

"I live to serve," Sir Guillam said glumly.

Sir Eleanor sighed. "Oh, this can only go well..."

Arthur turned to Merlin. "You are certain these creatures cannot be reasoned with?"

"They aren't terribly bright, even for dragons," said Merlin. "But they are quite definitely sensible enough not to listen to any human ever again. They're coming here to kill not just me, but anyone who might have heard of their foolish behaviour. Dragons have their pride, and have always been heavily into revenge."

"Then we have no choice but to slay them both," said Arthur. He smiled at me. "And then afterwards, we can harvest their insides to make our medicines."

"Really?" I said.

"Oh, dragon bits make for all kinds of effective remedies," said Sir Guillam. "Though the rendering process does tend to get a bit whiffy."

"You see?" said Merlin. "There's some good to be found in everyone. Now, Sire, if I could have just a quick word in private, about tactics?"

"Tactics?" said Arthur. "Has it really come to that? Can't we just use our tried-and-true method of hitting them really hard until they stop moving?"

"You haven't seen these dragons," said Merlin. "They are big, big, and really big, with a side order of extra bigness. You could hit them with a house and they'd barely notice."

"Oh, very well," said Arthur. He heaved himself up out of his chair, despite everything his armour could do to hold him where he was, and the two of them moved off a way to talk quietly.

Amanda looked after them, apparently lost in thought. I looked at the knights, and found they were all staring at me.

"So," said Sir Guillam, trying for the light touch and not getting anywhere near it. "What is it you do, Sir Jack, exactly?"

"Please," I said. "Just Jack. It's my job to deal with magical threats. Make them safe, to protect people."

"Just like us, then," said Sir Guillam. "Someone gets in a bit of bother, and we step in to help them out."

"Suddenly and violently," said Sir Eleanor.

"A hero is defined by what they do when it matters," said Sir Llanfair. "Are you ready to fight alongside us, Jack?"

"I would be honoured," I said. And I meant it.

Sir Llanfair looked across at Arthur and Merlin. They hadn't raised their voices, but there was an awful lot of arm-waving going on.

"What is there to argue about?" said the elf knight. "See a dragon; kill it."

"Depends on the kind of dragon," Sir Guillam said wisely. "I once had to fight this really nasty specimen that could spout fire from both ends. I had to drag it into the nearest river and drown it."

"I once encountered a dragon that boasted it could repair any wound," said Sir Llanfair. "So I cut it into small pieces, burned them separately, scattered the ashes in a several different rivers and said *Let's see you come back from that*. It didn't."

"My dragon was demanding a tribute of young maidens to devour," said Sir Eleanor. "So I found an innkeeper who'd been

convicted of poisoning her guests, filled her with her own poison,
tied her up and gagged her, and presented her to the dragon as
tribute."

"You always did fight dirty, El," said Sir Guillam.

"Best way," said Sir Eleanor. "It helped that I had a good teacher."

"My best student," said Sir Guillam.

They all looked at Sir Brendan, and the empty suit of armour
solemnly spread his arms wide, to indicate the size of the one that
got away.

I was fascinated by how casually they talked about fighting
dragons. Not for glory, or to be a hero, but because that was their job.

"It sounds like you have a real dragon problem," I said. "Is it very
widespread?"

"They aren't all bad," said Sir Guillam. "And they do keep the
other predators under control. As long as dragons don't bother
human settlements, we mostly leave them be. It's a big world; there's
room in it for everyone."

Sir Brendan's armour nodded his agreement.

"You'll have to excuse Jack and me for a moment," said Amanda.
"We need to talk."

We got up from the Round Table, and moved a polite distance
away.

"You were starting to look a bit out of your depth," said Amanda.

"A ghost knight?" I said. "Really?"

"When it comes to death, a magical world allows for a lot more
options," Amanda said calmly. "Though in Brendan's case, it's mostly
down to stubbornness. Arthur has offered to release him from his
vows so he can move on, but Brendan won't hear of it. And there are
times when a dead knight can come in very handy."

"Like when?" I said.

"For dealing with troublesome hauntings, of course," said
Amanda. "Sir Brendan scares the hell out of other ghosts. All they've
got are sheets and a few chains to rattle; he has a suit of armour and
a really big sword blessed by the Church."

And then everyone stopped talking and looked round, as the
seneschal came hurrying in. It caught me by surprise, because I
hadn't realised he'd left. He took a moment to regain his composure,
and then bowed formally to the king.

"The dragons have been spotted, Sire. At the speed they're flying, we can expect their arrival in the extremely near future."

Arthur smiled at his knights. "Time to go to work."

He strode out of the chamber and his knights followed after him. The sound of their boots on the wooden floor was like a drum roll of honour. I started to follow them, but Amanda stopped me. Merlin was coming over. He drifted to a halt before us and then smiled absently, as though trying to remember what had been on his mind when he started moving.

"Hello! I'm Merlin. Any questions?"

"Why the Victorian clothes?" I said, because you've got to start somewhere. "And especially, why the monocle?"

"I have a complicated relationship with Time," said Merlin. "I collect the flotsam and jetsam of popular culture, from all across Time. Because I can. Would you like to see my collection of lava lamps? No? Didn't think so. No one ever does. I am surrounded by Philistines. Oh well, let's take a peek at what's occurring outside." He paused, and shot me a knowing look. "When we get out there, try not to get caught underneath the dragons. They aren't exactly noted for their toilet training, and we probably wouldn't be able to dig you out for some time."

He gestured dramatically, and a standing mirror taller than all of us appeared out of nowhere.

"Well?" it said loudly. "What is so important I had to be dragged away from my shows?"

Merlin sighed. "I created this mirror to allow me to see the future more clearly. And all it ever wants to do is watch soap operas."

"You don't know what you're missing," the mirror said haughtily. "All human life is there."

"I want to see the dragons," said Merlin.

"And I want a pony. You promised me a pony! Oh all right, don't look at me like that. You know I hate it when you sulk. I suppose we can take a quick look while the adverts are on."

Our reflections vanished from the mirror, replaced by a view of two dragons hurtling over empty countryside. Big leathery creatures, with wide membranous wings and gargoyle faces, they seemed to plough through the air by sheer force of will, only staying up because they intimidated the ground into keeping its distance. Their mouths were so full of teeth I couldn't work out how they closed them, and their deep-set eyes burned like living flames.

"How are we supposed to get a sense of scale without any context?" Merlin said crossly. "Pull back, dammit!"

"Yeah, I've got something you can pull..." muttered the mirror.

The image retreated in a series of jerks and stutters, and finally showed the two dragons flying over a small town. Their combined shadows plunged the entire area into darkness.

"Those are big dragons," I said.

Merlin nodded unhappily. "I had hoped my memory was at fault over their size, but apparently not. And they do strike me as just a bit peeved..."

"You buried them alive," said Amanda. "How did you think they were going to feel?"

"I sort of hoped one of them would kill the other, thus reducing the problem by fifty per cent."

"Are you done with me now?" said the mirror. "Only they're just about to reveal who shot JR!"

"It was the alien on the grassy knoll," said Merlin, and dismissed the mirror with a wave of his hand. It made a rude noise as it disappeared, taking its view of the disturbingly large dragons with it. Amanda laughed softly at the expression on my face.

"You should see some of the really big ones..."

"I think I'm coping pretty well," I said. "I'm not panicking, or sprinting for the horizon, or ... Actually, I can't think of any other sane option."

"If you have to, put your head between your knees," Amanda said briskly. "Makes it so much easier to kiss your arse goodbye." She turned to Merlin. "Would I be right in assuming that the reason you didn't kill the dragons back in the day, was because you couldn't?"

"Got it in one," said the sorcerer.

"But...you're Merlin!" I said.

He smiled, just a bit tiredly. "Reports of my powers have been greatly exaggerated. Usually by me. Dragons are magical creatures; they have to be, or something that size would never get off the ground no matter how hard it flapped its wings. You can't fight magical creatures with magic; the two forces cancel each other out.

That's why Arthur sends knights to deal with them, because cold steel always works. And anyway, it's important that men kill monsters. To prove to themselves that they can."

"I taught you that," said Amanda.

Once we'd left the castle and made our way back to the grassy plain, there was a strained feeling to the atmosphere, like the unnatural calm before a cataclysmic storm. Arthur and his knights were studying an empty sky that wasn't going to remain empty much longer. They each had a heavy steel helm tucked under one arm, and a long sword buckled at their side.

"How long before the dragons get here, Merlin?" said Arthur.

The sorcerer consulted his pocket watch. "They're running a bit late. Must be strong headwinds."

"Any last words of advice?"

"Try not to get killed."

"Bit late for me," said an echoing voice, and I realised with a bit of a start that it came from inside the empty suit of armour.

I was so busy staring at Sir Brendan I actually missed the moment when the dragons came sweeping over the horizon. Their shadows immediately plunged the grassy plain into an artificial twilight. The temperature dropped, and all the birds stopped singing. Arthur put on his helm, and the knights followed his example. I looked at the massive creatures blocking out the sun, and then at the small group standing ready to oppose them with nothing but cold steel and firm resolve. I turned to Amanda.

"How can they hope to kill things that big?"

"This is what they do, Jack," said Amanda. "It's their job."

"It's suicide," I said. "Look . . . If Merlin isn't going to get involved, it's down to you."

"My magic wouldn't affect the dragons any more than his."

"I didn't come all this way just to watch King Arthur and his knights get torn apart and eaten by flying lizards on steroids!" I said. "You have to do something!"

"No," said Amanda. "You have to do something. That's why I brought you here."

I looked at her. "You expect me to fight dragons?"

"Of course. That's what a hero does."

"I am not a hero."

"Not yet," said Amanda. "But you're getting there."

The dragons were almost on top of us. I rummaged quickly through my backpack, searching through gas grenades, enchanted nunchuks, and a pistol made from bone that fired ghost bullets. (No use against the living.) In the end, the athame all but forced itself into my hand, though how I was going to get close enough to do any real damage without being chewed up and spat out eluded me for the moment. Unless one of them bolted his food, and then maybe I could stab at its heart on the way down. I hefted the athame, took a deep breath, and moved forward to stand next to Sir Guillam.

"Mind if I join you?"

"Always room for a good man," the knight said cheerfully. His voice echoed a little as it emerged from the Y-shaped slit in the front of his helm. "Tell you what, I'll knock them down and you can carve them up."

"Sounds like a plan to me," I said.

"To make God smile, have a plan," said Arthur, and all the knights chuckled briefly.

The dragons came sweeping down at incredible speed. We raised our weapons and braced ourselves. And a series of brilliant energy beams shot past us and enveloped the huge creatures in a cloud of crackling energies. The dragons plummeted from the sky, and slammed into the ground so hard it rocked under our feet like an earthquake. Arthur and his knights stood solidly in their armour, but Sir Guillam had to grab my arm to steady me. I glanced back at Amanda, to make sure she was all right, but she seemed entirely unaffected. Merlin had lifted up his feet and was hovering cross-legged in mid-air. The dragons lay sprawled on the grassy plain like leathery mountains, their massive wings slumped like collapsed tents. Their fiery eyes stared unseeingly.

"What the hell just happened?" I said.

"Beats me," said Merlin, dropping elegantly back to earth.

"Are they dead?" I said.

"No," Merlin said judiciously. "Just had all the fight knocked out of them. They'll wake up, eventually. Unless we do the sane thing and cut their heads off first. And then beat them flat, with sledgehammers."

"Where did that attack come from?" said Arthur. "And who do we have to thank for this unexpected salvation?"

"I'd hold off on the thanks," said Amanda. "Whoever fired on the dragons is currently hiding from us behind a cloaking field."

"A concealing glamour," Merlin explained to Arthur.

He gestured sharply and Miriam and Emil Morcata appeared, standing at the head of an army of Grey aliens. There were hundreds of the ugly things, each of them a good seven feet tall and entirely naked, the better to show off their unnatural natures. The arms and legs were weirdly jointed, the chests were hideously concave, and the oversized heads had the familiar all-black eyes, no nose, and slit mouths. They were also sexless, like the Men In Black. Something about the Greys gave me the same feeling of instant revulsion as a scuttling spider. It took me a moment to realise they were all carrying unfamiliar but very powerful-looking weapons.

Amanda moved in beside me. "They're just Halloween bogeymen, created to terrorise people and keep them in line. But I don't like the look of those weapons, Jack. If they're powerful enough to bring down dragons..."

"Particle accelerator guns," said Merlin, just a bit unexpectedly. "Future tech. Of course, it all gets horribly out of hand. Shame about what happens to Los Angeles. Or Arizona Bay, as it is on the new maps."

I made myself concentrate on what was in front of me. "What are Miriam and Emil doing together?"

"I saw them the exact same moment you did, Jack," Amanda said calmly. "So I really don't know any more than you do."

"I take it you have reason to believe that their bringing down the dragons was not an act of charity," Arthur said dryly.

"Whatever's behind this, you can bet the bill will be a lot higher than you're willing to pay," I said.

"Only one way to find out," Merlin said brightly. "Somebody needs to go over there and talk to them. I would volunteer, but I don't do that."

"I am king," said Arthur. "I will talk to them."

"Do you want me to write you a speech?" said Merlin.

Arthur looked at him. "I still remember your last effort: *Welcome to our home. Please don't kill us and sell all our mistresses into slavery.*"

"Short and to the point, I thought."

"Stand there and don't say a word," said Arthur. "I'll take care of this."

"No," said Amanda.

The king looked at her. "No?"

"Jack and I know these people," said Amanda. "They'll talk to us."

"That sounds annoyingly sensible," said Arthur. He turned to Merlin. "You're the one who remembers the future. Why didn't you warn me this was going to happen?"

"Because I didn't know," said Merlin. "And I should have. I think someone has been messing with my head. Which is odd, because that's usually me."

Amanda and I started toward Miriam and Emil.

"Any problems, shoot us a meaningful look and we'll come running," said Sir Guillam.

"I'm just in the mood to slaughter a whole bunch of goblins," said Sir Eleanor.

"Never knew you when you weren't," said Sir Llanfair.

I kept a careful eye on the Greys as we drew nearer, but none of them so much as twitched a muscle. Which actually made them even creepier, like so many trapdoor spiders waiting to pounce. I did my best to keep that out of my face. Amanda just strode along, humming something cheerful. We finally came to a halt before Miriam and Emil. He gave me a smug look, so I ignored him and spoke directly to her.

"Hello, Miriam. We do keep bumping into each other, don't we?"

"I'm here on Department business," she said. "You've been a bad boy, Jack."

I had to raise an eyebrow. "Why is the Department mad at me?"

"You shouldn't have sided with her," said Miriam, indicating Amanda with a jerk of the head. "You belong to the Department."

She stopped then, because I was smiling. And I just knew it wasn't a nice smile.

"I have always been my own man."

"That can be a very lonely position," said Miriam.

"I'm not alone. I'm with Amanda."

"And that's the problem."

"How were you able to find us?" I said.

"You took one of our books," said Miriam. "We have ways of tracking them."

"And I told you I wasn't finished with you," said Emil.

Miriam turned to look at him. "You speak out of turn again, and I will feed you to the Greys."

Emil bristled at her tone, but subsided. Which was interesting.

Miriam turned back to face me. "Emil's people have made common cause with the Department."

"Because you both serve the secret masters?" I said.

Miriam smiled briefly. "Everyone does, whether they know it or not."

"I'm surprised George isn't here," said Amanda.

Miriam didn't even glance at her. "He isn't with the Department any more. I've taken control, with Emil as my second-in-command."

"You mean your enforcer," I said. "He has the look."

Emil started to say something. I looked at him, and he thought better of it.

"I set policy, and Emil sees that it's carried out," said Miriam. "Every Department needs someone like him, if they want to get anything done."

"How did you get here?" I said.

"That's classified."

"Where did you get the energy weapons?" said Amanda.

Miriam looked at her for the first time. "Wouldn't you like to know."

"I'd like to know," I said.

Miriam smiled coldly at the unmoving dragons. "Science one, magic nil."

I nodded at the army of Greys, standing motionless in their ranks. "Why the alien attack dogs?"

"Men In Black are fine when it comes to intimidating an inconvenient witness," said Miriam. "But when the Department really wants to bring the hammer down it sends in the Greys. They're here to put an end to Camelot, by killing everyone associated with it."

I stared at her, remembering the Men In Black at Boudicca's court. And when I finally spoke, my voice was so cold and dangerous it even disturbed me.

"When did the Department decide it was in the atrocity business?"

"The secret masters have decided that the memory of Camelot is still too strong, if someone like you can reach it so easily," said Miriam. "Once we've destroyed the dream, the effect will reverberate throughout history. No more myths and legends, no more tedious musicals..."

"You can't do that!" I said.

"Of course I can," said Miriam. "And the outrage in your voice is all the justification I need. Camelot can't be allowed to have that kind of effect on people."

"Then why fire on the dragons?" said Amanda.

"To make sure the weapons really are everything we were promised," said Miriam. "And because it was fun."

"Enough talk," said Emil. "Let's get this party started."

"In a minute!" said Miriam. "Don't be in such a hurry, Emil. You must learn to savour these little moments. And before we do anything...I want a word with you, Jack." She glared at Amanda. "In private."

"Don't mind me," said Amanda.

Miriam moved away, gesturing sharply for me to go with her. I glanced at the motionless Greys, and went after her.

"I warned you not to side with that woman," said Miriam. "You have no idea what she is."

"She's not the one who's allied herself with an army of killer aliens," I said. "How did George get forced out?"

"He wasn't prepared to embrace the big picture. So his retirement was brought forward."

"How can you want to destroy something as wonderful as Camelot?"

"Are you kidding?" said Miriam. "Entitled aristocrats swanning around in armour, telling everyone else what to do?"

"It isn't like that!"

"Grow up, Jack."

"I can't let you destroy Camelot."

"You can't stop me," said Miriam. "But if you surrender, I'll take you back and speak on your behalf to the secret masters."

"Why would you do that?"

"Because it's not your fault, the way you are. You've been lied to your whole life, while I've always known how the world really works."

I gestured at the motionless dragons. "How do they tie in with your *No such thing as magic*?"

"Just overgrown reptiles, who should have had the sense to die out with the dinosaurs," Miriam said briskly. "Don't change the subject, Jack. You need to make a decision while the offer's still on the table."

"Camelot is important," I said. "It matters. And I will fight to protect it."

"You'd throw away your life, for a medieval fantasy?"

"Some dreams are worth fighting for."

"Take the offer, Jack!" Miriam said angrily. "You don't have to die here!"

"Why do you care?"

"Because you matter to me!"

She waited, but I couldn't say what she wanted to hear. Her mouth tightened, and her gaze became cold and impersonal.

"You can't say I didn't try."

"That was kind of you."

"I don't do kind," said Miriam.

We walked away from each other, back to the lives we'd chosen. Amanda put a comforting hand on my arm.

"You did your best, Jack."

I shook my head. "I really thought I could get through to her."

"She likes you, but ambition was always going to be more important," said Amanda. "Just the fact that she was willing to talk was a promising sign. After the fighting is over, you should definitely try again."

"You really believe we can beat an army of Grey aliens, armed with weapons from the future?"

"I find it helps to maintain a positive attitude, in situations like this," said Amanda.

We went back to Arthur, who looked at me steadily. "You could have walked away from this. Saved yourself."

"But that never even occurred to him," said Amanda. "Isn't he wonderful?"

I looked at the silently waiting Greys, and they stared back with their dark unreadable eyes.

"We don't have a hope in hell, do we?" I said quietly.

"Got to be easier than two dragons the size of mountains," said Sir Guillam.

"Really, the woman did us a favour," said Sir Llanfair.

"We should send her a thank-you note," said Sir Eleanor. "Maybe a basket of fruit and some nice flowers."

The elf knight looked at her. "Are you joking? I can never tell when you're joking."

"To be fair," said Sir Guillam, "elves aren't noted for their sense of humour."

"I can be funny," said Sir Llanfair.

"Of course you can," Sir Eleanor said crushingly. "We've seen what you wear to Court."

The knights limbered up, preparing themselves for battle. The elf knight's movements had an almost supernatural grace, while Sir Eleanor looked like she was ready to take on the whole Grey army by herself. Sir Guillam swept his sword back and forth, his every movement brutally efficient because he was the oldest of the knights and had the least energy to spare. The dead knight, Sir Brendan, didn't look any different from the others now he had his steel helm in place, but I had to wonder how much damage his armour could take before it finally gave up the ghost.

King Arthur stretched and stamped and swung his sword as though it was weightless. He seemed like a force of nature: implacable and unstoppable.

Sir Guillam nodded to Sir Llanfair. "Ready for the fray?"

"Always."

"Even against impossible odds?"

"Best kind."

"All right," said Sir Guillam. "You take the unbelievable number on the left, and I'll take the appalling odds on the right."

"What does that leave me?" said Sir Eleanor.

"You can finish off the ones we knock down," said Sir Guillam.

"No mercy?" said Sir Eleanor. "No quarter?"

"Look at them," said the elf knight. "Do those goblins look like they'd understand the concept, even if we explained it to them?"

"We should still make the offer," Sir Eleanor said stubbornly.

"No," said Sir Brendan.

Everyone turned to look at the dead knight. His voice echoed hollowly from inside his helm, as though in a church.

"They are here to destroy Camelot, the people and the dream. They are monsters."

"Well said, Brendan," said Arthur. "I can always rely on you to get to the heart of the matter."

And then a brilliant beam of light stabbed down from the sky, and George was suddenly standing between us and the Greys, holding a very large book. He glared about him.

"Everybody stand down! Don't make me have to tell you twice!"

"George?" I said.

He nodded briefly. "Not now, Jack. I'm working."

Miriam came hurrying forward to face him. "What the hell are you doing?"

"Keeping you from making a really big mistake."

"How did you even get here?"

George hefted his book. "Ever since I was put in charge of the Department library, I've been quietly sneaking the odd book home with me, when I didn't trust what the Department might do with it. Now do as you're told, Miriam, because there's enough power in this book to bring your entire army to its knees."

Miriam's gun was suddenly in her hand. "Don't make me do this, George."

"There's nothing you can do, Miriam."

She shot him at point-blank range, but the bullet slammed harmlessly into the book. Miriam kept firing until she ran out of ammunition, but the ancient leather cover just soaked up the bullets. Miriam looked like she wanted to throw the gun at George, but regained control of herself with an effort and put her gun away. George shook his head.

"You really are very predictable, Miriam. Now take your Greys home and put them back where you found them. Camelot is too important to be meddled with."

"That's not what our superiors believe."

"My Department does not bow down to the secret masters."

"It's not your Department any more," said Miriam. "It's moved on."

"Did you really think replacing me would be that easy?" said

George. "Now put a leash on Emil and we'll get out of here. I have a Department to run and you have some explaining to do."

Miriam moved in close to George, and lowered her voice. "Please, don't do this to me in front of everyone."

"I'm sorry," said George.

"I'm not," said Miriam.

She thrust a knife between his ribs, and twisted it. I started forward, but Amanda grabbed my arm as all the Greys turned their guns to target me. George tried to say something, but all that came out was a low shocked sound. The book tumbled from his hands, and disappeared before it hit the ground. Miriam jerked her knife out, and blood streamed down George's side. He dropped to his knees before Miriam and she cut his throat, stepping quickly to one side to avoid the jetting blood. George fell onto his face and lay still. Miriam looked down at him.

"Letting you retire early was all the mercy I had left in me." She turned to look at me, and her gaze was utterly cold. "I'll make you a final offer, Jack. Persuade the king to stand down, and he can save his precious castle. We'll just install a puppet ruler in his place."

Emil looked at her sharply. "Those aren't the orders!"

"I decide policy," said Miriam. "And there's more than one way to kill a dream. I like the idea of a Department functionary sitting on Camelot's throne, dismantling everything Arthur achieved." She smiled at the king. "Of course, all your knights will still have to die."

"Send your army against us," Arthur said calmly. "Whether we stand or fall, the dream of Camelot will endure."

Miriam turned her back on him, and walked away.

"Camelot's walls won't last one minute against the Grey's weapons," I said urgently to Arthur. "Get word to the castle. Tell them to leave by the back door, and then run for their lives."

"They wouldn't go," said Arthur.

I looked at him. "This isn't their battle!"

"Of course it is," said Arthur. "We all serve the dream in our own way. They won't run; just as they trust us not to."

"But if the Greys get past us . . ."

"Then the castle will fight to the last man and woman," said Arthur. "We don't battle evil because we expect to win, Jack. We fight because it's the right thing to do."

I turned to Merlin. "You remember the future. Who wins here?"

"Events are in flux," Merlin said carefully. "Now that unexpected elements have entered the world, history is up for grabs."

"Does this mean you're going to get involved, at last?" said Arthur.

Merlin looked thoughtfully at the ranks of motionless Greys. "I shall have to talk to Amanda. I've always valued her judgement in these matters."

"How long have you known her?" I said.

"All my life," said Merlin. He looked at me with something like compassion. "It's never wise, for mortal man to fall in love with magic. It rarely ends well for either side. Of course, I could be wrong. I often am."

He shook his head sadly, and wandered off to be alone with his thoughts.

"Merlin won't fight," said Arthur. "That's not what he does. There's no point in getting angry with him."

"You might as well get mad at the weather," said Sir Guillam.

"You do," said Sir Eleanor. "I've heard you."

Amanda walked away, without even glancing at me, so she could talk quietly with Merlin. Arthur took off his steel helm so he could look me in the eye.

"Mages can be very frustrating. They know so much, and can explain so little. Come stand with my knights, Jack, and we will do what we can."

I nodded stiffly. Arthur put his helm back on, and led me over to the knights. They were standing silently, facing the enemy like gleaming steel statues. Ready to take on monsters armed with weapons they couldn't hope to understand; because somebody had to.

"Would you care to stand beside me, Jack?" said the king.

"More than anything," I said.

I hefted my athame, and Sir Llanfair nodded approvingly.

"An eldritch thing, with a keen edge. A telling combination. Try not to stab me when the affray starts. It's bound to get a bit busy out there."

"I'll do my best," I said.

"Of course you will. You must let me examine the blade, once the battle is over. The workmanship is exquisite."

"You seem very confident that we'll survive," I said.

"Well, I expect to," said the elf. "But then, I'm wearing armour."

I couldn't tell whether he was smiling, inside his helm.

I looked at the alien Greys. I had intended to use the athame to make their guns disappear, the way I had with the Men In Black's clothes, but ever since I took the witch knife in my hand, I could tell there was a force in place, protecting them. The witch knife could still cut through anything physical. Not the best weapon when you're facing futuristic energy guns, but it would do.

Miriam's voice came clearly to us across the open space.

"Time's up! Emil, unleash the Greys."

Emil raised his voice, to show he was important too.

"Greys! Slaughter these fools, and then go to the castle and kill everything that moves. Today, we destroy a dream!"

"Likes the sound of his own voice, doesn't he?" said Arthur.

"Wait a minute!" I said loudly. "I've just thought of something!"

Emil started to argue, but Miriam shut him down with a look.

"I'm curious to see what Jack thinks he's come up with. And once I've proved how worthless it is, his friends' despair will be that much deeper."

"You're weird," said Emil.

I tucked the athame carefully into my belt, opened my backpack, and spoke to it quietly. "If you're listening, book, I'm hoping you're as powerful as you're supposed to be. Can you help? Not for me, but for Camelot?"

The book leapt out of the pack and into my hands. I shouldered the pack and walked toward the Grey army, holding the book out before me. I heard heavy footsteps, and when I glanced back Arthur and his knights were right behind me.

"You didn't think we'd let you do this on your own, did you?" said Arthur.

"Never crossed my mind for a moment," I lied.

Miriam frowned at the book. "That's your offer? I already have a library full of books!"

I didn't say anything. Emil gestured at the Greys, and they raised the weapons that had blasted two dragons out of the sky. My stomach turned over but I kept walking, gripping the book tightly so my hands wouldn't shake. Miriam shook her head disgustedly, and looked to Emil.

"I've had enough of this. Fry them."

Emil gestured to the Greys, and hundreds of energy beams flashed across the grassy plain. But somehow they were all dragged off course, and slammed into the book I was holding. The Greys' guns held enough destructive energies to blow up a dozen castles, but the ancient leather cover absorbed them all. The Greys fired and fired, and then lowered their weapons and looked to Emil for new orders.

"You don't need guns!" Miriam said harshly. "You have claws! Tear them apart! Do it!"

The Greys dropped their weapons and surged forward, holding their hands out before them like a praying mantis. The clawed fingers flexed eagerly, hungry for blood and slaughter. I stuffed the book back into my pack. It had done all it could. I pulled the pack into place on my back, and took a firm grip on my athame. King Arthur and his knights held their swords steady. I'd never felt more scared in my life, or more proud to be part of such a company.

Arthur and his knights broke into a lumbering run, their steel boots sinking deep into the earth. They charged right at the approaching Greys, and I went with them. They quickly built up a head of speed, despite the weight of their armour, and divots of earth flew in all directions. They were all singing the same battle song, inside their helms. Not a death chant, or a plea for strength from the Almighty; just a simple song on the glory to be found in fighting evil. I saved my breath for running.

We hit the Greys hard, our blades cutting down the horrid things like scythes through wheat. Dark blood flew on the air, and Grey after Grey collapsed without making a sound, but more of them leapt over the fallen bodies to get to us. We were soon forced to a halt by the sheer weight of Grey numbers, but our weapons still rose and fell in steady butchery. The knights' long swords flashed brilliantly, like summer lightning trapped in steel, while I hacked viciously about me with my witch knife, shearing cleanly through flesh and bone.

The Greys swept past us, turned, and hit us from behind. We formed a circle, shoulder pressed against shoulder. For all their numbers, the Greys could only come at us a few at a time, so we cut them down and trampled them underfoot, stamping black blood into the earth. But no matter how many we killed, there were always

more. The sheer effort of wielding the athame started to catch up
with me. My muscles ached, and sweat ran down my face. I had no
idea how Arthur and his knights were able to keep going in so much
armour. Vicious claws raised showers of sparks as they raked across
steel chests and arms, but I had no such protection. All I could do
was duck and dodge, and strike out at everything that came within
reach. Black blood soaked my knife arm, while red blood spurted as
alien claws savaged me again and again. A Grey darted in and opened
up a deep furrow in my forehead, and blood poured down, filling
my right eye. I sliced through the Grey's guts, and kept on fighting.
My muscles screamed with fatigue and I was desperately tired,
gasping for breath with every blow, but I was damned if I'd stop while
there was a single Grey left to threaten Camelot.

King Arthur and the Knights of the Round Table stood their
ground, and I stood with them. The grass at our feet churned into a
slippery morass of mud and blood. The Greys threw themselves at us
in waves: an endless supply of killing machines, just following their
orders.

Even in the midst of so much death and madness, I was still aware
of what was happening around me. Arthur and his knights might
wear similar suits of armour, but I could always tell them apart. I
kept a watch on all of them, because what they did gave me the
strength to keep going.

I saw a Grey leap high into the air, to attack Sir Eleanor from
above. She was so busy killing the Greys in front of her she didn't
even see it coming. But Sir Guillam did, and his long sword came
swinging round in a vicious arc that cut the Grey out of mid-air.
Black blood fell like rain as he sheared it through, and the pieces
dropped separately to the ground. But Sir Guillam was so busy doing
that, he didn't see the Grey that came at him from behind. Sir Eleanor
launched herself forward, to place herself between Sir Guillam and
the Grey. She parried its terrible claws with her steel arm, and sliced
its oversized head clean off its shoulders. Another Grey pressed
forward to take its place, and Sir Guillam butted it in the face with his
steel helm. The alien features shattered, and black blood spurted. Sir
Eleanor ran the creature through, and pulled her sword free just in
time to face another Grey.

Sir Guillam and Sir Eleanor moved quickly to stand back to back, guarding each other: the old tutor and his most accomplished student.

Sir Brendan's sword rose and fell with inhuman speed, cutting up Greys like sides of meat. He made no move to defend himself, and the Greys swarmed all over his armour, searching for weak spots. Not knowing he no longer had any. The dead of knight surrounded himself with piled-up corpses, and none of them rose to fight again as he had, because they had no honour.

Sir Llanfair danced among the Greys, too fast and graceful for them to get anywhere near him. His sword lashed out in sudden flurries that left Greys dropping unmoving on all sides. And then a group of them hit him from every direction at once and there was nowhere left for him to go. He cut them down with calm precision, his sword moving faster than the human eye could follow. So elegant, and so deadly. But the sheer force of numbers drove him this way and that, always keeping him a little off balance, and at last a flailing hand knocked his helm off, and the Greys went for his exposed throat. Sir Llanfair laughed in their faces.

While I fought and bled and couldn't help any of them. But I still kept fighting.

A series of lightning bolts stabbed down from the sky, to blast the Greys apart in showers of blood and gore. Ragged pieces pattered wetly to the ground. Merlin strode right into the midst of the fighting, throwing his lightning bolts this way and that, and no matter how many Greys died, not a single drop of black blood stained his fine Victorian clothes. The Greys threw themselves at him in waves, but Merlin strode through them like death incarnate.

Amanda walked calmly behind Merlin, guarding his back, and wherever she looked Greys withered and died. I remembered how many times I'd looked into those eyes, and a chill went through my heart.

A group of Greys charged straight at her; so many that some would be bound to reach her. I hacked my way through the battle to intercept them, and the Greys were so intent on Amanda they didn't see me coming. I killed them all, crying out with the effort of every blow, but Amanda didn't even glance in my direction. She just kept going, guarding Merlin's back.

I stood alone for a moment, ignored by the tides of battle as they swirled around me, so tired I could barely lift the athame. The only reason the Greys weren't pulling me down was because they were concentrating on more important targets. I watched King Arthur carve a bloody path through the heart of the Grey army. Their strength and speed and numbers meant nothing in the face of his calm determination: an unstoppable force that could not be slowed or turned aside.

His sword flashed supernaturally bright as it sent black blood flying in all directions. The Greys were coming at him from all directions now, and he had moved so far from his knights there was no one to watch his back. And I was tired, so tired. But he was Arthur, defender of Camelot, so somehow I found the strength to lift my witch knife one more time, and force myself forward.

By the time I reached Arthur the sheer press of bodies had forced him to a halt. The Greys crawled all over him, trying to pull him down. I hit them hard, cutting Greys away from the king like a gardener deadheading roses. Arthur threw off the last few with a great shrug, and pressed forward again. And I went with him.

Staggering and stumbling and gasping for breath, my blood splashed onto the churned up ground from too many wounds to count. With no armour and no protection I kept going, driven on by a simple dogged determination not to let Arthur down. I swept my witch knife back and forth, while vicious claws sank deep into my flesh and grated on bone. Sometimes I cried out in shock and pain, and then I would grit my teeth and cry bitter tears, before somehow finding the strength to cut down another Grey.

Because I was the Outsider, and this was my job. To protect people from the horrors of the hidden world.

My only advantage was that the Greys couldn't get at me from behind. The book was still in my backpack, and the Greys wouldn't go anywhere near it. Eventually the tides of battle swept Arthur away from me, and once again I was left alone. I stumbled to a halt, my head hanging down. Sweat coursed down my face and dripped onto the ground. I could barely feel the athame in my hand. And then I saw Miriam and Emil right in front of me, so I forced my head up, and headed straight for them.

I caught brief glimpses of the other knights at their work. One of the Greys had knocked off Sir Brendan's helm but the empty suit of armour just went on fighting without it. Sir Guillam charged a Grey with his steel shoulder, and drove it back so hard it took a dozen more Greys with it. Sir Llanfair fought with uncanny speed and inhuman grace, and Sir Eleanor's sword rose and fell like a machine. And King Arthur . . . was magnificent.

They all were. There were giants on the earth in those days. And I was with them.

Suddenly, the Greys broke. Faced with knights in armour who would not stop, a sorcerer who could throw lightnings, a woman whose very look was death, and one man who would not drop no matter how much they hurt him . . . They broke. One minute they were swarming all over us, and the next they were running for their lives. Miriam and Emil screamed after them, but the Greys weren't listening. It seemed even manufactured killing machines had their limit. Arthur and his knights, and Merlin and Amanda, were left standing alone in a morass of churned-up mud that squelched black blood every time they shifted their feet. Miriam and Emil looked at me as I headed toward them, and vanished. The fleeing Greys disappeared with them, including all the bodies we'd left scattered across the blood-soaked earth.

And just like that, the day was ours.

I stumbled to a halt. My heart was hammering painfully fast, and my clothes were ragged and torn and soaked in blood and gore. Arthur shook thick drops of black blood from his sword and sheathed it, and then he and his knights removed their helms so they could grin triumphantly at each other. I was relieved to see they looked just as sweaty and exhausted as I felt. Except for Sir Brendan, of course. The dead of knight was wandering calmly around the plain, searching for his missing helm. Arthur started toward me, grinning broadly, and his knights came with him.

"A great victory, Jack," Arthur said cheerfully. "And you helped make it possible."

"Honoured to fight beside you," said Sir Guillam.

"Indeed," said Sir Llanfair. "It takes real courage, to fight without armour."

"You would not turn your face from the enemy," said Sir Eleanor. "Which is all that can be asked of anyone."

"Say something complimentary to him for me," called Sir

Brendan. "You know, I can't see my helm anywhere. I think one of the nasty little buggers must have run off with it."

I tried to say something, but I had no strength left. I sat down hard in the mud, and the athame fell from my hand because I couldn't feel it any more. My head was full of a soundless roar and my sight was dimming, as though all the light was going out of the world. Arthur hurried forward and bent over me, his steel gauntlet heavy on my shoulder. He said something, but I couldn't hear what. Amanda pushed Arthur out of the way, so she could kneel before me. I tried to smile at Amanda. There were tears on her face, and her voice seemed to come from a long way away.

"Oh, Jack, what have I done to you?"

"It's all right, Amanda," I said. "It doesn't matter. I fought beside King Arthur. That's worth dying for."

"You're not going anywhere without me!"

She took my head fiercely in her hands, and new strength surged into me. Sight and sound snapped back into focus as my head cleared. I felt strong and well again, and nothing hurt any more. I laughed out loud from the sheer joy of being alive, and Amanda laughed with me. She threw her arms around me and held me tight, and I held on to her and never wanted to let go. The knights crowded around us as we finally broke apart, and Arthur grabbed my hand and hauled me up onto my feet. I ran my hands over my jacket, as I realised all the damage had disappeared along with the blood.

"How about that?" said Sir Guillam. "She even fixed your clothes!"

"Pity she couldn't do the same for the elf," said Sir Eleanor.

"It's a style thing," said Sir Llanfair. "You wouldn't understand."

Arthur looked at me steadily. "Do you have a title, Jack?"

"Yes," I said. "I'm the Outsider."

"Not good enough," said the King. "Kneel."

I knelt there in the mud, and he tapped me on both shoulders with the flat of his sword.

"Rise, Sir Jack. Knight of the Round Table."

I got to my feet again. I'd never felt happier, even though I was pretty sure I wasn't worthy of the honour. Sir Guillam winked at me.

"Everyone feels like that. You'll get used to it."

Amanda picked up my athame, and handed it to me. I slipped it into my backpack, and she smiled at me dazzlingly.

"I knew you'd love it here."

"Arthur . . ." said Sir Guillam.

Something in his voice caught our attention, and we all turned to look. The dragons were stirring. The Greys' energy weapons had brought the huge creatures down, but not killed them; now they were waking up. And remembering why they'd come here.

"Oh shit," said Sir Llanfair. It sounded so much worse in his perfect voice.

"Some days, things wouldn't go right if you paid them," said Arthur.

"Will you relax?" said Merlin. "I'm here."

He snapped his fingers at the dragons, and they both shrank rapidly in size until they were no bigger than songbirds. With distinct looks of surprise on their little faces. Merlin smiled smugly.

"Fighting off the effects of the energy weapons used up most of their magic, and that left them vulnerable to me. I think I'll keep them as pets."

"It's your job to house-train them," Arthur said sternly. "If I find one dragon dropping on my throne, they're stew."

George was lying alone on the blood-soaked grass. I drew Arthur's attention to the body.

"Bury him somewhere nice. He died honourably."

"Of course," said Arthur. "Was he your friend?"

"No," I said. "But he might have been."

Arthur nodded. "Come, we owe ourselves a celebration, for not dying after all."

Before I could say anything, Amanda took me by the arm and drew me gently to one side.

"We have to go, Jack."

I looked at King Arthur, laughing with his knights. "I don't want to leave."

"No one ever does," said Amanda. "But we still have much to do."

I nodded slowly, and let her lead me away across the grassy plain. She stayed close to me, and losing Camelot was that much easier as long as I had her. A thought occurred to me.

"What did you say to Merlin, to get him to enter the battle?"

She smiled. "I told him about you."

I didn't push her. It made as much sense as anything else.

"Where are we off to now? Will it be as amazing as this?"

"In its own way," said Amanda.

"Will I have to fight for my life again?"

"Your life, and others. But what else would you expect, from Sir Jack, the Outsider?"

CHAPTER SEVEN
YOU CAN'T SEE THE WOOD FOR THE TREES
WHEN THEY'RE ON FIRE

From a green and open plain, we stepped into a world of shadows. Huge trees towered all around us, their trunks broad as houses. Branches heavy with greenery closed together above us to form a canopy that shut out most of the light. We had arrived in a great green cathedral, a twilight world, where occasional shafts of sunlight dropped through the canopy like spotlights on a leafy stage. The air was full of birdsong, and rich with forest scents. It was like returning to a home I hadn't realised I missed so much.

"Where is this?" I said finally, and my voice seemed a very small thing in such a magnificent setting.

"Welcome to the twelfth century, and Sherwood Forest," said Amanda. "Home to Robin Hood and his Merrie Men."

I couldn't keep from grinning. "You take me to the best places. This is Sherwood? I've never seen anything like it."

"The forests of your time are small, tame things. Robin Hood's Sherwood covers acres beyond counting, and its secret paths and trails are known only to those who've left civilisation behind. We're in outlaw territory, the last refuge of those driven outside the law. This is where the wild people live."

"There is magic here," I said. "I can feel it, like a song my heart remembers."

"Sherwood is the last of the really old places," said Amanda. "Where nature and supernature still walk hand in hand."

"I hate to show my ignorance but I'm going to anyway," I said. "Most of what I know about this period I learned from watching television, and I'm ready to accept that Richard Greene in *The Adventures of Robin Hood* may not have been entirely historically accurate. A little background would not go unappreciated."

"I feel like I should be wearing a peaked cap with *Tour Guide* on it," said Amanda. "Very well...King Richard III, called the Lionhearted because he insisted, left his brother John to sit on the Throne and keep it warm while he went off to play hero on Crusade. Prince John repaid this trust by declaring himself king. Now no one is safe and no one has any rights, except to be taxed, exploited, and worked to death.

"Only Robin Hood and his followers stand against tyranny. Sherwood has become the last remaining safe haven for people driven from their homes by injustice, or taxes they have no hope of paying. Robin is the last champion of what England is supposed to be, and the secret masters hate him for it."

"Are we talking history or legend here?"

"Both," said Amanda. "Robin Hood was real, just like King Arthur, until the great rewriting removed him from history. But once again Robin survived as a story, because what he stood for meant so much to people that they refused to give him up. The outlaw who took from the rich to give to the poor, except it was never about the money. Robin took power from the rich, so he could give it back to the people."

"What's he like?" I said.

"I don't know," said Amanda. "I've never been here before."

I looked at her. "You knew Boudicca, and Hrothgar, and Arthur."

She shrugged. "I get around, but I can't be everywhere."

The look in her eye strongly suggested I shouldn't ask any more, so I just sighed internally and moved on.

"Robin Hood was always on the television when I was growing up. Riding through the glen every week, a hero and his one true love, fighting the good fight along with the best friends a boy could imagine. But how are we supposed to find the real Robin Hood in a forest that looks like it goes on forever? It's not like there are any signposts saying *This way to Robin Hood's secret camp! Be sure to visit our gift shop.*"

And then I stopped, and glowered around into the forest gloom. Amanda looked at me patiently.

"What's the matter, Jack?"

"I'm just trying to work out which way the next attack will come from," I said. "Because wherever you take me something unpleasant always turns up, determined to really ruin my day."

Amanda smiled. "I ask so much of you, but you never let me down."

She stepped closer and we stared into each other's eyes, but she didn't say what I was hoping to hear. Instead, she turned away and set off along a narrow trail that looked no different from any of the others. And I went after her, because there was nowhere else I wanted to be.

The trail meandered along between the massive tree trunks, as though it hoped it wouldn't be noticed if it didn't make too big an impression. I kept a watchful eye on the surrounding shadows, but the forest seemed surprisingly peaceful. Amanda didn't have anything to say, so after a while I went for a safe if somewhat obvious opening.

"What can you tell me, about the real Robin Hood?"

"The man who gave up everything to protect others," said Amanda, slipping easily into lecture mode. "He's actually more of a danger to the secret masters than Arthur ever was, because Robin Hood exists to challenge authority. He encourages people to think for themselves, and live their own lives."

"Yes . . ." I said. "But what's he like?"

"An outlaw and an adventurer, and everything a hero should be!" She broke off, as she realised I wasn't giving her my full attention. "You've got that worried look again, Jack, even though I keep telling you it doesn't suit you. What's wrong this time?"

"We're not alone," I said quietly, trying to glower in every direction at once without making it too obvious. "Something is moving along with us."

"Probably the local wildlife," Amanda said briskly. "They've just curious. If we don't bother them, they won't attack and devour us."

"I was thinking more about the secret masters," I said. "They've already hit us with the two biggest bogeymen of the modern age, the

Men In Black and the alien Greys. What does that leave, feral clowns?"

"Oh, I love clowns!" said Amanda, clapping her hands together.

"Then you are the only person in the whole entire world who does," I said. "Why are the secret masters so determined to stop us?"

Amanda shrugged lightly. "Now they've taken control of the Department, and brought in Emil's people, it would seem they're finally ready to start their endgame."

"What would that involve?"

"No more lurking in the shadows," said Amanda. "No more pulling strings. They're ready to take over."

"And do what?"

"Rule," Amanda said simply. "This isn't about politics, or philosophies. They just want everyone else to do what they're told."

"But who are they?" I said. "When are you going to tell me who is trying so hard to kill us?"

"When you're ready."

"I feel a sulk coming on," I said.

"And it's such an attractive look on you," said Amanda.

The trail wound back and forth, in no obvious hurry to take us anywhere. Time passed, in a great green haze. The huge trees didn't lose any of their overbearing presence, but I couldn't keep being impressed. It was wearing me out.

"Are we nearly there yet?" I said.

"Don't start," said Amanda.

"What makes Sherwood so important to everyone?"

"The forest is Robin's Camelot," said Amanda. "One of the legendary settings that inspire us to be better than we are. In Arthur's time the king protected people from monsters; here the king is the monster, and people are learning to protect themselves."

"Couldn't have put it better myself," said Robin Hood.

Amanda and I slammed to a halt as he stepped out onto the trail ahead of us. Tall and lean, and good-looking in a bluff country way, he had a mane of long blond hair and blue eyes sparkling with mischief. His clothes were a mixture of dull greens and browns, perfect camouflage for a forest. He carried a longbow slung over his shoulder, a quiver of arrows on his back, and a sword at his hip. A man who didn't feel safe even in his own outlaw hideout.

Half a dozen men clothed just like Robin stepped out of the shadows to surround me and Amanda. They all had arrows pointed at our hearts, and not one of them was smiling. I decided I'd had enough of being impressed, so I ignored the outlaws and fixed Robin with my best hard stare.

"Tell your men to point their arrows somewhere else, or I'll show them a trick Merlin taught me."

If you're going to bluff, go big. Robin's smile actually widened a little. He gestured for his men to lower their arrows, and they did so reluctantly. I nodded easily to Robin, as though I'd never expected any other outcome.

"Good ambush. The outfits really do help you blend in."

"Along with our woodcraft skills," said Robin. "I swear I spend more time training people how to move without being heard, than I do teaching them how to use their weapons."

I noted a certain amount of eye-rolling amongst Robin's men. They'd clearly had to listen to this lecture many times before.

"If you stopped us for tribute," I said, "I doubt we've anything on us you'd want."

"Relax," said Robin. "You're in no danger."

I looked at the outlaws. "Really?"

"They're just being protective," said Robin. "Even though I keep asking them not to. Put the arrows away, boys. These are the ones Herne told us about." He fixed Amanda and me with a charming smile. "You must forgive my outlaws. It's either that or shout at them a lot, and I just don't have the energy. You are to be our honoured guests, Jack Daimon and Amanda Fielding!"

He laughed at the surprise in our faces, but it was a kind and pleasant sound.

"Herne is our mage and advisor. He foresaw your arrival, and told me exactly where I needed to be to find you."

I looked at Amanda. "Herne?"

She shrugged. "Some local forest god..."

She broke off, because the outlaws were sniggering and elbowing each other. Robin didn't lower himself to join in, but looked like he wanted to.

"Herne isn't any kind of god," he said. "More like a supernaturally gifted pain in the arse. But there's no denying he knows things. He said it was important that I come and meet you, because you're going to save us."

"From what?" I said.

"He didn't say," said Robin. "Which is annoying in so many ways, and just typical of Herne. Sometimes I think he's the wisest man I've ever known; the rest of the time I'm convinced he's just another freeloader with a good line in impressive chat. But never mind him, until we absolutely have to. It's good to meet you."

"It's an honour to meet the legendary Robin Hood," I said.

"I'm no more a legend than Herne is a god," he said easily. "Just a man, trying to do what's right. Come with me, and I'll take you to meet Herne. Perhaps between us we can get some straight answers out of him." He looked round at his outlaws. "Why are you still here? Get back to camp and make sure everyone's safe, until I return."

His men nodded quickly, and disappeared back into the shadows as though they belonged there. Robin set off through the forest like a man strolling in his own private garden, and Amanda and I followed after him at our own pace.

Amanda leaned in close. "What were you going to do if your bluff hadn't worked?"

"Hide behind you," I said.

"So it was a bluff," said Robin. "I am relieved."

I shot him a reproachful look. "You have good ears."

"All part of surviving in the wild," he said easily. "Sherwood makes people into fighters, because they wouldn't survive here if they weren't. And of course, it does help to keep the sheriff out."

"What's he like?" I said.

"A cold man," said Robin. "Always thinking, and plotting. I sometimes feel the most useful thing I can do is keep that appallingly clever mind focused on me, instead of coming up with more schemes to oppress the people."

"Why is that so important to him?" said Amanda.

"Because he doesn't have anything else, except to be sheriff," said Robin. "And he's always worrying the people will rise up and take it away from him. Of course, if he didn't oppress them so much the thought would never occur to them, but I could never make him understand that."

"You know him well?" I said.

"We grew up together."

"You were friends?" said Amanda.

Robin frowned. "I thought so. He must be very lonely these days, because he's driven away anyone who might have cared. All that's left are the people who want something from him, and unfortunately he's smart enough to know that."

"I can't get any sense of where Herne is," Amanda said abruptly. "Which is . . . odd. Where are you taking us, Robin?"

"Herne has his own special hideout, deep underground," said Robin. "He prefers to live apart, which is probably just as well given how much he unnerves everyone. I don't think he means to; it's just that he doesn't see the world the way the rest of us do."

"What can you tell us about him?" I said.

"Oh, Herne has been around for ages," said Robin. "When I first led my people into Sherwood in search of a safe haven he was already here, waiting to teach me what I needed to know to protect people from the sheriff. How to create the legend of Robin Hood and his Merrie Men, that helps keep the authorities at bay, because it's a lot harder to fight a myth than a man. There are times when I wonder if Herne is the real legend of Sherwood Forest.

"Some say he was once a great noble, who shot a stag the king of the Fae had marked for his own. Oberon invited Herne to join him for a night of feasting, in his court under the hill. But when Herne emerged into the daylight again he found Oberon had taken his vengeance after all, because hundreds of years had passed in the world above.

"Others insist he's a sorcerer, and the son of the Fallen One. And some believe he's the spirit of the woods and as old as the trees. He is wise and powerful and knows many things, including some that haven't happened yet."

"Sounds a lot like Merlin," I said.

Robin shot me a warning look. "Don't use that name around Herne. He gets very tetchy. I think he's jealous of a legend even greater than his."

After a while, we came to a dark river that wound between the trees in a slow and purposeful way. Mists rose up from the surface of the waters, like a curtain between our world and another. All the birds had stopped singing, and the sudden quiet had an unnatural feel. Amanda frowned, but didn't say anything. Robin led us down the slippery mud of the riverbank to a hole wide enough to admit a coach and horses. He stopped before the opening, and looked back at us.

"This is where we step out of the world we know, and into Herne's underworld."

He gestured for us to follow him into the opening, and a cool blue light manifested to illuminate our way. We stumbled down a steeply sloping earth tunnel, with me close behind Robin, and Amanda so close behind me I could feel her breath on the back of my neck. The tunnel walls were tightly packed earth with no support timbers, just the occasional tree root curling out to block the way. Our feet slipped and skidded on the mud floor, and the ceiling was so low we had to keep ducking our heads. Almost as though the entrance to Herne's lair had been specifically designed to discourage visitors.

Eventually the tunnel opened out to reveal a huge underground cavern. Stalactites and stalagmites dropped down and rose up, like a forest confused by gravity, gnarled multicoloured columns, shining fiercely with their own phosphorescence. The cavern walls were studded with glowing stones, and gleaming veins of gold and silver. In the middle of it all was a great pool of water, darker than the night, that didn't reflect any of the cavern's light. It was like looking at a hole in the world.

Robin came to a halt, and Amanda and I moved in beside him.

"It doesn't look like there's anyone home," I said.

"Herne will make himself known, when he's ready," said Robin. "He does so love to make an entrance."

I studied the cavern carefully, trying to get some sense of who would want to live in such a place. Furs and rugs covered the stone floor, along with a few mismatched chairs and a great nest of crumpled blankets. Half-eaten meals had been left to congeal on wooden platters.

"We do our best to look after Herne," Robin said quietly. "He's very good at being magical and wise, but no use at all when it comes to practical things. I look down here at least once a week, just to make sure he's eating something."

He broke off as slow heavy ripples moved across the surface of the pool, as a man's head appeared out of the dark waters. Cool, thoughtful eyes fixed on me as the rest of the body rose up, untouched by any drop of water. Until Herne stood calmly on the surface of the pool, as though it was the most natural thing in the world.

Herne was Merlin, only decades younger than the last time I'd seen him.

He was wearing silver trousers tucked into calfskin boots, and a yellow silk shirt left open to show off a hairy chest. His shoulder-length hair was jet black, as was his drooping moustache and long sideburns. The outfit was topped off with a billowing leaf-green cape. He looked like the god of prog rock.

"Very distinctive," I said finally.

"The people here expect me to look like a sorcerer," Herne said proudly. "I saw this outfit in the future, and thought it would serve."

He walked toward us, and his feet didn't produce a single ripple on the surface of the waters. He stepped onto the cavern floor to join us, and made a point of bowing to Amanda and me. Robin relaxed a little. Since Herne knew us, we must be someone important.

"Good to see you again," Herne said happily. "I've been remembering this moment for ages."

"What have you been doing since we last saw you?" said Amanda. "And how many other people have you been?"

"Not in front of the civilians," Herne said quickly. "You are up to date on current events? Good, good, I hate it when they make me do the exposition. You've arrived at a significant moment. The sheriff has called on unnatural help to wipe out Robin and his people, once and for all."

"You never told me that!" said Robin.

"Didn't I?" Herne said mildly. "I know I meant to. That's the trouble with remembering things before they happen. Half the time cause and effect aren't even talking to each other." He turned back to Amanda and me. "The sheriff has made contact with the secret masters. Or possibly vice versa."

"The ones from here and now?" I said. "Or those in the future?"

"Hard to tell," said Herne. "I have a difficult relationship with Time. Like a problem relative you just have to put up with."

"Do you know who the secret masters are?" I said. "Or will be?"

"Yes, and no," said Herne.

"You haven't changed," I said. "And you have no idea how annoying that is."

"Trust me, he knows," said Amanda.

"And you're not much better," I said.

"But I'm loveable," said Amanda.

Herne pouted. "I can be loveable . . ."

"What are you all talking about?" said Robin, just a bit desperately.

"Damned if I know," I said. "You get used to it."

"Let's not get childish," Herne said reprovingly. "The point is the bad guys want Robin Hood out of the way."

"What have I done to upset these people?" said Robin.

"You have a mind of your own," said Herne. "And, you have accepted nonhumans into your band of outlaws."

"Why wouldn't I?" said Robin. "This is their Sherwood, as well as mine."

Herne beamed at me. "You see? He really doesn't understand why anyone would have a problem with that. Isn't he marvellous? Anyway, a terrible army is coming, to destroy Sherwood Forest and slaughter every living thing in it."

"It's going to do *what*?" Robin said loudly. "Why didn't you warn me about this before?"

"Because it wasn't the right time," said Herne. "Just be grateful I remembered to tell you at all."

"When, exactly, is this army going to arrive?" said Robin, in a voice brimming over with self-control.

"Hmm? Oh, quite soon actually," said Herne. "That's why Jack and Amanda are here. Yes! That's why I didn't tell you before! Because you couldn't do anything until they got here. And, I didn't want to worry you."

"You are too good to me," said Robin.

"I am, aren't I?" said Herne, nodding cheerfully. "You don't deserve me."

"I often wonder what I did to deserve you," said Robin. "Are Jack and Amanda here to save us from this army that's coming?"

"Well . . . yes, and no," said Herne.

Robin looked at me. "You're right. That really is irritating."

"Amanda's just as bad," I said.

"Who do you think I learned it from?" said Herne, just a bit unexpectedly.

"Can you at least tell me what kind of army we're talking about?" said Robin. "The sheriff's men, or King John's soldiers?"

"Unfortunately, none of the above," said Herne. "The secret masters create their own foot soldiers, designed to break their opponents' spirit before the fighting even begins. You must prepare your people, Robin. Horror is coming to Sherwood."

"How long do we have?" said Robin.

"Ooh . . . Hours!" said Herne.

He strode out of the cavern, snapping his cloak around him and leaving us to catch up as best we could.

When we finally emerged from the cave opening and back into Sherwood's twilight, Herne produced a pair of seriously dark sunglasses and put them on with a flourish. He caught me staring at him, and sniffed haughtily.

"You try living underground for centuries and see what that does to your pupils. Besides, I like shades. They're stylish, they're cool, they're . . . me."

He scrambled up the steep riverbank with surprising agility. Robin looked after him, and then turned to me and Amanda.

"I'm assuming what he says makes sense to you."

"Some of the time," I said.

"Well, that's good to know," said Robin. "Any idea on how you're going to save us all?"

I looked at Amanda, but she just shrugged and set off up the muddy riverbank after Herne.

"Nothing springs to mind," I said to Robin. "But I knew an invading army would turn up at some point."

"You can see the future as well?"

"No," I said. "It's just bitter experience."

I climbed the riverbank with as much dignity as I could manage, and Robin followed after me. Once we caught up with Herne and Amanda, Robin took the lead and we followed him through the great trees. Herne just wandered along, happily interested in everything but saying nothing, and after a while Amanda and I moved in on either side of him and slowed him down so we could talk privately.

"What are you doing here?" I said.

"It's my job to inspire Robin, just as I inspired Arthur when I was Merlin," said Herne. "I bring out the best in people, whether they like it or not. I don't receive nearly enough credit for all the heroes I make possible."

"Why do you look so much younger?" I said.

"The times change, and I change with them. My memory isn't the only thing that's out of synch with history."

"Why the new name?"

"Too much baggage associated with the old one," he said patiently. "Too many expectations."

"Can you still throw those lightnings around, to defend Robin and his people from what's coming?" I said bluntly.

"No," said Herne. "I draw my power from the genius loci of the land, the magical wellsprings of creation. And they're running out. That's why I came to Sherwood: the last living repository of ancient magic."

Robin dropped back to join us. "So, Herne used to be Merlin. Are the two of you anyone special?"

"No one you'd have heard of," said Amanda. "Jack and I are here to help. Settle for that."

"And people think I'm in charge around here," said Robin Hood.

A warm glow of torchlight appeared ahead of us. Guards stepped out of the shadows to challenge us, and then fell back again when they recognised Robin. They also knew Herne, though they didn't seem nearly as happy to see him.

Robin Hood's camp wasn't at all what I'd expected. No protective barricades, and no standing structures at all: just a wide-open clearing with bedrolls and blankets, stacks of weapons, and half a dozen cooking fires. People bustled back and forth, performing all the small necessary chores that keep a self-sufficient community going. A great cry of welcome went up to welcome Robin back, but he took it all quite casually, smiling and nodding as he made his way through crowds of men, women and children in ragged clothes. Hunger and hardship showed clearly in their bruised eyes and haunted faces.

Some of the outlaws looked suspiciously at Herne, and a few crossed themselves. They weren't too sure about Amanda or me either, but no one challenged our right to be there. Robin quietly spread word that trouble was on its way, and half the people broke off from what they were doing to arm themselves and join the perimeter guards. Interestingly, where Arthur would have given orders Robin just made it sound like simple common sense.

He led us to the far side of the clearing, where heavy sheets hung from tree branches to form a makeshift tent. Herne drifted away, lost in his own thoughts, and Robin shook his head.

"You have to make allowances for him. It's either that or end up as crazy as he is. Let him wander where he wants; my people will keep an eye on him, and make sure he doesn't get into any trouble. You look a bit disappointed by my camp, Jack. Have you been listening to those ballads? We always have to be ready to move on, so the sheriff's men can't find us. Even the best spies and informers can't reveal where we are, only where we used to be."

"Has the sheriff ever sent an army in after you before?" I said.

Robin frowned. "He usually has more sense. By the time his soldiers have travelled any distance, my best archers are always ready to teach the invaders that numbers and armour are no match for the silent death that strikes from ambush. Now, come and meet my Merrie Men."

"Why are they called that?" I said.

"Because there's nothing like killing bullyboys in chain mail to put a smile on your face," said Robin Hood.

He led us into the tent, to meet the outlaws who were almost as famous as he was. And just like Arthur's knights, they were nothing like the stories.

Maid Marion the Fair turned out to be Marion the Fae, a tall and stately elf with long silver hair, purple eyes and pointed ears. Slender as a greyhound and almost supernaturally beautiful, she wore a long gown made from camouflage material, but on her it looked stylish. The scabbarded sword on her hip looked like it belonged there. She grabbed hold of Robin the moment he entered the tent, kissed him soundly, and then pushed him away so she could glare at him.

"Why must you listen to that mad old sorcerer? You know he never tells you anything you want to hear."

"That's exactly what I need from him," Robin said calmly. "You shouldn't be so hard on the man, Marion. He's done a lot for us."

"For his own reasons. Which he has never seen fit to explain."

"Everyone comes to Sherwood for their own reasons," said Robin. "And Marion... Please don't try to kill him again. If you do and he notices, he might get upset, and I don't want to end up bedding down beside a really large frog." He smiled apologetically at me and Amanda. "Marion can be very protective."

"Somebody has to be," said Marion. "I don't want to end up bedding down next to a corpse. They get cold so quickly."

Everyone pretended they hadn't heard that.

Little John turned out to be a giant. (Outlaw humour.) Even sitting down, he still towered over everyone else, and took up the space where a back wall should have been. He looked like he'd be a good twelve feet tall on his feet, and wore more camouflage material than all the others put together. His entire body appeared to be made out of solid muscle, and he had a square face with skin like fissured stone.

"This is my living battering ram," Robin said fondly. "Slow to anger, but terrible in his rage."

Little John bowed briefly, and then fixed his gaze on Amanda. When he spoke his voice was a deep rumble, like approaching thunder.

"I remember you, lady. It has been long and long since you last walked among my kind."

I stared at Amanda. "Does everyone know you?"

"Everyone who matters," she said cheerfully.

Friar Tuck was the only one who looked the way I thought he should. A fat and jolly soul in a faded monk's habit liberally spattered with food and wine stains, he had a red face, a shaven tonsure, and a smile for everyone. He shook my hand heartily, his oversized paw swallowing mine without doing any real damage.

"Welcome to Sherwood, my boy!" he said. "Too cold when it isn't too hot, and raining in between. The food's monotonous, and you can't get a decent bottle of wine for love nor money and God knows I've tried. I have to perform communion with mead I make myself. You must try some, if you've a strong stomach. I also practice a little white magic on the side, but don't let that worry you."

He fixed Amanda with a thoughtful look, and didn't offer to shake her hand. "It seems to me that I have read about you, my lady, in some very old books. Are you what I think you are?"

"Oh, I'm so much more than that," said Amanda. "What kind of white magic?"

"Nothing I would be ashamed to admit to my God," said the friar. "I only ever use the magics of nature to protect people, but it was still enough to get me thrown out of the monastery."

Everyone in the tent had some kind of smile. Robin fixed the friar with a sardonic look.

"That is not why they kicked you out, Tuck."

The friar nodded wryly. "I always was a little too fond of the earthly appetites. I fear the final straw was when an outraged father came hammering on the monastery door, shouting my name. I thought it best for all concerned if I just slipped quietly away. Now here I am, doing penance for my many sins. Not at all the life of quiet reflection I had in mind for my later years, but good company makes it bearable."

"I am Will Scarlett."

The dry whispering voice came from a far corner, where Scarlett sat half hidden in the shadows. A rangy aristocratic sort, he had dark hair and eyes and a surprisingly pale face for someone who lived outdoors. He dressed all in black and didn't look in the least interested in shaking hands.

"What brought you to Sherwood?" I said, just to be polite.

He smiled slowly, showing pointed teeth.

"I'm a vampire. And like the good friar, I am here to do penance."

"But . . . it's still daylight," I said.

"It's never more than twilight in Sherwood," said Will. "I can live with that." He turned his cold dark eyes on Amanda. "You see me as I really am."

"Yes," Amanda said steadily. "Glamours have no power over my eyes."

She dropped a hand onto my arm and suddenly the dark and brooding aristocrat was gone, as my Sight showed me a decaying corpse in ragged grave clothes. He looked like what he was: a dead thing that had dug its way out of the ground to feast on the living. Amanda removed her hand and the illusion returned. Will looked at us coldly.

"How can we be sure you're not the sheriff's creatures, sent here to spy on us?"

I looked to Robin, but he just stared calmly back, interested to see what I would do. And that suited me fine. I'd spent most of my time among Arthur and his knights feeling seriously outclassed, but I could handle something as straightforward as a vampire.

I smiled easily at Will and gestured at the backpack on my shoulder. "I am the Outsider. Which means I don't take any crap from the supernatural. In this pack I have a crucifix blessed by a living saint, a wooden stake from the tree Jesus planted at Glastonbury, and a squirt gun full of holy water. But I think I'll go with an old reliable."

I reached into my pack, and brought out the athame. Its blade glowed brightly, as its presence filled the tent. Marion had to turn her face away, Tuck crossed himself, and Little John growled dangerously. Will sat very still.

"You know what this is," I said. "I could kill everyone in this tent before any of you could get to your feet . . . but that's not what I'm here for."

I put the witch knife back in my pack, and everyone relaxed a little. I looked at Robin, and found he was still smiling.

"That was a test," I said accusingly.

"Of course," said Robin. "I haven't lasted this long by trusting every stranger who wanders into Sherwood."

"Even though Herne vouched for us?" said Amanda.

"Herne . . . isn't always entirely reliable," said Robin.

"I told you that," said Marion.

"And I listen to absolutely everything you tell me," said Robin.

I turned back to Will. "Does everyone in the camp know you're a vampire?"

"Of course," said Will. "They know they have nothing to fear from me. I don't drink . . . people."

"Will is one of our strongest weapons," Robin said firmly. "I trust him implicitly."

"Yes, well, that's you, Robin," said Tuck. "I'm the one kept busy blessing improvised crosses."

"It does help that we're surrounded by trees," Marion said solemnly. "So we're never far from a wooden stake if we need one."

"Stop teasing him," said Robin.

"Tell him to stop being a vampire," said Marion.

Robin shook his head. "I swear no one around here listens to a word I say."

Will surprised me then, with a brief bark of laughter. "Remind me again of the particular qualities you bring to our little group?"

"I have no special abilities," said Robin. "So I have to settle for being smart. And that is why I'm the leader of this merry band of outlaws and renegades."

"We let you be leader so the sheriff's men will always aim at you first," said Tuck. "Allowing the rest of us a chance to get away."

"And if we should happen to fall on hard times, we can always turn you in for the reward," said Marion.

"We wouldn't do that," said Little John, in his deep rumble of a voice.

"I'm relieved to hear it," said Robin.

"Not with the amount as low as it is," said the giant.

Everyone laughed, including Robin. And then he brought the Merrie Men up to speed on what Herne had told him. They all listened intently. They might not care for Herne, but they trusted his warnings.

"Apparently we only have a few hours before this unknown army enters Sherwood," said Robin.

"Let them come," said Marion, her long-fingered hand dropping to the pommel of her sword. "We will bury their bodies among the tree roots, to nourish the forest."

"Has anyone seen my club?" rumbled the giant. "I'm sure I had a club when I came in here."

Tuck frowned. "Herne wouldn't be putting the wind up us if it was just another incursion by the sheriff's men."

"I like it when he sends in soldiers," said Will. "They break so easily."

Robin set to making plans, so Amanda and I left him to it. We took a stroll around the camp, but there didn't seem to be anything we could do to help, so we ended up warming our hands at one of the cooking fires. The twilight was darkening into night, and there was a definite chill on the air. Herne came over to join us. Somewhere along the way he'd lost his sunglasses, and the light from the dancing flames invested his face with sinister shadows.

"Having fun?" he asked. "Making new friends? Good, good... Try not to develop a close relationship with anyone; a lot of these people aren't going to survive what's coming."

"Do you know who's going to die?" I said.

"No, or I'd stay well clear of them," said Herne. "I remember the shape of the future, but not the details. And having you two around disturbs the pattern even more, because you don't belong here."

"I thought we were supposed to save the day?" I said.

He shrugged. "Apparently."

I turned to Amanda. "What makes Robin Hood and his Merrie Men so special that they have to be removed from history?"

"Because this is the last time all the different races will gather together in common cause," said Amanda.

"The Merrie Men are all that remain of their kind," said Herne. "The last elf, the last giant, and the last vampire. All the others are gone. I do miss them. They were so colourful."

"Hopefully, you're the last of your kind," said Marion.

None of us had noticed the elf coming over to join us. She glared at Herne, who seemed quite used to it.

"There has never been anyone like me," he said calmly. "And never will be again." He paused, to look at Amanda. "Unless you know otherwise."

She ignored him, staring into the flames, so I turned to Marion. "Are you really the last of the elves?"

"If there was another of my kind anywhere in this land, I would know it," said Marion. "The Faerie War destroyed the Light and the Dark."

"How did you survive?" I said.

She smiled bleakly. "Just lucky, I guess."

"Little John walked all the way here from Cornwall," said Herne. "He couldn't find anyone who'd even heard of another giant for generations. As for Will Scarlett..."

"Taking my name in vein?" said the vampire, appearing suddenly beside Marion. She jumped a little, and punched him hard in the ribs. He didn't seem to feel it.

"There used to be so many of my kind," he said, staring at the shadows outside the camp. "Haunting the forests of the night, feared by all. But I haven't talked with anything like me in a very long time."

"What do you feed on?" I said bluntly.

"Deer," said Will. "Their blood is very nourishing. Full of iron."

"And the occasional sheriff's man?" I said.

"No," said Will. "I can't afford to be tempted."

Robin joined us, and Marion moved in close beside him. Their hands found each other without either of them having to look.

"Everyone is getting ready to fight," said Robin. "Have there been any sightings?"

"No one has entered the forest," said Marion.

"They won't hide themselves," said Herne. "When the horror begins, you'll know."

Everyone looked at him, and he shrugged. "Don't shoot the messenger."

"Don't tempt me," said Marion.

"I think it's time we all had something to eat and drink," said Robin.

I looked at him incredulously. "How can you even think of eating, when people are coming to kill you?"

"People are always coming to kill me," Robin said reasonably. "That's the outlaw life."

He went off to oversee the cooking. Not because anyone needed his help, but because they found his presence reassuring. Herne also moved from one cooking fire to another, tasting things and offering carefully considered recommendations, which were universally ignored. Marion stalked the camp perimeter, keeping the guards on their toes. Their startled shrieks could be heard all over the camp. Tuck rolled a great barrel of mead across the clearing, refusing every offer of help. Will Scarlett disappeared back into the shadows. Little John sat down in the middle of the camp, and small children swarmed all over him as though he was the best toy ever.

Soon there was food enough for everyone, and I could tell from the looks on many faces that this wasn't something they were used to. We all sat down around the fires, and Amanda and I were given places of honour next to Robin and Marion. There were no plates or cutlery; food was just dumped in people's laps, and everyone used their hands. I did my best not to be a wimp about it. Mead came in rough wooden cups: a thick golden brew with things swimming in it. Everyone was eating and drinking and talking at the top of their voices, all at the same time.

And afterwards, there was dancing. Musicians raised a joyous noise, and people went whirling and stamping around the blazing fires. Dancing for the sheer joy of it, for the hell of it, for the simple delight of being alive. Bare feet pounded on the packed earth, and hair flew wildly as heads whipped back and forth. Dancing because what else was there to do, in the face of what was coming.

At first, I was too self-conscious to join in. I've never been much of a dancer, and this felt like the outlaws' moment. I watched Amanda dance, swinging energetically from one partner to another, her face gleaming with sweat as she laughed out loud. It seemed to me that she had never looked more beautiful, or more alive. Suddenly she burst out of the crowd to stand before me. She thrust out a hand and I took it, and she pulled me into the heaving throng.

I don't know how long we danced, stamping our feet to the rhythm of the music. She never let go of me and I never let go of her, and I had never felt so happy. At some point the music slowed down, and all across the clearing couples held each other close, lost in each other's eyes. I held Amanda in my arms, and she turned her face up to mine; when we finally kissed it felt like the moment my whole life had been leading up to.

The music stopped. People moved away in pairs to be on their own, perhaps for the last time. Amanda stepped back out of my arms, looked searchingly into my face, and then turned abruptly and walked away. I stood there and watched her go. I could have called after her, but I didn't. Because if she didn't want to be with me, I didn't want to be with her.

It was cold and dark and I had never felt so alone.

I sat down beside a guttering fire. Herne dropped heavily down beside me, and we sat together for a while, staring into the dying flames. I wondered how long we had, before the sheriff's army arrived to put an end to everything. I looked at Herne.

"Can't you tell me anything about what's going to happen?"

"You and Amanda complicate things," Herne said tiredly. "You're like a blind spot in my memory."

"Why?" I said.

"Why do you think?" he said testily. He gestured at Amanda, standing at the edge of the clearing and staring out into the darkness. A nearby fire left her half in light, half in shadow; splendid and mysterious like a spirit of the forest, or some ancient goddess come down to earth to meddle with human lives.

"Who is she, really?" I said.

"You'll find out," said Herne.

"I think I love her," I said quietly.

"Of course you do."

"Well?" I said. "How is that going to work out? Does she love me?"

Herne sighed, and looked at me with eyes older than the centuries. "She is so much more than you could possibly imagine. Loving her, being loved by her ... is like a moth diving into the sun."

"Well," I said, after a moment. "There are worse ways to go."

Robin sat down beside us. He was still smiling.

"I live for nights like this," he said. "Dancing on the edge, savouring every moment, because you know you'll never feel so alive again. Sometimes I think if I could only get the sheriff to come and join us for a night like this, we could put an end to all our quarrels."

"He wouldn't feel the same," said Herne.

"But if I could just show him that he doesn't have to be so alone ..."

"It's what he's chosen," said Herne.

Robin shook his head stubbornly. "There's good in every man, if you just dig deep enough. I have to believe that."

"Of course you do," said Herne. "That's what makes you Robin Hood."

"He is a legend," Robin said sharply. "I'm only a man. Have you had any other visions about this army that's coming? How big is it?"

"Big," said Herne. "Really big. Horribly and devastatingly big ..."

"All right, all right!" said Robin, stopping him with an upraised hand. "I get the point. Isn't there anything useful you can tell me?"

"I don't know," said Herne. "Ask me questions, and see what happens."

"What kind of help has the sheriff received, to make him so confident?" Robin said carefully. "What kind of army will we be facing?"

"Nightmares," said Herne. "Death on the march. Something bad is going to happen to Sherwood."

Robin beat a fist against his thigh in a slow rhythm of frustration. "If the sheriff has called on unnatural forces . . . are there other powers, that we could reach out to?"

"There are some who might listen if I call," said Herne. "Ancient beings from when the world was young, wild and playful, always looking for something new to interest them. They might agree to get involved just for the fun of it. The real problem lies in getting rid of them afterwards."

Robin frowned. "You mean the old gods, from before Christianity?"

"Older even than that," said Herne. "Beyond good and evil, because those are limited human concepts. Like the pookah, who danced in the forest before men ever came here. The pookah is wild delight, the laughter in the woods and the joy in the night. Love and madness and everything in between, who dabbles in the glory and damnation of human hearts for its own entertainment. It likes to play with us, but it doesn't always play nicely, and sometimes it breaks its toys."

"Call one," said Robin.

"I knew you were going to say that," said Herne. "So I did it yesterday."

"Then where is it?" said Robin.

"It'll make itself known when it's ready," said Herne. "Or it won't. It's like that."

Robin stared into the guttering flames of the fire. "We're going to have to do this on our own, aren't we?"

"You have me, and Amanda," I said.

"Ah yes," said Robin. "Our promised saviours. Can you fight?"

"I fought beside King Arthur and the knights of Camelot, against an army of monsters," I said steadily. "And we were still standing when they turned and ran."

Robin looked at me. "Camelot was hundreds of years ago . . ."

"We took a short cut," I said.

Robin nodded slowly. "If you stand with us, the odds are you'll die with us."

"I would be honoured to stand with you and the outlaws of Sherwood," I said. "The odds don't matter. We don't fight to win; we fight because it's the right thing to do."

"To hell with that," said Robin. "I always fight to win, because innocent people will die if I don't."

And that was when a messenger came stumbling into the clearing, a young man so exhausted by hard running two guards had to support him. They brought him straight to Robin.

"The sheriff has set fire to the forest!" the messenger said loudly. "He sent people in with torches, and now a great wind is fanning the flames and driving them deep into Sherwood!"

We were all on our feet in a moment.

"Where did he set these fires?" said Robin.

"All along the boundaries! The sheriff has vowed to burn the whole forest to ashes, and he has enough men with him to see it done."

"Of course," said Herne. "With Sherwood gone, there'll be nowhere left to hide. And burning down an entire forest is an excellent way to show everyone just how far he's prepared to go to get his own way."

"It's not too late," said Robin. "We can take water from the rivers, cut down trees to keep the flames from spreading . . . And if all else fails, we can still escape. Find a new haven, and start again."

"The sheriff has thought of that," said the messenger. He looked ready to collapse, but he made himself stand straight so he could tell Robin what he needed to know. "He has people watching the boundaries, collected from all the nearby towns and villages, with orders to kill everyone who tries to leave the forest. And they are ready to do it! No one knows why. Either we stay in Sherwood and burn alive, or the very people we fought for will cut us down."

Robin stared at him. "Why would they betray us, after everything we've done for them . . ."

"There are special orders, where you and the Merrie Men are concerned," the messenger said miserably. "You are to be taken alive, dragged through Nottingham in chains, and then publicly tortured and executed. So everyone can see the fate of outlaws."

"The sheriff always was a bad loser," said Robin.

He had his guards lead the messenger away to be cared for, and then called out to his people. Men and women came running from all over the clearing. Robin quickly explained the situation, and the outlaws hurried off to spread the word. Robin stood for a long moment, thinking hard, before finally turning to Herne.

"Is this what you saw coming?"

"Some of it," said Herne.

"Why didn't you warn me?"

"Because it wasn't the right time. And it wasn't like there was anything you could do," Herne said reasonably.

"Can the sheriff really prevent us from escaping?"

"If you spread your people widely enough, some might get away," said Herne.

It wasn't the answer Robin wanted, but he nodded quickly and strode off to begin the evacuation of Sherwood. No one asked questions. They just packed up their few belongings and headed into the trees. Robin called for the messenger, and he came hurrying back. He'd been given a mug of Tuck's mead, and was looking a lot more collected.

"Has the sheriff come in person?" said Robin.

"He's holding a position by the northern boundary," said the messenger. "So he can watch the forest burn, and laugh."

"The nearest boundary ... Which means he wants me to come to him," said Robin. "It's always been all about me, as far as the sheriff is concerned." He clapped the messenger on the shoulder. "Thank you, friend. You put your life at risk to warn us."

"Anything, for Robin Hood," said the messenger, standing straight and tall despite his exhaustion.

"Then do me one final service," said Robin. "Find a way past the fires and out of the forest, and tell everyone that Robin Hood and his outlaws never stopped fighting."

The messenger shook his head fiercely. "I came here to fight alongside you!"

"Of course you did. But I need this more."

The messenger nodded stiffly, and left the clearing. Robin turned to Herne.

"You were never a fighter. Go back to your cave. The fires won't reach you there."

Herne nodded slowly. "We will never see each other again. A shame. I shall miss our conversations."

Robin smiled. "And I will miss you, old friend. Let's see if I can finally be the legend you wanted." He raised his voice again. "Marion! Tuck, Will, Little John! I need you!"

The Merrie Men came hurrying forward from every side. Marion moved in close beside Robin, where she belonged, one hand resting on his shoulder and the other on her sword. Tuck had a long wooden staff. Will Scarlett was smiling widely, his whole body seized with a dangerous tension. Little John loomed over everyone, even taller than I'd expected. He was carrying a club that looked big enough to drive a man into the ground like a nail into wood.

"It's time to kill the sheriff," Robin said calmly. "I've given the man every chance because he was my friend once, but he's gone too far. Are you with me?"

Marion drew her sword. "Always, my love."

"You took me in, when no one else would," said Little John. "I will make your enemies remember why men were right to fear giants."

Tuck hefted his staff. "I can crack a few pates with the best of them, and I've been working on a few new magics to confuse and bedevil our enemies."

"I'm thirsty," said Will Scarlett, and we all shuddered just a little.

Robin looked around at his Merrie Men, but the words wouldn't come. So he just smiled and nodded, and strode off into the woods. The outlaws went after him, and suddenly the only people left in the clearing were me, and Herne. I looked at him steadily.

"Why didn't you go with Robin? There must be something your magics could do."

"Robin doesn't need me any more," said Herne. "Events have been set in motion, and the future is inevitable. It always was. I've remembered this for so long, I thought it would be easier to accept, but it never is. The ending of a dream . . . He doesn't know it, because I couldn't tell him, but this is Robin Hood's last adventure in Sherwood. My work here is done. I shall retire to my cave now, and sleep the sleep of ages. So I can wake up as someone else, to inspire some other hero."

"Are you running away to hide, because you know the sheriff is going to win?" I said harshly. "Are Robin and all his outlaws going to die?"

"There's nothing more I can do," said Herne. "My power comes from the magical wells of Sherwood, and the sheriff's people are burning it down." He smiled tiredly. "Off you go, Outsider. You don't need me; you have Amanda."

"Do I?" I said.

"Well, that's up to you, isn't it?" He yawned suddenly. "Pardon me. I need to get my head down for a century or two. See you later, alligator."

He ambled off into the trees, and the shadows swallowed him up. Amanda suddenly appeared out of the shadows, to face me.

"I know you love me," she said. "And I love you, as much as I can."

"Then what's the problem?" I said, as steadily as I could.

"You keep asking what I really am," said Amanda. "And we're getting closer to the moment when I'll have to tell you. But once you know, I'm afraid you won't love me any more."

"How I feel about you isn't going to change," I said.

"It will," said Amanda. "Because once you know the truth, you'll never be able to see me the same way again. Do you still want to fight alongside Robin Hood and his Merrie Men?"

"Of course," I said.

"Then we'd better get a move on."

She strode out of the clearing without looking back to see whether I was following. And this time I went with her.

I was surprised to find the night had come and gone while we feasted and danced, and grey shafts of early morning light were filtering down through the overhead canopy. Robin and his Merrie Men were completely out of sight, but Amanda plunged down one trail after another without hesitating.

It wasn't long before I smelled smoke on the air, and heard the crackling of fires. Soon we were having to detour around whole areas of burning forest. Flames jumped from branch to branch, igniting one tree after another, until a harsh light filled the woods bright as day, and the air grew so hot it smarted painfully on my bare face and hands. We finally found Robin and his Merrie Men standing together in an open clearing, staring into the trees ahead. Robin barely shot us a glance as we joined him.

A growing thunder of running feet drew steadily nearer. We braced ourselves, and then a host of forest wildlife was running straight at us, panicked by the advancing fires. Deer and boars and wolves streamed past us, not even recognising us as anything more than obstacles to their flight. Waves of smaller creatures streamed after them, shooting across the clearing. Robin smiled briefly.

"It would appear we're the only ones in this forest foolish enough to walk toward certain death. But we're not far from the edge of the forest now. And, hopefully, the sheriff. If this is the end of my story, I'd hate for him to miss it."

"Lead the way," I said. "I'd like a few words with the man myself."

"Of course," said Marion. "You're going to save us."

"I'm the Outsider," I said. "It's what I do."

But when we finally reached the forest boundary, and all of us except Will Scarlett stepped out of the trees and into the morning light, the sheriff wasn't there. Instead, Miriam and Emil were waiting for us, backed up by row upon row of armed villagers. Robin and his people looked blankly at the motionless figures, while Miriam smiled mockingly at me.

"About time you showed up, Jack."

The villagers were dead. Men, women and children stood silently, with empty eyes and slack mouths, not moving and not breathing. Their clothes still showed bloodstains from the wounds that killed them. Some had swords and axes, but most carried scythes and other farm implements. Friar Tuck put his hands together and murmured prayers for the dead. Robin turned to me, and when he spoke his voice was colder than I'd ever heard before.

"You know this woman?"

"I thought I did," I said.

"She serves the secret masters," said Amanda. "That has a way of rubbing off on people."

"Why isn't the sheriff with you?" Robin demanded of Miriam.

"Oh, he wanted to be here," she said lightly. "He said he had a right to be present, at the end of the legend of Robin Hood. But when he called on my masters for help, they sent me and Emil; after that there was no more need for a sheriff."

"He died bravely, if that matters," said Emil. "Wouldn't scream no matter what I did to him."

Robin started forward, but Marion grabbed his arm. Emil looked disappointed.

"He was my friend and my enemy," Robin said harshly. "That made him mine to kill, not yours. Who are you people? Name yourselves!"

"Cattle don't need to know who the butcher is," said Miriam. She smiled brightly at me. "What do you think of my new army, Jack?"

"A whole new low," I said. "What were you thinking, Miriam?"

She shrugged. "Men In Black and alien Greys are all very well when it comes to intimidating people, but when you need something the whole world is afraid of you can't go wrong with the living dead. Shock troops, in every sense of the word."

"I knew these people," said Robin, his voice thick with anger. "How can you justify what you've done to them?"

"I have always been able to do whatever it takes, to win," said Miriam. "After what I've done here, no one will ever dare rise up against authority again. The fire will destroy Sherwood, the living dead will kill any outlaws who try to escape the flames, and everyone will know who did this, and why."

"My people don't die that easily," said Robin.

"No doubt they're brave enough, when it comes to shooting soldiers in the back from ambush," said Emil. "But how do you think they'll cope when the people coming to kill them have faces they know?"

"Don't smile," I said. "There's nothing funny about this."

"Really?" said Emil. "I think it's hilarious."

"I didn't have any particular reason to kill you, until now," I said. "But after this I'll think of something special, just for you."

He looked into my eyes, and saw I meant every word. He tried to say something, and couldn't.

"Don't tease the hired help, Jack," said Miriam.

"How many of my people have you made into liches?" said Robin.

"The entire populations from every town and village bordering Sherwood," said Miriam. "I had them all killed, and then I made them all stand up again, with the help of this very useful book I found in the Department library."

"I thought you were all about the science?" I said.

She shrugged. "I'm sure I'll come up with a rational explanation later."

I turned to Amanda. "Can't you do anything?"

"Even I can't bring back the dead," she said quietly. "And men have to fight monsters themselves, remember?"

Robin took a deep breath, and made himself smile easily at Miriam. Putting on the legend, to hide the man's pain.

"Well, it's been nice talking to you. Actually it hasn't but I was brought up to be polite. We will defeat your army the same way we always have: by using the forest against them. Back into the trees, my Merrie Men."

They were gone in a moment, as though the forest had swallowed them up. Miriam and I looked at each other, but neither of us had anything to say. Amanda tugged urgently at my arm, and I let her lead me back into Sherwood.

We ran after the outlaws, darting in and out of the burning trees. The appalling heat was closing in from all sides, and every breath seared my lungs. The air was thick with smoke. We fought our way through the inferno, and eventually caught up with the outlaws. They were crouched down on their heels, where the air was fresher, discussing tactics. Robin nodded to me.

"You seem to have some knowledge of the risen dead," he said. "How do we put them down?"

"Destroying the head usually works," I said. "Or an arrow through the eye, as long as it reaches the brain."

"I can do that," said Robin. "How fast do these liches move?"

"Depends on what kind they are," I said. "Knowing Miriam, she'll have gone for the speeded-up version."

"You go on," Will Scarlett said calmly to Robin. "I'll hold them here."

Robin didn't argue. "Fight hard, Will. And die well."

"Been there, done that," said Will.

"Go with God, my son," said Tuck.

"If he'll still have me," said Will.

Robin set off, and the other outlaws went with him. I stood before Will, and searched for something to say. He nodded understandingly.

"You don't believe in last stands. You think there's always something more you can do. But there's nothing like being killed, and having to claw your way out of your own grave, to teach you that sometimes you just run out of options. I want this, Jack. One last chance to feel like a man again."

"Maybe it takes an undead, to teach the dead fear," I said.

He smiled. "Nice thought. Now get the hell out of here. They're coming."

Amanda pulled at my arm, and we moved quickly to the edge of the clearing. I stopped, to look back. The dead came running through the forest, weaving blindly past blazing trees. Their clothes caught fire, but they didn't care. Will waited patiently for the dead to come to him, and then crushed their skulls and broke their necks with casual blows. He picked up the dead and threw them at trees with such force their backs broke. He knocked bodies down and trampled them under foot. Smiling happily all the while. It must have felt good, so good, to let his rage run loose after having to keep it caged for so long. But in the end the dead just swarmed right over him and dragged him down. Will Scarlett disappeared under a pile of seething corpses, and was still struggling when they hauled him away.

Amanda and I moved deeper into the forest. After a while I heard Will start to scream.

"What are they doing to him?" I said to Amanda.

"They've dragged him out into the sunlight," she said.

I plunged blindly through the burning forest, stumbling along and fighting for every breath. Trees were going up on every side like blazing torches, and the smoke was so thick I could barely make out the way ahead. I stopped to peer about me, and then had to bend right over because my head was swimming. Sweat dripped from my face onto the scorched earth, where it evaporated immediately. Amanda waited patiently.

"The fires are getting closer, Jack."

I just nodded.

"Try your Sight," she said. "Let's See what's happening to the others."

I nodded, and Amanda put her hand on my arm.

Robin and Marion were running easily through the great trees, pacing themselves. The dead were close on their heels. Robin lured them into all his most secret traps and pitfalls, but no matter how many fell there were always more to take their place. Robin and Marion finally entered a clearing and came to a sudden halt, as dead men and women emerged from every side to block their way. There was no triumph in their slack faces, no hatred in their empty eyes. Death had come for Robin Hood and Marion the Fae, and it was a cold, heartless thing.

"We're surrounded," said Robin.

"I had noticed," said Marion.

Robin slipped the bow off his shoulder, and notched an arrow to the string. Marion hefted her sword. Robin smiled at her.

"The last stand of Robin Hood. I always knew I'd die in Sherwood."

"And I always knew I'd die with you," said Marion.

"Watch my back?"

"Forever and a day."

The first dead man started toward them and Robin put an arrow through its left eye. The head snapped back, and the dead man crashed to the ground and didn't move again. More dead surged out of the treelines, charging across the open space from every direction at once. Robin fired arrow after arrow and every shot hit home, until his quiver was empty. He shouldered his bow and drew his sword. He shared a quick smile with Marion, and then they moved to stand back to back. And waited for the living dead to come to them.

They came with grasping hands and remorseless strength, clawing at the outlaws with cold determination. Robin hacked and cut with elegant style, laughing out loud. Happy to be living his legend at last: facing impossible odds and refusing to be beaten. His blade cut down everything that came within reach, but soon enough the dead found their way past it and cold hands clawed at Robin. They tore his skin and spilled his blood onto the parched earth floor, but he wouldn't cry out. He didn't want to worry Marion.

The last of the Fae guarded his back with more than human ferocity, refusing to let any of the dead get past her to the man she loved. He never knew how many wounds she took, standing her ground and refusing to be moved. Her blood splashed on the ground, and mixed with his.

More and more dead emerged from the trees, and the human outlaw and his elven love fought on; like the legends they were.

The scene changed abruptly, to show Little John brought to bay in another clearing. Roaring flames consumed the surrounding trees, which toppled slowly and crashed to the forest floor like burning logs. New fires were springing up everywhere, and smoke curled thickly on the heated air as the dead poured into the clearing to face the giant. Many of them were half consumed by the fires they'd passed through, unknowing and uncaring, and smoke curled up from their charred and blackened forms. Little John towered over them like a bear beset by dogs, and when they came for him he struck them down with his massive club. A few crawled forward to clutch at his legs, and the giant stamped on their heads. His club rose and fell, doing terrible damage, and soon the clearing was littered with awful broken things that would never rise again. Little John stood his ground and swung his club as though it was weightless, and not one of the dead could get close enough to lay hands on him.

The giant fought off an army, and looked like he could do it all day.

My Sight switched to Friar Tuck. He had his back set against a tree as yet untouched by flames, and was sweeping his staff back and forth before him. The dead stood back, out of range, watching with empty eyes. And then one of them reached out unnaturally quickly, snatched the staff out of Tuck's hands, and threw it away. Tuck cursed the living dead in God's name, but they couldn't hear him.

He spoke some Words in a language I didn't recognise, and the grass in the clearing reached up to wrap itself around dead ankles. The dead just kicked their feet free, and moved forward. Tuck spoke more Words, and tree branches writhed like snakes before dropping down to seize hold of the dead. They broke the branches' grip easily, and closed in on Tuck.

He faced them unflinchingly, his great hands closed into fists. A fat old man who loved life, and never dreamed that one day he would have to fight death with his bare hands. He hurried through his prayers, and then lashed out as best he could. He was still cursing the dead when they dragged him down.

Amanda took her hand off my arm and we were back among the choking smoke and the roar of blazing trees. I raised an arm to protect my face from the heat and looked around for a trail that would take us away from the fires, but there didn't seem to be one. I turned to Amanda, who seemed as cool and collected as ever.

"You have to do something."

"I can't," she said flatly. "The power it would take to overcome something like this would reveal my presence to the secret masters. And then they'd know who and what I am. I can't risk that. My cause is too important."

"You'd let Robin and his outlaws die?" I said.

"That's why I brought you here, Jack. To do what I can't."

"What can I do?"

"Outthink the opposition." She broke off, as she concentrated on something only she could hear. "Someone's coming."

I glared around me, straining my eyes against the thickening smoke. I started to reach for my backpack, but I couldn't think of anything in it that could help. I looked at Amanda.

"You should go. You know this forest better than me."

"We've come this far together," she said. "I think I'll stick around, for a while."

Her smile warmed my heart. We stood side by side, and waited to see what would come for us. In the end a young man emerged alone from the smoke, its shirt hanging open to show the bloody hollow where its heart used to be. The messenger Robin had sent away hadn't got far, after all. It looked at us with empty eyes.

"This is Miriam," said the dead man. "Speaking to you on the supernatural channel. I see you, Jack! Surrender to me, and I'll let Robin and his people run. I want you more than I want them."

"Don't do it," Amanda murmured to me. "You can't trust her."

"I have to," I said. "Robin has to survive this, to be the legend we came here to save."

"If you go to her," said Amanda, "I can't go with you."

I looked at her for a long moment, but her gaze didn't waver.

"Just as well, then, that Miriam only wants me," I said, as steadily as I could. "Look after yourself, Amanda."

I walked over to the dead man, and it took hold of my arm in an iron grip. It dragged me into the burning forest, and I wouldn't let myself look back.

There were fires everywhere. Roaring flames consumed the massive trees, and shot high into the sky. The interlocking branches of the canopy had already burned away, and for the first time in centuries morning light fell uninterrupted into Sherwood. The air was thick with black smoke and floating smuts. The dead man dragged me past one blazing tree after another, walking right through flames it couldn't feel. And all I could do was try not to cry out as the fires burned me.

We finally left the forest and emerged into the light, all seared flesh and charred clothes. I'd had to clench my eyes shut against the awful heat, and it took me a while before I could force them open again. It seemed like I hurt everywhere, and I didn't dare look down to see how bad the damage was. I made myself concentrate on the scene before me.

Emil was sitting at his ease on a shooting stick, while Miriam walked among the last few rows of dead men, studying them interestedly like a science project. I looked around, but couldn't see so much as a patch of darkened grass to show where Will Scarlett had met his end. Miriam finally deigned to take an interest in my arrival, and gestured for my dead captor to haul me forward. Before I could say anything, two more dead men emerged from the trees, hauling Friar Tuck along between them. They came to a halt beside me. Tuck's face had been beaten to a pulp of blood and bruises, and he was barely able to stay on his feet, but he still managed a small smile for me.

"I never was much of a fighter, but I think I crushed a few of the things when I fell on them."

I glared at Miriam. "You said you'd let Robin and his people go, once you had me!"

She shrugged easily. "But now the good friar is in my hands, I might as well make use of him."

"That wasn't the deal!"

"I'm changing the deal," said Miriam. "We need one Merrie Man to make an example of, and the last one didn't leave anything behind. I think we'll send the good friar on a little tour, so everyone can see what happens to those who defy authority. He'll make an excellent example, for as long as he lasts."

I strained against the dead hand holding me, but couldn't even loosen its grip.

Miriam ignored me, giving all her attention to Tuck. "Oh, the things we're going to do you . . . Emil, show Robin Hood's man what happens to people who defy us."

Emil got up off his shooting stick, and sauntered over to stand before Tuck. He smiled easily, and punched the friar in the face. Tuck's head snapped back, blood spurting from a broken nose. He barely had time to cry out before Emil hit him again, and again. I fought against the dead man's grip, and yelled at Emil to stop, threatening him with everything I could think of, but he just kept going until the friar hung limply in the dead men's grip. Emil grabbed Tuck by an ear, and twisted it cruelly.

"Wake up! I've only just started!"

I looked desperately at Miriam. "Why are you doing this? I thought you only wanted me!"

"Yes," said Emil, turning away from the barely conscious friar. "I'd like to know the answer to that one. Taking the Outsider prisoner was never part of our orders."

"I'm in charge," said Miriam. "And I will run things however I see fit."

Emil looked at her for a moment, and then turned back to Tuck, hanging slumped between the dead men. Blood dripped steadily from his ruined face. Emil smiled.

Miriam walked over to stand before me. I couldn't read the expression on her face.

"Work with me, Jack, and all this unpleasantness will stop."

"It'll never stop," I said. "This is what the secret masters want for all of us."

"Why do you have to be so difficult?"

"Because sometimes, it's the only way to live with yourself."

"Told you," said Emil. "The Outsider was never going to turn."

"I know what I'm doing!" said Miriam.

"This is just a distraction from what we were sent here to do," Emil said flatly. "If you don't kill the Outsider, I will. And then I'll tell our masters that you aren't up to the job."

He produced a long thin knife from his sleeve, and turned it back and forth. The blade shone very brightly in the early morning light. Emil chuckled softly.

"You have been a thorn in everyone's side for far too long, Outsider. And you really shouldn't have threatened me."

He raised the tip of his knife to my face, and I tried not to flinch.

Miriam drew her gun and shot Emil in the head. Blood and brains flew on the air. The blade dropped from Emil's hand, and then his knees gave out and he fell unmoving to the ground.

"The things we do for love," said Miriam. She smiled slowly, and aimed her gun at me. "No more arguments, Jack. Let me save you from this madness, and make you part of a better world."

I looked at the gun. Death had never seemed closer, or more real. I took a deep breath, and let it out slowly.

"I think I'd rather die, than live in the kind of world you want. So go ahead, Miriam. Pull the trigger."

"It's her, isn't it?" said Miriam. Her eyes were gleaming with tears she wouldn't shed. "I never had a chance with you, because she got there first. Well . . . If I can't have you, no one can." She aimed the gun between my eyes, and her hand was very steady. "I would have given you everything, and loved you all my days . . ."

"You don't know what love is," said Amanda.

Suddenly she was standing right there beside me. Miriam backed quickly away, so she could cover both of us. Amanda smiled at me.

"Sorry I had to leave you on your own, Jack. I knew she'd never speak freely in front of me, and you needed to make this decision for yourself."

"I thought I was supposed to save the day," I said, as steadily as I could.

"You did," said Amanda. "You kept Miriam and Emil distracted, and turned them against each other, by refusing to be what either of them wanted. I'm so proud of you, Jack."

She snapped her fingers, and the dead man holding me dropped to the ground. The dead men holding Tuck let go, and all three of them fell. The rows of dead men standing in the background quietly collapsed. Leaving Miriam all on her own.

"The dead are at peace now," said Amanda. "Every single one of them . . . wherever they are."

"How did you do that?" said Miriam.

"All this time, and you haven't worked out what I am?" said Amanda. She put her arm through mine, and smiled sweetly. "I'm the free spirit, and the laughter in the woods. I'm the help Herne called for. I'm the pookah, darling."

Miriam aimed her gun at Amanda, but her hand wasn't as steady as it had been. Amanda snapped her fingers, and Miriam disappeared. I looked at where she'd been, and then at Amanda.

"Where did you send her?"

"To her death," said Amanda. "Does that bother you?"

"It should," I said. "But after everything she did, and everything she was prepared to do ... No. The world is better off without her."

"That's what I thought!" Amanda said cheerfully.

"Don't smile," I said. "She really did love me."

"Well," said Amanda. "You are very loveable."

She turned around and blew out the burning trees, like so many candles. Blackened trunks steamed slowly in the early morning light. I didn't need Amanda to tell me that all the fires in Sherwood were out.

"I thought you were worried about attracting the attention of the secret masters?" I said carefully.

"We'll be gone before they can get here. I only held off this long because I wanted you to see me as human for as long as possible." She shrugged quickly. "Selfish of me, I know, but that's part of being human, isn't it?"

"You really are a pookah?"

"I'm *the* pookah, darkling. There's only ever been one."

"Okay ..." I said.

"And you're not freaked out about it?" Amanda said anxiously.

"What do you think?" I said. And then I kissed her.

I held her close and buried my face in her hair, and she snuggled up against me, and I never wanted the moment to end. But eventually she pushed me away, and I let her. Because both of us knew there were things that needed doing. I suddenly realised my burns didn't hurt any more, and when I looked down they were gone. Even my scorched clothes had been restored. Amanda smiled brightly.

"I'm not just here for the bad things in life."

"What about Robin, and the outlaws?"

"See for yourself."

She put a hand on my arm, and I Saw an entirely unharmed Robin and Marion standing back to back in their clearing, surrounded by fallen dead bodies. Marion kicked a few, just to be sure. And then I was looking at Little John as he shook unmoving bodies off his huge frame, wondering what the hell just happened. All through the forest, trees were healing and sprouting new leaves as the smoke quickly dispersed, while a whole lot of outlaws stared dazedly around them, surprised they were still alive after all. And then my Sight shut down, and all I could see was Amanda.

"Is there anything you can't do?" I said.

"Oh, lots and lots," she said calmly. "It's very frustrating."

"What happens to Robin now?"

Amanda shrugged. "His legend is safe, but his story is over. Just as Herne predicted. With the sheriff dead and the secret masters defied, Robin can stay in Sherwood or go to Nottingham and become sheriff, whichever he thinks will do the most good. So, our work here is done! Let's go."

"What about Tuck?" I said. "We can't leave him here like this."

She looked at the friar, lying unconscious on the grass.

"I should have got here sooner, shouldn't I? Ah well..."

Tuck's wounds healed in a moment and he sat up suddenly, a look of astonishment on his restored face. I extended a hand to Tuck, and hauled him onto his feet. He looked at the restored Sherwood, and blinked a few times.

"I seem to have missed out on a few things... Did we win?"

"Of course," I said. "That's what legends do."

CHAPTER EIGHT
THE BARGAINS WE MAKE

One moment Amanda and I were walking through the dark green twilight of Sherwood forest, and the next I was inside a cage. Thick iron bars pressed in from every side, and the top was so low I was forced into a half crouch. My first startled movement was immediately punished so viciously I had no choice but to stand still, because the inside of every bar was studded with razor-sharp spikes.

Trapped in a cage with no door, where even the slightest movement brought sudden pain and a rush of blood. Caught halfway between standing and crouching, unable to properly support my weight with either my back or my thigh muscles. I knew I couldn't maintain this stance for long . . . But I had no choice.

I turned my eyes but not my head, and there was Amanda in a second cage, just a few feet away. It was smaller than mine, just enough to force her into the same hideously uncomfortable position, but she didn't seem at all disturbed. Instead, she was studying the spiked bars in a cool and thoughtful way. I had to call her name twice before she turned her eyes in my direction.

"What is it, Jack? I'm thinking."

"Where are we?" I said, keeping my voice carefully calm. "And what the hell is going on?"

"I arrived here the same moment you did," she said patiently. "All I can tell you is, this isn't where we were supposed to be going next."

I took a deep breath, and then gritted my teeth as a row of spikes stabbed me in the back. I could feel blood running down under my jacket. I took a moment, to make sure my voice would be calm and steady.

"Any idea why we're locked up in these S and M birdcages, without even the benefit of a nice mirror and some cuttlefish?"

"Obviously, someone has interrupted our journey," said Amanda. "I knew I was taking a risk when I revealed my power in Sherwood, but I didn't think they'd strike back this quickly."

"Who could be powerful enough to put you in a cage?"

"Good question," said Amanda. And then she went back to frowning at the bars of her cage.

My back and leg muscles were aching fiercely from the strain of holding the same position. I tried to reach for my backpack, but there wasn't enough room to raise my arm. I tried shrugging the pack off my shoulder, but only succeeded in stabbing myself repeatedly. Blood pattered steadily onto the floor of my cage, and I had to stop and breathe heavily.

"What are you doing, Jack?" said Amanda.

"If I can just get to my athame, I can cut through these bars," I said.

"We're not going anywhere," said Amanda. "Like animals caught in a trap, we will wait for the hunters to come to us. And once we know who they are, we'll make them sorry they ever thought of this."

I would have nodded, but I didn't dare. A heavy spike was already threatening my forehead, and two more extended right in front of my eyes.

"These cages have the Department's sense of humour stamped all over them," I growled. "But they stink of desperation. The secret masters must have realised we're closing in on them."

Amanda's eyes turned in my direction. "You think we're getting close?"

"Aren't we?"

"Well," she said. "I don't know about close. Closer, maybe."

One of my thighs twitched heavily from the stress of holding the same cramped position for so long, and my shoulder jerked in response. A spike punched through my leather jacket and gouged my upper arm. Blood coursed down my sleeve and dripped from my fingers. I swore under my breath, and forced myself to hold still.

"I should have known the Department would put someone new on our trail," I said. "Now that Miriam and Emil are dead."

"The world is better off without them," Amanda said absently.

I took a moment, before I answered her. "Did you have to kill Miriam? I think I could have brought her around, if things had been different."

"But they weren't," said Amanda. "She would never have stopped coming after us, Jack. I knew how you felt about her. That's why I killed her; so you wouldn't have to."

I didn't have an answer to that, so I looked past the bars to check out our surroundings. A wooden stage swept away in both directions, ending in heavy curtains at the wings. Beyond the stage a great open space ended in curved tiers of seats that made up the far wall, and when I glanced up I could just make out a thatched roof. Oil lamps shed a pleasant golden glow, but it seemed to me there were far too many shadows: all of them deep and dark and menacing. I tried to raise my Sight so I could examine them, only to find something was blocking it. A brief panic flashed through me. No one had ever been able to do that before. I swallowed hard, and hung on to my self-control with both hands.

"I know where we are, Amanda . . ." I said steadily. "This is the modern version of Shakespeare's Globe theatre, in London. I came here a few years back."

"Oh yes," Amanda said politely. "Which play did you see?"

"I wasn't here for that," I said. "I'd been summoned in my official capacity. Most theatres are lousy with ghosts, but the Globe had to go one step further. Actors were being possessed, night after night, just when they came to their big speech. They would suddenly start belting it out in the old bravura *pin them to the back of the stalls* style, and then just snap out of it, with no memory of what had happened.

"I shooed everyone out, and when I was sure I had the place to myself I took the stage and launched into what I could remember of Hamlet's soliloquy. I must have been seriously awful, because the possessing spirit descended on me like the wrath of God, but no one gets inside my head but me.

"I called for whatever it was to show itself, and a ghost manifested right in front of me: tall and stately, with a straight back and a noble brow, dressed in the height of Victorian finery. He was delighted someone could finally see him, and we ended up having a nice little chat. Maximillian Lionheart was an old-time matinee idol who really didn't care for the modern style of acting, all method and mumbling and lack of passion. He said he only wanted to show today's audiences what a real performance was, but really he was just missing his time in the spotlight. Acting had been his whole life, and he wasn't ready to move on and leave it behind.

"I examined the ghost carefully with my Sight, and discovered he had a demon on his back. The nasty little thing had its claws dug in deep, so it could feed on his pain and need. I produced a pair of mail gloves from my backpack, specially knitted by the bearded nuns of St Baphomet's. The gloves let me grab hold of the demon, and rip it right off the ghost's back. I stuffed the nasty wriggling thing into my backpack, along with the gloves, and then used my athame to cut a door into reality that opened onto the hereafter. I told Max the light spilling out was the biggest spotlight ever, and that the greatest audience of all time was waiting for him. He thanked me profusely, drew himself up, and walked proudly through the door."

"Is there a reason you're telling me all this?" Amanda said politely.

"It helps take my mind off being trapped in a cage full of spikes," I said.

"Of course," said Amanda. "How did you get rid of the demon?"

"I curdled its ectoplasm, distilled it into a spirit bottle, and then buried it in consecrated ground," I said harshly. "Haven't you anything useful to tell me?"

"We're not in the modern theatre," said Amanda. "This is the original Globe, in the year sixteen fifteen."

"How are you always so sure about the date?" I said. "Do you have a built-in calendar?"

She smiled briefly. "Something like that. How much do you know about this period, Jack?"

I thought for a moment. "Elizabeth died in sixteen oh three, so James is on the throne. Not a great fan of magic, as I recall . . . Hey, wait a minute. Someone told me the original Globe burned down in sixteen thirteen?"

"It did," said Amanda. "Which means we are trapped inside a building that shouldn't even exist. Interesting, isn't it?"

"Are we still in the past that was, before the rewriting?" I said.

"Of course."

"So what's it like here?"

"All the magical races have left this world," said Amanda, "and most of the old monsters with them. But there are still some magical wells here and there, and those who draw power from them."

I waited, but she had nothing more to say. I went back to studying the open area beyond the stage. There was fresh sawdust on the ground, but nothing to suggest anyone had walked across it recently. A quick glance confirmed the tiered seats were just as empty. Amanda and I had the Globe Theatre all to ourselves. But why cage us here, and now?

"Are you sure about the date?" I said.

"Oh please," said Amanda. "I am always right."

I raised an eyebrow. "Merlin said that, at Camelot."

"He got it from me."

"If this really is sixteen fifteen," I said, not giving an inch just on general principles, "then we won't be meeting Shakespeare. He went home to Stratford-on-Avon after his theatre burned down."

"But what need have you for Willy Shakes-rags, when you have me?" said a loud and cheerful voice.

A tall, well-made fellow came striding out of the left-hand wings. He had long red hair, a handsome face, and a rogue's smile. Dressed to the height of Elizabethan fashion, he swirled his cloak around him in suitably dramatic style. I could just make out the hilt of a sword hanging scabbarded at his side. He swaggered to a halt before Amanda and me and grinned broadly, as though everything was bound to be fine now that he'd turned up.

"Christopher Marlowe, and it please you," he said, favouring us with an elegant bow accompanied by some sweeping arm work. "Renowned playwright, poet, and wit about town. Also spy, duellist, and intriguer to the trade. Call me Kit."

"I'm Jack Daimon," I said. "The Outsider."

He raised a neatly trimmed eyebrow. "I am the current Outsider, sir. I was not aware Dr. Dee had raised another to my position."

"I'm not from around here," I said. "This is my companion, Amanda."

Kit nodded to her politely. "Delighted, I'm sure."

"I attended the first performance of your *Doctor Faustus*," she said. "I liked the fireworks."

Kit shook his head mournfully. "My speeches were fireworks enough, and had no need of adornment, but the groundlings will have such things. And the theatre owners insisted."

"I didn't know you were the Outsider, as well as a playwright," I said.

"Tasked to deal with all unnatural threats to Crown and country," said Kit. "A man of secret power and unknown influence, and yet somehow here I am, trapped and confined in this theatre just like you."

"You're not stuck inside a cage," I said.

"My prison may not be as obvious as yours, but I assure you it holds me just as securely." Kit took a moment to study the vicious spikes lining the inside of my cage, and then dropped me a knowing wink. "I have memories of a certain bawdy house in Deptford where you'd have to pay good coin to be treated in such a fashion."

"I'm not here by choice," I said.

Kit shrugged. "Well, we can't all be interesting. What did you do, to earn such pointed treatment?"

"Amanda and I have enemies," I said. "Can you get us out?"

"Alas, I see no lock to pick," said Kit. "Nor any trace of a door that I might force."

I tried to keep the disappointment out of my face. My body was aching all over from the stress of holding myself still.

"Do you have any idea who might be behind this?" I said.

Kit shrugged, which seemed to be his default response to most questions. "I also have no shortage of enemies. Ex-lovers, creditors . . . critics. And of course in my time as Outsider, I have made enemies both monstrous and inhuman."

"How did you get to be the Outsider?" said Amanda.

"The role was thrust upon me," said Kit. "Gloriana required it, and I never could say no to her."

"I should hope not," said a loud and commanding voice.

Queen Elizabeth I came striding out of the wings to join us. She was barely average height, and thin enough to look half-starved, but there was no denying she had presence. Hard and unflinching, she came storming across the stage as though perfectly prepared to walk right over or even through anything that got in her way, because that was how she had survived so long, surrounded by enemies without number and friends she couldn't trust. She was wearing a voluminous gown of creamy silk studded with any number of semi-precious stones, along with massive puffed sleeves and a tall open collar. Her aged face was painted stark white, touched here and there with fierce dabs of cosmetics, under a rather obvious red wig. She advanced on us like a galleon under full sail, and finally slammed to a halt facing Kit. She swayed for a moment, as she struggled to regain her balance against the accumulated momentum of her gown, and then nodded briefly to Kit before fixing Amanda and me with a cold stare.

"I find myself imprisoned on this stage by unknown forces," she said bluntly. "Do you have any knowledge of who is responsible for this outrage?"

"We only just got here," said Amanda.

The queen turned to Kit, who offered her one of his best shrugs.

"Sorry, Auntie. I'm as much in the dark as you." He smiled at the look of surprise on my face. "Oh yes, Gloriana is indeed my kith and kin; though of course I was never officially acknowledged, being born on the unacceptable side of the blanket."

Elizabeth dismissed him with a sniff, and glowered around the Globe.

"At least our prison is known to me. I spent many a happy time here, attending master Shakespeare's plays. Incognito, of course."

"Everyone knew who you were really," said Kit.

"Not officially!" the queen said loudly. She took a moment to settle herself, before turning to me and Amanda. "My fondness was always for the comedies. Too much affliction in my life, to properly enjoy a tragedy. And while I appreciated the histories, and funded the writing of most of them at one remove or another, I knew far too much about the real nature of events to ever be comfortable with master Will's more poetic versions." She stopped, to snap a look at Kit. "What are you frowning at, boy?"

"You seem so much older than I remember," he said slowly. "And why are you wearing that awful wig?"

The queen started a sharp retort, and then stopped herself. "It is good to see you again, Kit. It seems to me that there is something important I should remember about you, but I cannot bring it to mind, just at the moment..."

"Would this be a good time to inquire why you were so keen for me to take over as Outsider?" said Kit. "You know I never wanted the responsibility."

"You never wanted any form of honest endeavour," the queen said tartly. "Always too busy scribbling, or keeping unfortunate company in the alehouses. My old Outsider was gone, and I needed someone in the position I could trust."

"You flatter me, Auntie," said Kit. "Many descriptions have been lobbed in my direction, but trusted was rarely one of them."

"I had faith in you because you never sought to take advantage of our connection."

"I knew better than to try," said Kit. "I like to think I did good work. Like the time I uncovered a shape-shifting Spanish spy, who had taken the face and form of your current favourite so he could get close enough to assassinate you." He grinned at me. "I burst in on them just in time to prevent an intimate encounter of entirely the wrong kind. I ran him through with only moments to spare."

"How can I forget?" the queen said coldly. "When you take such delight in constantly reminding me?"

"Then perhaps we could discuss how I put down the terrible death cult of the witch Sycorax," said Kit. "By proving to her followers that all her powers were nothing more than expertly staged illusions. She tried to run, but her own people dragged her down and tore her apart. In the occult game, you're only ever as good as your last miracle."

Elizabeth sniffed loudly. "It takes more than half a dozen followers to qualify as a death cult."

"Then how about the screaming skulls of Stepney, or the werewolves of Wapping?" said Kit. "As your Outsider, I have stamped out all manner of supernatural threats. All for indifferent pay and no public praise."

"You would have been tried and executed long ago, boy," said the queen. "If not for my protection. As an invert, a rabble-rouser, and a Catholic sympathiser!"

Kit bowed to her. "I do thank you for that, Auntie."

She favoured him with a brief smile. "So you should, boy."

Kit looked thoughtfully at the queen. "Might I inquire what brought you to this place?"

Elizabeth frowned. "Strange . . . I can't seem to remember."

"My memory is also oddly obscured," said Kit. "But worry not, Gloriana; I will stand between you and all harm."

"I wouldn't expect anything less," said the queen. "But why am I here without my bodyguards? I have enemies everywhere."

"Only one who could be responsible for our present troubles," said Kit. "The hero and villain of my greatest triumph: Faust."

"He's real?" I said. "Not just a character in a play?"

"Master Shakespeare produced his histories, and I mine," Kit said coldly. "And just as dear Will shaped his characters to fit the needs and prejudices of his audience, so I gave the groundlings a man they could cheer and hiss. Faust made himself a legend; I just polished his story a little." He nodded to Elizabeth. "At your instruction, Auntie."

"I funded master Shakespeare's histories because I needed them to shape the people's vision of England," said the queen. "But our legends shape us too. I wanted Faust's story better known, as a cautionary tale."

"So he really was real?" I said. "The man who sold his soul to the Devil, in return for knowledge?"

"Oh, indeed," said Kit. "Though the character I created was far more interesting than the cold-hearted scholar I was introduced to. A pity I had to abandon him to the Pit at the end, but Auntie would have her moral ending."

"So what really happened to Faust?" I said.

Kit shrugged. "He disappeared. And whether he went to the Devil, or to Spain, no man can say. But now I would wager he has returned, because only Faust could have enough power to hold all of us here."

I gave Amanda a look. "It's going to be Merlin again, isn't it?"

Amanda sniffed loudly. "Not unless something has gone terribly wrong with history while I wasn't looking."

"Have you met Faust?"

"She has not," said a new voice. "Even at my most arrogant and assured, I still knew better than to have anything to do with a creature like her."

Faust walked unhurriedly out onto the stage. A dark and saturnine presence dressed in blood-red leathers, he had the look of a man with no illusions about life, because he had good reason to know better. He stopped before Amanda in her cage, and looked her over as though contemplating some interesting new specimen. He barely glanced at me, before nodding to Kit and Elizabeth.

Kit arched an elegant eyebrow. "My dear Faust, how is it that thou art out of Hell?"

"You always were too fond of your own words," said Faust. "Reports of my damnation were greatly exaggerated. Mostly by you."

"Why would a man like you serve the secret masters?" asked Amanda.

"Why does a man do anything?" said Faust. "Because it profits him."

"Is that why you sold your soul?" I said.

Faust nodded. "For knowledge and power, and much good they did me."

"I don't think I believe in Hell," I said.

"It believes in you," said Faust. "Don't judge me, Outsider. I merely made a bargain, like everyone on this stage. And what happened to me is what happens to all of us, when we bargain with the wrong kind of people."

"Wasn't the name Hell a bit of a clue?" I said.

"Where else can you go, when they're the only game in town?" said Faust.

All my muscles were screaming with pain from being locked in the same awful position for so long, but I was damned if I'd admit it. I kept my voice carefully calm.

"Did you have to make these cages so unpleasant?"

"The secret masters were very specific about the nature of this trap," said Faust. "They wanted you so troubled and distracted you'd be unable to plan a means of escape. Take it as a compliment, that they see you as so cunning and so dangerous."

He turned to Kit. "You made your bargain when you turned my life into an entertainment, in return for the queen's protection. But what in God's name possessed you to change my name to Faustus? You made me sound like some second-rate street conjurer!"

Kit shrugged. "I needed a name with more drama to it."

"At least I had the courage of my convictions," said Faust. "What do you believe in, scribbler?"

Kit smiled. "I believe in wine, tobacco, chocolate, and good-looking young men. And, sometimes, the satisfaction to be found in a well-written piece. Enough for any man, I would have thought."

Faust turned to Elizabeth. "You gave up all hope of love and marriage and family, so you could be queen all your days."

"I kept England safe by not marrying," said Elizabeth. "It's called duty. You wouldn't understand."

"You made your bargain, and I made mine," said Faust. He turned abruptly to face me. "You agreed to assist Amanda, in return for her love. But the joke is on you, Outsider; a creature like her knows nothing of love."

"You know nothing about her," I said. "Why did you make your bargain, Faust?"

"I was the Outsider before Kit," said Faust. "I yearned to understand all the amazing things I uncovered, because I needed something in my life to give it meaning."

"Most people find that in each other," said Amanda.

"I never cared for people," said Faust. "Why should I? They never gave a damn about me."

"I understand that life as the Outsider can be solitary," I said. "But it doesn't have to stay that way. People can always surprise you."

"That has not been my experience," said Faust. "I needed something I could believe in, and I found it in the magic that gave me knowledge and power."

"But did it make you happy?" I said.

"It got me everything I thought I wanted," said Faust. "But none of it was worth what I paid to get it. So here I am, tired of life but scared of dying because I know what's waiting for me. That's why I made a new bargain, with the secret masters. My service in this matter, in return for more years of life."

"Why choose the Globe as the setting for your little drama?" said Kit.

"Because this is one of the few places I remember being happy," said Faust. "Shakespeare's plays showed me life as it should be: where love is real and dreams come true. So unlike the grey disappointments of my existence."

"What about my plays?" said Kit.

Faust barely glanced at him. "Too grim."

"Has anyone else noticed that we're not alone here?" I said carefully. "Everything outside this stage has been swallowed up by shadows, and I can hear things moving in the dark."

Everyone turned to look out from the only island of light in a sea of shadows. The sounds of surreptitious movement came clearly to us, as hidden things pressed up against the other side of the shadow.

"Why didn't we notice this was happening?" Kit said quietly. His hand had dropped to the sword under his cloak.

"I did," said Faust.

"Then why didn't you say something?" said the queen.

"Because for me, the shadows are always full," said Faust.

"Why are these things here, Faust?" I said quietly.

"To make sure events turn out the way they're supposed to."

"For the secret masters?" I said.

"For Hell," said Faust. "Both sides want you two dealt with, but neither trusts the other."

Amanda raised an eyebrow. "Dealt with?"

"You're going down," said Faust. "All the way down. To dwell in the Houses of Pain forever."

"I won't let you hurt her," I said to Faust. And there must have been something in my voice, because everyone turned to look at me.

"How will you stop me?" said Faust. He sounded genuinely interested. "It's not like you can reach any of your toys."

I smiled at him, deliberately cold and condescending. "You keep boasting about how powerful you are, Faustus. Show me something. Something real."

"I have already provided you with two miracles," said Faust. He gestured at Kit Marlowe and Queen Elizabeth. "Kit died in a pointless duel, and Gloriana was finally allowed to die of old age when the secret masters decided they didn't need her any more."

The queen stared in horror at Kit, lines of emotion running so deep in her face they cracked her makeup.

"Oh my dear nephew . . . How could I have forgotten?"

"Now I now why you look so much older," Kit said quietly. "My dear Gloriana, I honestly thought you'd live forever." He glared at Faust. "Why bring us back? Did you feel the need for an audience?"

"I wanted someone who would appreciate the drama of the occasion," said Faust. "And . . . you were the closest things I had to friends."

Kit looked at him for a moment. "Can't say I saw that one coming. Really?"

Elizabeth frowned at Faust. "I barely remember you."

"We met several times," said Faust.

"I'm sorry," said the queen. "I meet so many people . . ."

"Who summoned the winds that sank the Armada's ships?" Faust said loudly. "Who uncovered your enemies at court, and set them at each other's throats? I bent the laws of this world to my will, because I believed you were worth defending." He turned sharply to Kit. "And all those hours we spent talking together, as you turned my story into fable and put wonderful words in my mouth. I never felt so understood, by any man. Your play is a wonder that will survive the ages. Though I could have done without the clowns."

Kit winced. "The theatre owners insisted."

"Faust!" I said loudly, and he turned to face me. I smiled on him as kindly as I could. "You didn't choose this setting on a whim. You came to this theatre to see great stories acted out: heroes and villains, and all the passions of the world writ large. That's real power, to make something out of nothing, that will survive long after we are gone. Not the petty magics you traded your soul for."

"I made my bargain," said Faust. "And I am bound by the terms of it."

"Are you?" I said. "In this place, people believed they could be better than they are. That villains can be defeated, and everything will turn out right in the end. Imagine yourself a better man, and you will be."

Faust turned slowly, to look at Kit and Elizabeth.

"I made your life into a story that will never be forgotten," said Kit.

"Through Shakespeare I created a story of England, for the people to live up to," said Elizabeth.

"That's why you brought us here," said Kit. "Not just as friends, but because you respected what we created."

"You needed someone you trusted," said Elizabeth. "To talk you out of this."

"Hell cheated you," said Kit. "Be a man; cheat Hell back."

Faust gestured for them to be silent, and they were.

"This is your chance to be free, at last," I said.

"How?" said Faust.

And with that one word, everything changed.

"Some bargains were made to be broken," I said. "In my backpack there's an athame. A witch knife, that can cut through anything. Take it, and cut your ties to Hell, and the secret masters. Believe in a better Story and be a part of it."

Faust stretched out his hand, and suddenly he was holding my athame. He smiled briefly at me, and then turned to face the shadows. He looked suddenly taller, and more substantial.

"I defy you. My soul was given to me by God; you have no power over it. No matter how foolish I may have been."

A roiling crowd of demons burst out of the shadows, and headed straight for the stage. Malign and malformed, they stood like men but had the teeth and claws of animals. Faust sniffed loudly.

"That's all you've got? I think I'm insulted."

"They're basing their forms on memories of the groundlings," said Amanda. "That's all they have to draw on, as long as I'm here. Can you see them off?"

"They won't listen to me, and I can't make them," said Faust. "You can't use Hell's power against Hell's creatures."

Kit drew his sword, and moved quietly forward to place himself between Queen Elizabeth and the demons.

"I did promise I would protect you from all harm, Auntie."

"I never doubted it for a moment," said the queen.

The first wave of demons scrambled up onto the stage, and Kit laughed happily as he went to meet them. The demons leapt at him like starving wolves, all hate and hunger, and Kit's sword flashed brightly as he cut and hacked at them. It was one man against an army, but the demons burst into flames and fell apart wherever the glowing blade touched them. Kit threw me a glance.

"Did you think you were the only Outsider to wield an athame?"

More demons surged up onto the stage, and Kit danced lightly among them, cutting throats and piercing hearts with practiced grace and style. He stamped and lunged, always darting back out of reach before the demons could lay hands on him. Burning corpses fell to the stage, already fading away to nothing. But for all his skill and strength and endless courage, still the forces of Hell pressed forward, and step by step Kit Marlowe was forced backwards.

I decided I'd had enough. I'd followed Amanda's advice, and endured the torments of the cage so I could get a clearer idea of what was going on, but I was damned if I'd let this go any further. I eased my hands into my jacket pockets, ignoring vicious jabs from spikes I couldn't avoid, and brought out the blessed and cursed knuckle-dusters I'd tucked away earlier. I slipped them on, and then lashed out with my armoured fists. Spikes tore into my arms and blood spurted through the torn leather, but the bars before me cracked and bent and fell apart. I kicked them out of the way, forced myself through the gap, and then lurched out onto the stage, hurting and bloody but free at last. I took a moment to stretch luxuriously, and then strode forward to show the demons what a seriously annoyed Outsider could do.

I waded right into the fight, striking down demons and trampling them underfoot. Impacts from the blows juddered painfully up my wounded arms, but I didn't give a damn. Up close the demons smelt of blood and sulphur and spoiled milk, and their eyes burned with inhuman malevolence. They came at me with teeth and claws, but after the cage's spikes, that was nothing. I introduced the demons to my blessed and cursed knuckle-dusters, and it would be hard to say which hurt them the most. I smashed in snarling faces and shattered skulls, punched out hearts and broke spines, and it felt good, so good, to have an enemy I could get my hands on.

I moved in beside Kit, and we both laughed out loud as we fought the good fight, because there wasn't a demon out of Hell who was any match for two Outsiders with blood in their eyes. A few got past us, but Gloriana produced a long pin from her sleeve and stabbed each demon as it came within reach. They died without a sound, fading away to nothing before they could even fall to the stage.

"Unicorn horn," said the queen. "Courtesy of Dr. Dee."

"He always did keep the best toys for himself," said Kit.

And yet for all the demons we destroyed and sent screaming back to Hell, there never seemed to be any end to them. They just kept boiling out of the shadows and surging up onto the stage, and there was a limit to what even Kit and I could do. We stood back to back as the demons surrounded us, and I could feel the strength going out of my blows. The cage had taken more from me than I realised. But still I threw my armoured punches, and Kit's blade sliced through demon flesh as though it was nothing more than mist. The demons were pressing in close now, their clawed hands ripping through our clothes. Sometimes I cried out, and sometimes it was Kit, but still we stood our ground and refused to be beaten.

Suddenly, Amanda's cage exploded. Shards of shattered iron flashed through the air, cutting the demons down like shrapnel, while miraculously missing me and Kit. Amanda stepped lightly out of the wreckage, and brushed herself down.

"I've waited long enough. The secret masters aren't coming, and I have things to do."

Faust stared at her. "How did you do that?"

"Oh, please," she said. "Like anything in this world could hold me."

She strode forward, and the surviving demons backed away. I realised with something like awe that even demons out of Hell were afraid of Amanda. They turned abruptly and jumped off the stage, racing back into the shadows. In just a few moments they were gone: an army from Hell routed by one small woman with an implacable gaze. Kit lowered his sword, and I lowered my knuckle-dusters, and we leaned heavily on each other as we shared a tired grin.

Elizabeth looked narrowly at Amanda. "Why were they so scared of you?"

"Because they can see what I really am," said Amanda. She turned to Faust. "We've done all we can; now it's up to you."

Faust nodded slowly. "Thank you for buying me time to put my thoughts in order. There's only one way I can set myself free. Let us hope . . . that one good act pays for many bad ones."

He thrust the athame into his heart, and fell dead onto the stage. A great howl of thwarted rage rose up from the shadows and suddenly they were gone, leaving the whole of the Globe Theatre spread out before us. Kit and Elizabeth moved forward to stand over Faust's body. They both reached down a hand, and after a moment Faust sat up. He took their hands in his, and they hauled him onto his feet. He smiled at Kit and the queen, and they smiled at him, and then they walked off together, leaving Faust's body lying on the stage. They faded away before they could reach the wings, and so did the ghost of the Globe, and all that it contained.

✣ ✣ ✣

Amanda and I stood alone in the open air, in the empty space that once held a theatre. My wounds were healed, my muscles no longer ached, and I just knew my athame was safely back in my pack. I nodded to Amanda.

"Can we move on now?"

"There's nothing left to keep us here," said Amanda.

There was something in the way she said that . . . I looked at her carefully.

"Was Faust really strong enough to drag us off course, or did you let it happen, because this was another lesson you wanted me to learn?"

Amanda smiled brightly. "Who can say?"

I sighed, quietly. "Where are we going next?"

"To witness the birth of the scientific age," said Amanda.

"Well," I said. "It's about time."

"It always was," said Amanda.

CHAPTER NINE
THERE ARE MANY WAYS TO HELL

From the ghost of a long gone theatre, we came to a dead house in a dead place. A crumbling old mansion, set on a grim grey moor. The sky was overcast, the sun barely out, and a freezing wind was doing its best to cut right through me. All the windows had been bricked up, and the only door was a featureless slab of wood. The old dark house looked more like a prison than home: the kind of place where old sins and family secrets could be kept securely hidden from the outside world. Where a locked door was meant to keep people in, as well as out.

"I don't think I want to meet whoever chose to live in a place like this," I said.

"You're not the first to feel that way," said Amanda. "Which is why the house has been left abandoned for so many years."

"Then what are we doing here? And where is here?"

"The north of England, in the early nineteenth century," said Amanda. "When the secret masters tried to prove once and for all that science ruled the world, by creating life using the scientific method rather than any natural means. Welcome to the house of Frankenstein."

I looked at her sharply. "Wait just a minute; are you telling me Frankenstein was real? That his monster was real? Come on, Amanda; legends are one thing, but we're talking about a work of fiction now."

"Just another half-remembered dream, of the way things used to be," Amanda said patiently. "Another story that refused to be forgotten, because it had important things to tell us."

I studied the old house carefully. "If there's nobody home, what are we doing here?"

"There's still something in there, that you need to see."

I nodded. I was getting used to that. "What's with the windows?"

"Frankenstein didn't want anyone to see what he was doing," said Amanda. "Of course, that led to all kinds of stories. Local people still believe this house contains a gateway to Hell."

Something in the way she said that made me look at her. "An actual entrance, to actual Hell?"

Amanda met my gaze unflinchingly. "Frankenstein opened a door to a dimension of absolute chaos and utter horror. And the door is still there, because it was never properly closed."

"Then what's stopped all Hell from breaking loose?"

"I did," said Amanda. "I went in and closed the door. Unfortunately, I wasn't able to finish the job."

"Why not?"

"Because the man I had helping me then wasn't up to it. He lost his nerve."

I had to raise an eyebrow. "I wasn't your first choice?"

"At that point, I still thought of the Outsider as an enemy." Amanda kept her gaze fixed on the old house rather than look at me. "Charles was a good man, with good intentions, but that wasn't enough."

"Wait a minute. You're the pookah, one of the great old powers. Why do you need anyone's help to close a door . . . or to put history back the way it was?"

"There are rules," she said flatly. "Humans rewrote history, so a human has to be part of its restoration. The door to Hell was opened by a man, so a man has to be there to help me secure it."

"What did my predecessor do, that was so bad?"

"When I tried to seal the door permanently, Hell threw an army of demons at us. Faced with all the horrors of the Pit, Charles broke and ran. I had to face the demons alone, drive them back through the door, and then close it as best I could. I need you to help me finish what I started, or history is doomed to remain the way it is."

"Why?" I said.

"Because Hell likes things the way they are."

There are times when you realise there's no point in asking any more questions, because you're never going to get an answer that will satisfy you. Or even one you can live with. I gestured at the featureless front door.

"I'm not seeing a handle, never mind a lock...I suppose I could kick it in."

"I wouldn't," said Amanda. "That door was designed to hold off angry mobs with torches and battering rams."

"How did you get in the last time you were here?"

"I appeared with Charles in the main hall, right in front of the door to Hell. Which might have been part of the problem. He never got a chance to prepare himself."

"Against what?"

"Soldiers of the Pit," said Amanda. "Monsters, from the underworld."

I nodded, back on familiar ground. "I can do monsters. And I can definitely do doors."

I took the athame out of my pack, and thrust it into the top left-hand corner of the door. The witch knife sank all the way in to its hilt, and I dragged the blade down through the thick wood, sawing a line from top to bottom. I jerked the knife free, slammed it back in on the other side, and cut another line facing the first. Then all I had to do was join the lines at top and bottom, and a whole section of the door toppled slowly backwards, to land on the floor beyond with a deafening thud.

"Sorry about the noise," I said. "Bit of a giveaway, that we're here."

"Hell knows everything," said Amanda.

I shook my head. "Really not helping..."

I put away the witch knife, and stepped through the opening. Light spilled in after me, revealing the beginnings of an intimidatingly wide corridor. The walls were bare stone, and there was no sign of any furniture or fittings, as though whoever lived in the house couldn't be bothered with fripperies like style or comfort. The air smelled dank, and stale, and there was a definite sense of foreboding. Amanda pushed impatiently past me, and snapped her fingers. A ball of light appeared hovering over our heads, its shimmering glow bright enough to illuminate the whole length of a corridor whose sheer size and scale actually took my breath away for a moment.

"Look at that..." I said. "You could drive a truck down there and not bump into the walls!"

"Frankenstein's family always did think big," said Amanda. "Which was probably part of what made him the way he was."

"All right," I said. "We're in. Now what?"

"Just follow the light," said Amanda. "It'll take us straight to Hell."

I looked at her. "Smile when you say that."

We set off, and the ball of light sped away before us, bouncing along like a dog set off its leash. Amanda peered happily around her, studying everything with great interest, as though we were just tourists visiting a stately home. Everything was perfectly still and silent, as though nothing had changed since the house was abandoned, because it was still shocked and traumatised by what Frankenstein did within its walls.

"Something really bad happened here," I said quietly.

"Frankenstein turned his family home into a charnel house, and made his name a byword for blood and horror," said Amanda. "But that's science for you."

I stopped abruptly, so she had no choice but to stop with me. The ball of light shot on without us, realised we weren't following, skidded to a halt, and hurried back to bob impatiently over our heads. I looked steadily at Amanda.

"I need to know what happened to my predecessor, Charles."

Amanda nodded. "Of course you do."

She put her hand on my arm, and suddenly we were in the middle of a huge hall, staring at a door standing upright and unsupported, surrounded by shadows and silence. Two figures stood facing the door. One was Amanda, though her face seemed colder and more focused, and the other was a handsome young man in a smart suit, holding a glowing sword. *Carcosa's Doom*, the present-day Amanda whispered in my ear. *A grown-up version of your athame. Charles liberated it from the Department's armoury when no one was looking.* I watched the earlier Amanda approach the door, her face set and intent. It swung slowly back, revealing a darkness so absolute even my Sight couldn't penetrate it. Amanda stopped, and Charles moved quickly to stand beside her, sword at the ready. And then all the forces of Hell burst out of the dark and into the light, and Charles started screaming.

Hideous, nightmare shapes, constantly growing and shrinking and taking on new attributes, as though searching for some form that could survive in our rational world. Impossible tangles of many-jointed legs and thrashing tentacles, sex organs lined with teeth that vomited streams of maggots. Mouths that never stopped screaming, and eyes that had seen all the horrors the Houses of Pain had to offer.

Everything that had ever scared humanity, made real, and hungry.

Amanda stood her ground, staring Hell in the face, and wherever she looked demon shapes exploded. Charles finally stopped screaming, but only because he didn't have the breath to keep it going. He raised his sword and cut and hacked hysterically at the demons. The glowing blade sliced through everything it touched, leaving misshapen bits and pieces to writhe and hump on the floor, still trying to get to him. Carcosa's Doom couldn't kill any of Hell's foot soldiers, because none of them were alive.

Forced to confront things he had never wanted to believe were possible, Charles didn't just look scared and horrified, but actually broken on some fundamental level. As though the demons' very existence was an affront to his reason. Shocked tears streamed down his face, and his flailing attacks grew wilder and more desperate. Suddenly he threw his sword aside and turned to run. Amanda stopped him with a gesture, freezing him in mid-step.

She headed straight for the open door, and the demons retreated, unable to face what they saw in her. Step by step she forced the monstrous things back, just by being her, until the last of them had retreated through the door, and there was nothing in it but the concealing darkness. Amanda stared unflinchingly into Hell, and the door swung slowly shut. Amanda turned her back on it, and walked over to Charles. She stood before him, staring dispassionately into his face, and then she picked up the discarded sword and stabbed him through the heart. The glowing blade punched out of his back in a flurry of blood, but Charles didn't make a sound, because he couldn't. Amanda pulled the sword back and Charles collapsed, to lie unmoving on unpolished floorboards in a slowly spreading pool of blood.

✣ ✣ ✣

My Sight shut down. I was back in the empty corridor, and Amanda's hand was no longer on my arm. I felt as though she'd just stabbed me through the heart. I stared accusingly at Amanda, and her gaze didn't waver in the least.

"You killed him!" I said.

"I sacrificed him," said Amanda. "It was the only way to hold the door shut, in the face of so much pressure from the damned. We could have sealed it permanently, if he hadn't run."

"So Charles' death was his own fault?"

I could hear my voice rising dangerously. Amanda stared back at me, her eyes full of all the understanding in the world.

"Now you know why I showed you all those other places and people, Jack. So you could learn how to face overwhelming odds, and become the kind of man I needed you to be."

I couldn't say what I wanted to, so I said something else.

"Where did you find Charles?"

"Hiding in George's shadow. A field agent who'd grown disenchanted with the Department's aims and practices. Charles swore he was ready to do whatever it took to bring about a better world. But when the time came, he didn't have what it took. You won't have that problem."

"So all this time you've been preparing me," I said. "Honing your weapon."

"I needed a partner I could depend on."

"Would you sacrifice me, to close the door?"

"Wouldn't you want me to?" said Amanda. "Rather than risk Hell breaking loose, and running wild in the world?"

We looked at each other.

"I need to See what Frankenstein did," I said.

"Then follow me," said Amanda.

We set off down the corridor again. The ball of light bounced along ahead of us, happy to be moving again. I couldn't look at Amanda. I was still having trouble coming to terms with how quickly she'd turned on Charles. I had to wonder how she persuaded him to follow her into a place like this. Did she tell him that she loved him?

Amanda finally came to a halt halfway down a side corridor, before a door that had been left standing open. I moved cautiously forward, and peered inside. The room was still and silent and full of shadows. The shimmering ball dropped down to project its light through the open doorway, and the shadows retreated a little.

"It's not much, but it's not home," said Amanda. "This is where Frankenstein achieved his life's ambition. Only to see it turn to ashes in his hands."

I stepped carefully into the room, with Amanda right there at my side, entirely calm and composed, as though nothing had happened between us. The ball of light ducked under the door's lintel and then shot up to bob against the ceiling. Its shimmering light revealed only a large empty space, with nothing left behind to suggest what might have happened in it. But something about the room's atmosphere made my skin crawl, as though we were surrounded by unseen horrors.

"The ghosts of yesterday are never far away, in the house of Frankenstein," Amanda said quietly.

"Is this where he made his monster?" I said.

"The creature was always going to be monstrous," said Amanda. "He took after his father."

"A living man, pieced together from dead leftovers."

"It was supposed to be science's greatest triumph," said Amanda. "But in the end, Frankenstein had to cheat to get what he wanted. You can sew dead tissues together as neatly as you like, but no matter how much electricity you shoot through them, your creation is never going to do anything but lie there. Dead is dead. So Frankenstein found another way."

"The door to Hell," I said.

"Exactly. Hell's energies sparked the creature to life, not lightning from the heavens. And so it woke up angry, a thing that knew it shouldn't exist. Are you sure you want to see this?"

"I need to know," I said.

Amanda's hand dropped gently onto my arm, as though apologising in advance.

Now the room had a feverish aspect, like a hothouse in a hospital, forcing life into unwilling patients. It stank of spoiled meat and acrid chemicals. The walls were sweating, and sudden rushes of moisture coursed down over detailed anatomy charts. There were no examination tables, no trays of surgical instruments, no baroque scientific equipment, just half a dozen mud-smeared coffins piled up against the far wall, their lids cracked open to get at the contents.

Two men stood opposite each other, glaring into each other's faces like boxers in a ring. Or perhaps just father and son, caught up in the argument of generations.

One of them was tall, slender, aristocratic. In his exquisitely tailored suit, complete with old school tie and a fresh carnation in the buttonhole, he might have just stopped off on his way to some fashionable gathering. His face was lean, harsh, driven, dominated by cold grey eyes and a jutting nose. His hands caught my attention; delicate and long-fingered. Surgeon's hands.

I knew his name. Everybody did.

Facing him was a huge towering figure wrapped in a long coat barely big enough to contain him. Because this man never had anything that didn't come from someone else. The skin of his face was stretched unnaturally taut, like an actor who'd overdone the Botox. His lips were black, distended with congealed blood, and his eyes were different colours. Long stringy hair hung down around his face, as though trying to hide its terrible aspect from the world. Huge bony hands hung at his sides, clenched into fists.

I knew who he was, who he had to be. The man forever known by his creator's name.

Frankenstein and his creature. The unnatural father, and the son built from corpses instead of a woman's love. They stood facing each other in a room haunted by death and life, and neither would look away.

"You are such a disappointment to me," said Frankenstein, in a high clipped tone. "Not at all what I intended."

"I didn't ask to be made!" The creature's voice was rough and harsh, as though talking was always going to be painful.

"The lament of every ungrateful child," said Frankenstein. "I had hoped my creation would be more original."

"You never wanted a son," said the creature. "Just a successful experiment. You made me to make a point."

Frankenstein shook his elegant head. "If I had known you would be the result, I would have tried harder. You were to be my perfect Adam, the forerunner of a new and noble race. Instead, I have a thing of rags and tatters, without grace or gratitude."

"Oh, I have so much to be grateful for," said the creature. "You made me strong, and filled me with enough rage to know what strength is for. I will remake the whole world in my image: cold and unforgiving."

"The world is not yours to play with," said Frankenstein. "You are simply a mistake that must be corrected. I shall take you apart and return you to your separate beginnings and do better next time."

The creature laughed. It was an ugly, humourless sound. "You can't kill me. What was never born can never die."

"I know all there is to know about life and death," Frankenstein said coldly.

"No," said the creature. "Not yet."

He slammed a hand in under Frankenstein's breastbone, burying it to the wrist. Frankenstein's shocked gasp was interrupted by a torrent of blood from his mouth. The creature jerked his hand back, and it was full of something crimson and purple, spurting blood. He held it up before Frankenstein's dying eyes.

"Well, what do you know," said the creature. "You did have a heart, after all."

He crushed it to a bloody pulp, and Frankenstein fell dead to the floor. The creature opened his hand, and let the dripping mess fall onto his creator's face.

The vision disappeared, as Amanda took her hand off my arm. The room was empty again, though still heavy with concealing shadows.

"Have you seen enough?" said Amanda. "Frankenstein's creature is long gone, but the door to Hell is still waiting for us."

I turned on her. "You wanted me to See this! So I'd be outraged enough to do what you want!"

"If that's what it takes," said Amanda.

"You ask so much ..."

"But none of it's for me. It's all about rescuing humanity from the prison the secret masters made for all of you to live in."

"You're a pookah," I said roughly. "Why should something like you care about us?"

She smiled, perhaps just a bit sadly. "Because you're so loveable."

✣ ✣ ✣

The main hall turned out to be a huge affair. It took some time to cross, while our footsteps echoed back from the distant walls. The ball of light shot up to bob against the high-raftered ceiling, so it could spread its illumination across the open space. The door to Hell was still standing upright and alone in the middle of the hall, and approaching it felt like staring down the barrel of a loaded gun. I circled the door cautiously, only to be a little thrown when I discovered the other side wasn't there. A door that could only be seen from the front because its opposite side was somewhere else. I moved back to stand in front of the door and then looked to Amanda, who was courteously giving me some space. Or perhaps just maintaining a safe distance.

"Are the demons still there?" I said. "Waiting for the door to open?"

"They're always waiting," said Amanda.

"All right," I said. "How do we close this thing permanently?"

"First we have to talk to the door's guardian," said Amanda. "The one I left in place to hold back the demons. Someone who would never stop fighting them, because he could never be killed."

A chill ran through me. "Charles? He's still here?"

"I bound his spirit to this place, so he could do in death what he failed to do in life. Stand his ground and do his job."

"That's cold, Amanda..."

"It was necessary," she said. "Charles! Make yourself known to us, there's a dear."

And just like that a young man in a smart suit was leaning against the door to Hell. He looked real enough, but his shirt front was soaked with blood from where he'd been stabbed. The ghost of Carcosa's Doom hung at his side. He ignored me, fixing Amanda with his cold, cold eyes.

"Yes, my dear, my only love; I'm still here. I'm always here. I can't even go for a little stroll around the castle to pass the time. Not that I'd want to. There are other ghosts here, and you wouldn't believe the noise they make. Still, there are always visitors dropping by. And I get to fight them back, night after night, saving the world over and over again. I should get a medal."

"You've done a good job, Charles," said Amanda.

"It's not like I was given a choice!" Charles started away from the door, his eyes dangerous, only to stop abruptly as she met his gaze unflinchingly.

"I had to have someone to guard the door," said Amanda. "And you were all I had to work with."

"You have no idea of what I've been through," said Charles. "Torn apart, over and over, only to be pulled back together again by your magics. Did you think it wouldn't hurt, just because I don't have a body?"

"I'm sorry," said Amanda, and her voice sounded genuinely soft and kind. "I should never have expected so much from you."

Charles nodded slowly, as the anger went out of him. "I really did love you. I think I would have volunteered, if you'd asked."

Amanda smiled. "You've come a long way, Charles."

He didn't smile back at her. Instead, he turned abruptly to look at me. "So, you're my replacement. Don't make the same mistakes I did. Don't believe her, don't trust her, and above all don't love her. She can't love you back, because she only looks human."

"You always did talk too much, Charles," said Amanda.

She snapped her fingers, and the ghost blinked out of existence.

"Where did you send him?" I said.

"To his rest," said Amanda.

"How much of what he said was true?"

"That's for you to decide," said Amanda.

"Can you really love me?" I said. "If you're not human?"

The smile she showed me then was a small and fragile thing. "I'm a lot more human than I used to be. That's what hanging around with people does to you."

A sudden intuition tapped my shoulder like a warning, and I turned quickly to stare at the door.

"Something's coming. Getting closer. I can feel it."

"I know," said Amanda.

"What do we do?"

"You stand your ground," said Amanda.

I tore my gaze away from the door to stare at her. "Just me?"

"It's the ritual," said Amanda. "You have to fight what comes through and force them back so I can close the door forever."

Before I could say anything the door to Hell swung back, but instead of the dark I saw an endless labyrinth of suffering, like an infinity of living butterflies pinned to a display board. I turned my face away, and fell back a step.

"Jack," said Amanda. "Please. Hold your ground."

I stopped where I was. "How am I supposed to fight something like that?"

"Demons have to make themselves physical to have an effect in this world, and what is physical is vulnerable," Amanda said steadily. "Just buy me some time, Jack, to do what needs doing."

"Is that what you told Charles?" I said.

"Yes," said Amanda. "He should have listened."

I forced myself to face the door again. The chaos had vanished, and the darkness had returned. As though something didn't want me to see what was coming.

"I can fight monsters," I said. "It's what I do."

"There are all kinds of monsters," said Amanda. "Hell will send whatever scares you most."

"You are really not helping, you know that?"

"Would you rather I lied to you?"

"Yes!" I said.

"Lies are Hell's business," said Amanda.

Two oversized white gloves appeared out of the darkness. They gripped the doorframe on both sides, and then hauled their owner out of the dark and into the light. A clown in multicoloured silks stood slouching before me, with a gaudily painted face but no eyes, only empty sockets crusted with dried blood. The red, red mouth stretched wide in a horrid grin, revealing jagged broken teeth. The gloved hands opened and closed menacingly.

I punched the clown in the face so hard my fist smashed all the way through and out the back of its skull. For a moment the clown just stood there, and then it stepped carefully back, pulling its shattered head off my fist with a certain wounded dignity. It took another step back into the dark, and was gone.

"I never liked clowns," I said.

"I could tell," said Amanda.

I looked at my fist, but there wasn't a trace of blood on it, or even a smear of greasepaint. A movement in the dark caught my eye, but when I turned to face it what stepped out was worse than any monster. A middle-aged man stood before me, smiling easily, looking exactly the way I remembered him.

"Dad?" I said.

"Of course I went to Hell," said Tom Daimon. "Hell is where all the well-meaning people go, when they don't understand how the world works."

"Why are you here?" I said. "Why did Hell send you?"

"Because I'm the one person you'd trust to tell you the truth. Listen to me, son. The thing that only looks like a woman has been using you, right from the start. You were doing such a good job as my successor, removing all the last traces of magic from the world, that she decided you had to be stopped. She made up this whole other history nonsense, just to distract you from doing your job. She only pretended to care for you so she could defuse you."

I drew the athame from my pack, and held it out before me. The blade was shining so brightly I could barely look at it.

"What do you want, Dad?"

"I remember that knife," he said. "And how it can cut through absolutely anything. We want you to use it, Jack, to cut the ties that bind and let us out. Let all of us out."

"Why would I do that?"

"Because Hell isn't what you think it is," said Tom Daimon. "Hell is the last true repository of free will. Think what this world could be like, without all the stupid rules and regulations. If everyone was free to achieve everything they ever dreamed of."

I shook my head. "I've seen what happens to people when they throw away the rule book. I saw what abandoning her moral compass did to Miriam. I could have liked her, if she hadn't lost her way."

"Would you like to talk to her?" said Tom. "Ah . . . Amanda didn't tell you where she sent your little friend, did she? There are lots of people you know, just waiting to come back through this door. Because all the best people end up in Hell. Join us, Jack. I promise you'll feel right at home. And we'll have all the fun in the world."

"That's enough!" I said. "My father was always all about his duty. He would never have gone along with this bullshit. How stupid do you think I am?"

The demon with my father's face shrugged easily. "It was worth a try."

"But thanks for coming," I said. "It was good to see my dad again, if only for a moment. And, you reminded me of something I'd forgotten."

The demon wasn't smiling any more. "We could have done this the easy way, Outsider. But if it's blood and horror you want..."

He disappeared back into the darkness, but before an army of living nightmares could come boiling out I cut at the door with my athame, and the glowing blade sheared clean through the doorframe and all the darkness it contained. The door to Hell vanished, and it felt like a terrible weight had been removed from the world. I laughed shakily, and nodded to Amanda.

"All I had to do was cut through the ties and bindings Frankenstein put in place, and the door to Hell was no longer anchored here."

Amanda clapped her hands, and grinned broadly. "It took you long enough to work that out."

I stared at her. "So all that stuff about buying you time..."

"Was just something you needed to hear, to get you to stand your ground."

She walked forward to stand before me, until our faces were so close I could feel her breath on my lips. Her eyes were impossibly bright, and in them I could see everything I ever wanted.

"I've brought you as far as I can, Jack," she said. "Now it's time for you to tell me what's really going on."

I nodded slowly. "I have been thinking about this, and putting things together. Stop me if I miss out anything important. You set all of this in motion when you arranged for Richard Dadd's painting of 'The Faerie War' to be rediscovered and put on display in the Tate. As bait, to attract my attention. So you could meet me, apparently accidentally, and then... what? Seduce me into doing what you wanted?"

"I had to do something," said Amanda. "The Department had kept the Outsiders so busy doing its dirty work, that your family had destroyed most of the remaining vestiges of magic. And once the last of them was gone, the rewriting of history could never be undone."

"You took me on a tour of England's magical history so I could appreciate what would be lost. You wanted me to care enough to fight for it."

"I did set out to make you fall in love with me," said Amanda. "But somewhere along the way I fell in love with you, Jack. You became so much more than I expected: a hero and a legend in your own right. I couldn't be more proud of you."

"What happens to us?" I said. "If we do bring back the magical world?"

"I don't know," said Amanda. "But wherever we end up, I want to be with you. Always."

"Good," I said. "Because that's what I want too."

She came forward into my arms, and we held each other for a long time.

Eventually, I pushed her away. Because there were still things that needed doing.

"Where do we go now?" I said.

"To the one place in the present where magic can still be found," said Amanda. "Because it never went away."

CHAPTER TEN
FIGHTING FOR A BETTER WORLD

Standing stones, under a night sky. A horned moon and a scattering of stars. Ancient stone monoliths set in a circle, with openings like doorways. The past made real, and solid. Bright security lights poured in from outside the circle, flooding the scene with flat colourless light. The present, trying to intimidate the past.

"Stonehenge," I said. "I should have known."

"It's good to be back," said Amanda. "I always feel at home here."

I looked at her sternly. "Are you about to tell me you were here when it was built?"

"No," said Amanda. "But I did help with the design."

"Okay ... When, exactly, are we?"

"Right back where we started," Amanda said happily. "We have returned to the very day we left. Our journey is almost over, Jack."

I looked out past the Stones. "I never did understand why they felt the need to surround Stonehenge with barbed wire. It's not like anyone was going to steal it."

Amanda looked down her nose at the security barrier, and sniffed loudly.

"The last repository of magic in the world, and they've put it in a cage. So the secret masters can watch it wither and die."

"I'm not seeing any security guards," I said carefully.

"They're here," said Amanda. "They just haven't shown themselves yet."

"Why not?"

213

"Because they're waiting to see what we'll do."

"All right," I said. "What are we going to do?"

"Bring an end to this sick, miserable mistake of a world," said Amanda. "And put things back the way they should be."

"I'm still not clear why you need me to help you do that," I said.

"There are rules, Jack, even for beings like me. Perhaps especially for beings like me. Things must be done the right way, if they're to mean anything. That's what our little road trip through history was all about: teaching and preparing you, for this place and this moment. So you can stand in judgement on what the world should be."

"You should listen to her," said a cheerful young voice. "She knows what she's talking about. In fact, that's pretty much her job description."

I turned sharply, and was surprised to find a boy of about twelve standing a few feet away, particularly when I was positive he hadn't been there just a moment ago. He was wearing a smart school uniform and cap, and leaning on a tall wooden staff. He had a typical schoolboy face, but his eyes were so much older. He smiled at me, and nodded familiarly to Amanda.

"Took you long enough to get here."

She smiled fondly at him. "We had a lot to do."

"At least you could take short cuts," said the boy. "I had to come the long way round."

There was something about the way the boy spoke, and those old, old eyes . . .

"Merlin?" I said.

He grinned broadly, his ancient eyes sparkling with mischief. "Good to see you again, Jack. I've been remembering this moment all my life."

"You age backwards?" I said.

He shrugged. "Trust me, it wasn't my idea. It came with the job. But I quite like being this young. No one expects anything from me, and my only real worry is where the next toffee is coming from. I'm looking forward to being born, so I can get some rest at last." He looked at Amanda. "You do know this is a trap?"

"Of course," said Amanda. "Did you bring what I'm going to need?"

"Of course," said Merlin.

"This is just typical of magic," I said. "I don't know what's going on, I haven't a clue what you're talking about, and just looking at Harry Potter here is freaking me out big time. At least I know where I am with science."

"Do you?" said Amanda. "Do you understand how your computers work? Or any of the machines you depend on every day? You're constantly at the mercy of specialists who might or might not be available when you need them. That didn't happen by accident, Jack. It was deliberately set up to isolate and control people.

"Magic can be used by anyone, or it can just be experienced, and enjoyed for its own sake. Science is a way of life; magic can be lived. Of course magic can be scary as well as marvellous, but anything else would just be boring, wouldn't it?"

And that was when hundreds of heavily armed figures burst out of the darkness and into the light, closing in on us from every direction at once, until we were surrounded by Men In Black and alien Greys.

"Looks like they emptied the barracks, just for us," said Merlin. "Which is something of a compliment, if you think about it."

Some of the spindly creatures in shabby black suits went skittering up the standing stones, like so many oversized insects. They clung to the sides and crouched on the crosspieces, covering us with their guns. The Greys took up positions between the stones, carrying the same futuristic weapons they'd used to shoot dragons out of the sky.

"The word overkill comes to mind," I said. "And not in a good way."

"We've finally reached the endgame," said Amanda. "The secret masters' last chance to stop us."

"Please tell me you have a plan," I said.

"Of course she has," said Merlin. "She plans like other people breathe."

A handful of Greys stepped aside, to let a single figure through. A large man in a smart city suit, with a face that was classically handsome but essentially characterless. A plastic surgeon's idea of perfection. Jet black hair and eyebrows gave him a sardonic air, but whatever he might be thinking didn't disturb his perfect face in the least.

All along I had been convinced that when I finally came face to face with the leader of the secret masters, it would be someone I knew. Some familiar face who'd been hiding in plain sight all along. But I was positive I'd never seen this man before in my life.

"Jack," said Amanda. "Allow me to present to you: the man behind the secret masters."

"The only master, for some time now," said the big man, in a smooth and cultured voice. "Call me Caliban: the child betrayed by his father."

I stared into his different-coloured eyes and realised that I had seen him before, after all.

"Frankenstein's monster. I should have known."

"Ease back on the m-word," Merlin said quietly.

"Yes, be polite, Outsider," said Caliban. "I'd hate to have to tear you limb from limb, when there are still things I want to say to you."

"We could start with why your people didn't just shoot us on sight," I said.

"Don't give him ideas," said Merlin.

"Jack Daimon," Caliban said heavily. "The Outsider who turned on his own kind. All for a smile from a pretty face."

"I'm not the only one who's changed," I said. "You didn't always look this good."

Caliban shrugged. "In this modern age, we can all have the face we want."

"How are you still alive, after all these years?"

"What was never born can never die," said Caliban. "The energies of Hell have no limit."

"How ironic," Amanda said sweetly. "That science's most famous son can only exist by depending on magic."

"Speak one more word that I don't care for," said Caliban, "and I will rip your tongue out."

"Don't speak to her like that," I said. And there must have been something in my voice, because he stopped and looked at me thoughtfully.

"If you could only see her as she really is, Outsider."

"You have a handsome new face," I said. "But you're still the monster your father made you."

"I owe nothing to that man!" Caliban's voice cracked like a whip.

"He disowned me, for the sin of not being perfect. For being the ugly conclusion of his limited skills." He broke off, and made himself smile coldly at Amanda. "I knew I could count on your arrogance to bring you here, even though you had to know I'd be waiting. Unfortunately for you, I saw to it that all magic was drained from this setting long ago. There's nothing left in this place that you can use to protect yourself."

"Why are you so keen to protect science?" I said. "Given that it produced something like you?"

"Only science can protect humanity," said Caliban.

"From what?" I said.

"From Hell," said Caliban. "My father opened a door to a whole other dimension of magic, to give me life. The door may be gone, but Hell's armies are still there, waiting for their chance to break through and fill this world with chaos and madness. I'm damned if I'll let that happen. I have dedicated myself to the destruction of magic, because no one knows better than me what it leads to."

"How can you save humanity, by building a prison for everyone to live in?" I said.

"We need strong walls to keep everything else out," said Caliban. "Consider your companion, Outsider. How do you think we look, to something that existed before humanity even appeared? We don't matter to her; we're just mayflies, come and gone in a moment. Things she can use to get what she wants."

"It's only by living so long that I have learned to appreciate life in all its forms," Amanda said calmly. "Short or long, it must be savoured, because none of it lasts."

"You do," said Caliban. "And so do I. I will never allow creatures like you to have power over me."

"Is that why you killed your creator?" said Amanda. "To make sure no one could ever tell you what to do?"

I looked at her. "All of this, because his father didn't love him?"

She shrugged. "It's a very human motivation."

"Enough!" said Caliban. "The last hope of magic ends here, tonight. Once you're dead the world will work perfectly, like clockwork, and I will hold the only key."

"And you'll be safe at last," I said. "No one will be able to hurt you, ever again."

"Everyone will be safe," said Caliban. "How does it feel, Outsider? To know you've been working for the wrong side all along?"

"That's what I was about to ask you," I said.

Caliban shook his head. "I should have known you wouldn't listen. But I had to try."

"Why?" I said.

"Because we have so much in common."

I looked at him. "Run that by me again."

"We both know what it's like to be always alone, cut off from the very humanity we're trying to protect."

"You want to lock everyone up for their own good. I want to set them free."

"You'd damn us all, for something that only looks human!" said Caliban.

He raised a hand to the waiting Men In Black and alien Greys.

"Can I just ask," I said quickly, "why you only brought homunculi to back you up? I saw plenty of human guards in the Department library."

"Men are weak," said Caliban. "I wanted something I could depend on."

"For someone who claims to be so keen to protect humanity," I said, "you don't seem to have much time for them."

He smiled his cold smile. "I know them so well."

"Is that why you've surrounded yourself with monsters?" I said.

"Hell is always waiting," said Caliban. "You need monsters, to fight monsters."

"And to keep people under control," I said.

"A world of science has to follow the rules," said Caliban. "Unlike your companion. How much has she told you, about what's really going on?"

"Enough," I said.

"Do you know you're not her first patsy?"

"She told me about Charles."

"But did she tell you about me?"

I glanced at Amanda, but she had nothing to say. Caliban laughed softly.

"Did you never wonder exactly how history was rewritten? It all comes down to the book in your backpack. Oh yes, I know it's there;

I can feel its power and its presence. Amanda approached me long ago, to help her in her fight against the secret masters. Who were really nothing more than a bunch of scientists with ideas above their station. She thought I must hate science as much as she did, because of the part it played in my creation."

I looked at Amanda. "What makes the book so important?"

"It's the key to everything," Amanda said calmly. "Older than humanity, older even than me, its contents shape and form to the world and everything in it."

"How did that happen?" I said.

She shrugged. "It was decided where all the things that matter are decided: in the Courts of the Holy, on the shimmering plains." She smiled suddenly. "Don't look so shocked, Jack. You know Hell is real, so why not Heaven? The book tells the Story of all this is, or what should have been, before the secret masters got their hands on it."

"They were all set to recreate the world according to their needs," said Caliban. "But Amanda and I tracked them down."

"And then you betrayed me," said Amanda. "You killed them all, and used the book to rewrite the world according to your needs."

"To keep us safe, from the madness of magic," said Caliban. "Afterwards, I hid the book in the Department library. The only place with enough protections to keep you out. Until the Outsider helped you steal it." He looked at me coldly. "I am the one who's been pursuing you all this time, to take back what is mine. The book that makes anything possible. Because I'm damned if I'll let you undo all of my good work."

He smiled triumphantly at Amanda, only to break off as he realised she was smiling back at him.

"I knew what kind of trap this would have to be," she said calmly. "For you to find enough courage to emerge from the shadows at last. But after everything you've done I needed to be here, to see you punished. Small of me, perhaps, but that's what comes of living among people. You're quite right, there isn't a scrap of magic left in Stonehenge. That's why Merlin is here."

She gestured at the schoolboy, standing patiently to one side. Caliban looked at him, and Merlin bowed mockingly.

"Ta-da!"

"What can you do, boy?" said Caliban.

"I draw power from the magical places of the world," said Merlin. "And I've spent centuries visiting all the ones that remain, and draining their power."

"The great sorcerer," said Caliban. "Reduced to playing tourist, and grubbing after the dregs of magic. It doesn't matter what you have. I brought insurance."

He gestured sharply and two Men In Black hurried forward, carrying something heavy. They unrolled it to reveal Richard Dadd's painting of "The Faerie War."

Caliban gestured proudly at the canvas. "George gave orders for it to be destroyed, but I had Miriam intercept the painting on its way to the furnace. It still contains the terrible thing you saw in the Tate, Outsider, so it seemed only fitting that I should feed you to it."

"The painting is here because that's what I wanted," said Amanda. "I went to a lot of trouble to put it into the Department's hands, knowing you wouldn't be able to resist using it. There never was any monster in the painting, Jack, just me, hiding behind one of my masks." She saw the expression on my face, and shrugged apologetically. "No one was ever in any real danger."

"You abducted and terrified innocent people!" I said. "You saw the state they were in, after I got them out of that painting!"

"Sometimes, I have to take the long view," said Amanda. It was as close as she could come to an apology.

"But how could you be inside the painting, and in the Tate at the same time?" I paused, to glance at Caliban. "Yes, I know; you're impatient to get started. But I would like to get some answers straight in my head before I get it shot off."

"Be my guest," said Caliban. "Don't let me hurry you."

"I was Richard Dadd's muse," said Amanda. "My power made his painting possible. Which meant I could store a small part of myself in the work he created, waiting to be set in motion at the right time."

"You really do plan ahead," I said.

"Like you wouldn't believe," said Merlin.

"But what I saw in that painting was monstrous, hideous..." I stared at Amanda, as a thought struck me. "Is that what you really look like?"

"Of course not," said Amanda. "That was just a big spooky scarecrow, so I could get you moving and motivated."

"You could just have asked for my help," I said.

"I couldn't risk you saying no." Amanda turned back to Caliban. "I wanted the painting here, because I knew I'd need an army of my own to fight yours."

She gestured at "The Faerie War," and when we all looked the scene had changed. The fighting had stopped, and piles of elven dead lay scattered all across the broken ground. A dozen cold-eyed survivors stood together, staring out at us. Their War was finally over, and all it had cost them was everything.

"This was never meant to be just a painting," said Amanda. "It was always a gateway to another place."

"No wonder Marion thought she was the last of the Fae," I said. "None of the War's survivors came back, because you had them trapped inside the painting."

"Hush, darling," said Amanda. "Working."

She gestured at Merlin, and he tapped his staff on the ground. Magical energies crackled on the air, and the elves strode out of the painting and into Stonehenge. The two Men In Black holding the canvas dropped it and fell back. Amanda smiled easily at the elves, and they bowed formally in return.

"We thank you, lady, for this release," said one of the elves. "How may we repay you?"

Amanda gestured at Caliban. "Save the world, from this man and his army."

"You think a handful of elves can stand against my forces?" said Caliban.

Amanda was still smiling. "The rest of my army hasn't arrived yet."

I looked at her. "There's more?"

"Of course," said Amanda. "You made some good friends on our journey through history, Jack. Friends with armies of their own. Why don't you call them?"

I thought about that, and smiled. I took the athame out of my pack, and the blade glowed palely with the last of its stored energies. Magic enough, for a few small miracles. I concentrated my Sight through the blade, looking back into the past. And then I raised my voice, in the ancient amphitheatre of Stonehenge.

"Queen Boudicca! King Arthur! Robin Hood! Across the years I call to you, because I need your help. To save not just me and the woman I love, but the true path of history itself."

And from across Time, they came. From the past that was, to the history that replaced them, came the armies of yesterday.

A tall warrior woman in leather armour, with a blue-painted face and hair packed with clay, strode out from between two standing stones as though they were a gateway, followed by a great host of her warriors. I nodded to Queen Boudicca, and she nodded cheerfully back.

"Thanks for coming," I said.

Boudicca grinned. "What are friends for?"

"Exactly!" said a loud familiar voice. A large figure in steel armour strode out of another gateway, followed by every knight of the Round Table. King Arthur took off his helm, so he could smile at me.

"After everything you did for Camelot, how could I not be here, Sir Jack the Outsider."

"Damn right!" said a merry voice, and Robin Hood appeared, backed by his entire band of outlaws.

I smiled and nodded to all of them, as though I didn't have a care in the world now they were here, and then looked round at the Men In Black and the alien Greys, still covering us with a multitude of weapons.

"Numbers are fine," I said quietly to Amanda, "But we are seriously outgunned. Isn't there anything you can do?"

She was shaking her head before I'd even finished speaking. And then she looked at me expectantly. I sighed, and didn't even try to keep it internal.

"I am getting really tired of you always leaving it to me to save the day."

"But that's what you're here for, Jack. And this is the very last time."

"Promise?"

She shrugged. "If you don't come up with an answer we won't be here for another try."

I looked at the athame in my hand. Its light was barely flickering, on the verge of going out.

"Enough magic for one last trick," I said.

Caliban sneered at me. "But not enough to stop my forces, Outsider."

I covered the distance between us in a moment and set the edge of my knife against his throat. I showed him a cold smile of my own.

"Sometimes, a knife is just a knife. Tell your people to drop their weapons."

"If you harm me, my people will shoot you down."

"You won't be here to see it," I said.

He glared at me with his mismatched eyes, his perfect lips pressed together. I applied a little pressure, and a trickle of blood coursed down his throat as his skin parted under the knife's edge. Caliban yelled to the Men In Black and Greys to drop their guns, and they did. I looked around to check all of them had obeyed, and Caliban seized the moment to step quickly back out of reach.

I turned to the friends who'd come so far to help me.

"See the bad guys, with the shabby suits and the Grey faces? Kill them all!"

Queen Boudicca raised her battle-axe and charged the Men In Black. Her warriors went streaming after her, howling their wolfish battle cries. They crossed the ground so quickly, advancing from a standing start to a full charge in just a few moments, that they were in and among the Men In Black before they had a chance to grab for their dropped guns. Swords and axes flashed brightly in the moonlight, as the warriors of the woad hacked their way through the Department homunculi. The Men In Black fought back with vicious strength and speed, but they had relied on those advantages for so long they had no thought of tactics. They went one on one, head to head, and didn't even think to guard each other's backs. Vicious claws tore through leather armour to savage the flesh beneath, but for every warrior that dropped there was an army waiting to avenge them. Boudicca's wolves threw themselves at the Men In Black, howling like demons in the night.

The battle spread out to cover the whole of Stonehenge. Two armies that knew nothing of mercy slammed together, and keen-edged swords cut down Men In Black, while swinging axes stove in rib cages and sent severed heads rolling across the ground. Knots of struggling figures formed and reformed, and blood splashed across the standing stones. The warriors of the woad pressed forward, even as more of the spindly creatures came scrambling down the sides of the stones, or launched themselves from the crosspieces.

Boudicca led from the front, laughing out loud as her battle-axe split skull after skull. A group of Men In Black cut her off and swarmed around her, intent on dragging her down and butchering her in front of her people, to break their spirit. But the Queen of the Iceni would not fall. She stood her ground and howled defiant curses into their bony faces as she held them off long enough for her warriors to burst through the Men In Black, reach her side and force the enemy back.

It was a glorious slaughter, and Boudicca and her warriors of the woad filled the shadows of the stones with their battle cries as they delighted in their enemies' destruction.

There was more than one front to the battle. A dozen elves went to war against an army of alien Greys, and didn't give a damn about the odds. They were in and among their foes in a moment, cutting them down with brightly glowing blades. The Greys had their own claws, and were inhumanly fast and strong, but the elves moved gracefully among the alien figures as though they were dancing between raindrops in a thunderstorm. Elven blades sheared through alien flesh as though it was nothing more than mist or smoke, and no elf was ever there when clawed hands struck desperately back in retaliation. The elves flickered through the packed Greys like deadly notions, come and gone in a moment, leaving butchered alien dead in their wake, and not one drop of their own blood to show where they had been.

Survivors of an apocalyptic war, they had learned to be very hard to kill.

King Arthur and his knights also joined the battle, slicing through the Greys like farmers in a field of wheat. Heavy swords hammered the Greys to their knees and punched through alien flesh, while vicious claws skittered harmlessly across the knights' armour. The Greys' usual tactic of swarming and overwhelming the enemy proved useless as the knights stuck close together, guarding each other's backs and blind spots. King Arthur had learned much from his clash on the field outside Camelot, and had taught his knights well.

Also believing that if they could just lop off the head the body would die, the Greys launched themselves at the king in wave after wave. Arthur stood his ground, his sword flashing brightly as he struck down Grey after Grey, but they forced their way close enough to grab hold of his arms. And while Arthur struggled to free himself, clawed hands prised at his helm. His knights fought desperately to get to him, but the Greys held them off through sheer weight of numbers.

Sir Brendan, the dead of knight, stepped back from the battle, and studied the scene dispassionately. He moved in beside a standing stone and put his shoulder against it. Steel boots dug deep into the ground as the empty suit of armour slowly forced the stone off balance and sent it toppling forward. The huge menhir came crashing down onto the main body of Greys attacking Arthur, and its awful weight hammered them to the ground. Shock waves from the impact sent everyone staggering, and Arthur seized the moment to break away from his attackers. He nodded his thanks to Sir Brendan, and the empty suit of armour moved quickly forward to guard his king's back. The two old friends went to war together, dealing out death and destruction to all who came against them.

Robin Hood and his outlaws worked their bows tirelessly, loosing shaft after shaft to strike down Men In Black and alien Greys. Body after body crashed to the ground with an arrow protruding from its eye socket. Some of the homunculi broke away from the main fight to charge the archers, but a wall of pointed death struck them down long before they could get anywhere near Robin and his people. The outlaws soon ran out of arrows, and then they put aside their bows and drew their swords, and went to join the battle with merry hearts. After fighting the living dead in a burning Sherwood Forest, nothing was ever going to give them pause again.

Robin and Marion fought side by side, striking down their enemies with dashing style and elegant precision. Little John guarded their backs with his massive club, and sent crushed and shattered bodies flying in all directions. Friar Tuck guarded the giant's blind spots, his long staff flashing out to crack the skull of any Grey foolish enough to see him as an easy target. He still murmured prayers for the dead with every blow, because that was his job.

I started forward to join the fighting the moment the battle began, but Amanda's hand fell implacably on my arm, holding me where I was.

"You stay right where you are, Jack. Your friends can do this on their own, and I still need you to do the one thing they can't. They can win the battle, but only you can win the day."

I nodded unhappily, and threatened Caliban with my athame when he tried to get involved. And so we both stood our ground, and watched the tides of battle move this way and that.

It all ended quite suddenly. Trapped inside the standing stones and attacked from all sides at once, the last of the Men In Black and alien Greys fell to the armies of humanity, and a sudden hush fell across Stonehenge. Queen Boudicca, King Arthur, Robin and Marion, looked out over the piled up bodies of their fallen enemies, and sent up a great roar of triumph and celebration. They raised their swords to honour me, and I saluted them proudly.

Boudicca and Arthur gave quiet orders to gather up their fallen, and led their people back through the stone gateways, but Marion the Fae asked Robin to wait a moment. She walked over to where the twelve survivors of the Faerie War were standing quietly together, unhurt and unmoved by the slaughter, because they had known so much worse.

One of the elves bowed to Marion. "It is good to see you again, Princess."

"I would have fought beside you in the War," she said.

"We could not allow that. You were the last of the royal line."

"I thought I was the last of my kind," she said. "I have been alone for so long . . . You have nowhere left to go; our homelands are lost forever. But you could come with me. To join Robin and his outlaws, in Sherwood."

"Princess," said the elf. "We would be honoured, to have a home again."

Marion led the elves over to Robin, and he smiled easily.

"I always knew that some day I'd have to meet the in-laws."

Robin and Marion, the outlaws and the elves, walked between the standing stones and were gone. Caliban stared out across Stonehenge, his perfect face full of shock and disbelief as he took in the utter destruction of his forces. Amanda moved in beside me.

"Jack, give me the book."

"It's about time," I said.

"Yes," said Amanda. "It is."

I hauled the massive volume out of my backpack, and handed it to her. She leafed unhurriedly through the pages.

"*Things That Shouldn't Exist*," she said. "The latest in a long line of titles, for the last book to list every magical thing still remaining in the world of science, everything left over from the world that was." She closed the heavy volume with a snap. "Merlin, if you please? It's time."

"Of course, Mother," said Merlin. "Hello, I must be going."

He raised his staff and hammered it on the ground, and the staff exploded in a burst of light. There was no heat or force, but when the light faded away Merlin was gone. And then I heard laughing overhead, and looked up to see Merlin soaring across the night sky. He rolled over onto his back, so he could wave down at me.

"Catch you on the flipside . . ."

He disappeared into the darkness, and I turned to Amanda.

"What just happened?"

"All the magic Merlin collected has been set loose in Stonehenge," said Amanda. "Not a lot, but enough to work with."

Caliban turned suddenly, to hit us with his mismatched gaze. "I can still win the day, if both of you are dead."

I moved quickly to stand between him and Amanda. "Really not going to happen."

Caliban looked at the no longer glowing witch knife in my hand, and his smile had nothing of humour in it.

"That might have hurt me while it was a thing of power, but no ordinary weapon can stop me as long as I am driven by Hell's energies."

His eyes flickered away from me, and I looked round just in time to see one last Man In Black leap down at me from a standing stone. I threw myself to one side, and hit the ground so hard the witch knife went flying from my hand. The Man In Black crashed to earth right where I'd been standing, his long legs easily absorbing the impact. I scrambled up onto my feet and then stopped as I took in the long scar running around the figure's throat, held together by innumerable stitches.

"Slender? Is that you?"

The Man In Black snarled briefly. "I kept myself apart from the fighting, because I always knew you were the real enemy. You're

going to die here, Outsider, at my hands, and your precious cause
with you."

I shook my head. "You always were a bad loser."

Slender's mouth stretched wide, to show off his pointed teeth. His
long-fingered hands flexed hungrily. I glanced at my knife, but it had
fallen well out of reach. So I looked down my nose at Slender and
gestured haughtily, inviting him to do his worst. He launched himself
at me, clawed hands straining for my face. I grabbed one out-
stretched arm in a judo hold, turned sharply, and used his own speed
to slam him to the ground. Then all I had to do was twist the long
arm against the joint, and use the pressure to hold him where he was.
He thrashed helplessly, unable to break free.

"You were the one who told me the Outsider needed to know how
to fight, as well as defuse bombs," I said. "Or I might not last long
enough to get to the defusing. So I took a few lessons."

I released his arm, reached down and took his head in my hands.
I planted one foot in the small of his back to give myself some
leverage, and twisted his head right off. It came free in a stutter of
snapping stitches, and I held it up before me so I could look the last
Man In Black in the eye.

"Sorry, Slender. No more second chances."

I threw the head to the ground, and stamped on it. The skull
collapsed, and the headless body stopped moving.

Caliban started forward, but Amanda looked at him, and the
force of her gaze was enough to send him flying backwards. He went
skidding across the ground, and slammed up against the base of a
standing stone. He shook his head, and lurched up onto his feet
again.

"You can't hurt me! Nothing can, while Hell's strength burns
within me!"

He started forward again, heading for Amanda. She glared at him,
and he just kept coming. I moved quickly to intercept him, and
punched him in the face with all my strength. My fist jarred painfully,
but Caliban barely blinked. He lashed out at me, and I only just
ducked a blow that would have taken my head clean off. I hit him
again and again, but all I did was hurt my hand. Caliban didn't even
try to dodge my blows, absorbing the impacts as though they were
nothing. I shrugged the backpack off my shoulder to grab for

something useful, and Caliban snatched it away from me and threw it to one side.

I ducked inside his reach, and slammed a blow in under his sternum. It felt like punching a brick wall. I grabbed at Caliban's arm, trying for a judo throw, but he grabbed the front of my jacket, lifted me into the air, and threw me all the way across the clearing. I hit the ground hard, and rolled painfully over onto my side. And only then realised that I'd landed right in front of Dadd's painting, still standing upright. My witch knife was lying before me.

I didn't glance at Amanda. If she had helped out, she'd never admit it. I gathered what was left of my strength, and forced myself up onto one knee, facing Caliban. His smile was a cold and malignant thing.

"I'm going to break your bones, one at a time," he said. "And then leave you lying there, helpless, so you can watch as I take back my book and tear your precious love apart. I will thrust my hands deep into her guts, and savour her screams."

"Well," I said. "That makes this easier." I grabbed up the witch knife, and showed him my smile. "There should be just enough magic left in it, to summon a few old friends of yours."

I turned to Dadd's painting, that had always been a doorway to another world, and thrust my knife into the canvas. A moment's raising of my Sight, a last flicker of magic, and one portal became another. The painting disappeared, to be replaced by a very familiar door.

I scrambled to one side as it swung open, and a mess of leprous tentacles shot out, rotting and corrupt but full of hideous strength and purpose. They wrapped themselves around Caliban, pinning his arms to his sides. He fought the tentacles with all his unnatural strength, but it made no difference. Foot by foot, they dragged Caliban toward the door. Something in the darkness laughed happily, and I shuddered at the sound. Caliban looked back at me, but after everything he'd done and planned to do, I had no mercy left in me.

"Go to Hell," I said.

The tentacles hauled Caliban through the doorway, and his last despairing scream was suddenly cut off. For a moment there was only darkness, and then a human skeleton stepped out, with Caliban's face stapled to its skull. The colourless lips stretched slowly, in a smile that tore the skin.

"Hello again, Outsider. Thank you for the gift; we do so hate unfinished business. What do you wish of Hell, in return?"

"Not a damned thing," I said steadily. "Were you really planning to invade our world?"

"Always," said the demon. "But there's no rush. All the best people come to us anyway." Caliban's torn-off face smiled briefly. "Be seeing you, Jack."

The demon stepped back into the dark, and the door closed. I stabbed it with my athame and the door disappeared, taking the witch knife with it. I waited a moment, to be sure the door wouldn't be coming back, and then turned to Amanda.

"I did feel a bit sorry for him, at the end."

"Well," said Amanda. "You're only human. And now it's time for you to bring back magic, and save the world."

"But how am I supposed to do that?" I said. "How did Caliban rewrite history in the first place?"

"With this book," said Amanda, holding it out to show me. "Caliban found the description of the world in this book, struck through the word magic and wrote science in its place. That was all it took. Now it's your turn, Jack. Strike out the word science and write in magic, and all will be well again."

"How can one word change everything?"

"Because intent is everything. Ownership of the book gives you the power to work the change."

"Why?" I said.

"Because!" said Amanda. "Now get on with it."

I took the book from Amanda, but couldn't bring myself to open it.

"Do it, Jack," she said. "The history you know is just a nightmare the world is waiting to wake up from."

I lifted the front cover, and the book immediately cracked open to just the right place. Hundreds of carefully described items had been crossed through, in a variety of different inks. Generations of Outsiders at their work, not understanding what it was they were destroying. Some of it had been evil, like the box that killed my father, but . . .

On the facing page was a description of the world, in a language I couldn't read but immediately understand, because the book wanted me to. One word had been struck through, with the word *science* written in above it.

And it seemed to me that the world had been at war for too long, between the two opposing sides of Science and Magic. It was time for the war to end. So I took a pen from my pocket, and beside the word *science* I wrote *and magic* in a firm and steady hand. Because there had to be a better world than this.

Suddenly, it was a bright summer's day. The sky was impossibly blue, like Amanda's eyes, and wide-open grasslands blazed a brilliant green. The air was rich as champagne, and the sunlight felt like a blessing. The stones of Stonehenge were still there, the gaps between them now so many dimensional doorways, opening onto other realities. Fascinating and inviting, they looked like worlds you could spend a lifetime investigating, and never grow tired.

Wonderful creatures ran freely in the fields: unicorns and horses with wings, fauns and centaurs, talking animals and wee winged fairies. All kinds of old friends, lost but not forgotten because they lived on in the dreams humanity refused to give up. Off to one side stood a wonderful wood, where a boy and his bear would always be playing, and in the distance an emerald city shone like a precious jewel. And I just knew that somewhere there were islands, with pirates and treasures and lost civilisations, and all the other fairy tale lands of glamour and glory.

Magic had returned to the world, and it was marvellous.

The book was gone from my hands, its work done. I stared around me, drinking it all in, and Amanda laughed happily at the look on my face.

"Isn't it amazing?" she said. "Isn't it everything I promised you?"

"Yes," I said, and turned to look at her. "But what kind of life can we have together? I'm mortal, and you're not."

"Such things might have mattered in the world that's gone," said Amanda. "But anything is possible, in this best of all worlds. So let's just see what happens."

I grinned at Amanda and opened my arms, and she ran into them.

We finally let go of each other when a shadow fell over us. I looked up, expecting dragons. But instead, the sky was full of flying cars, people with jet-packs, and superheroes in colourful costumes.

"This is the future that should have been," said Amanda. "Where science has become magical. There is life on Mars, and dinosaurs roam the hollow earth, and everything you ever wished for is true! It's a glorious world, Jack, and I can't wait to share it with you."

"It's a shame Merlin isn't here to see it," I said.

"Oh, he'll turn up," said Amanda. "We're going to have a baby, Jack. A boy named Merlin. Only here, he won't have to age backwards."

A rainbow slammed down out of the sky, its glorious colours thundering like a mighty waterfall, and Amanda took my hand and led me toward it. The world was back the way it should have been, where everything was magical, and good things happened every day.

And we all lived happily ever after.